BASIC
Computer Programs
for Business
Volume 1

BASIC Computer Programs for Business
Volume 1

Charles D. Sternberg

HAYDEN BOOK COMPANY, INC.
Rochelle Park, New Jersey

Library of Congress Cataloging in Publication Data

Sternberg, Charles D.
  Basic computer programs for business.

  (Hayden microcomputer series)
    1. Business—Data processing. 2. Programming
languages (Electronic computers). I. Title.
II. Series.
HF5548.2.S7816   658'.0542   80-20732
ISBN 0-8104-5162-X (v. 1)

11 12 13   PRINTING

83 84 85 86 87 88   YEAR

Contents

BASIC
Computer Programs
for Business
Volume 1

1 Introduction

The cost of computing hardware has decreased so rapidly that the microcomputer has been placed within the financial range of even the smallest business enterprises. That they have not been more fully utilized indicates the lack of a readily available, comprehensive set of business programs that are easy to use and understand, inexpensive, and adaptable to the practical requirements of the small office. The objective of this book is to provide a set of business-application systems that will allow your computer to start paying for itself the moment it enters your office. Their range is broad enough to guarantee that the computer's potential may be exercised in the critical areas of your specific business. Their independence and modularity allow you to apply only those portions that are relevant to your business so that you do not have to pay for the overhead of unnecessary functions.

The applications have been designed for the typical business system that makes use of disk storage and printed output media; they do not rely upon other features that might not be so easily obtained. As you gain familiarity with computer use, you should find it progressively easier to make modifications to these programs to utilize the features of your particular machine.

The Book's Format

The computer applications given here have been formatted in a way that the author hopes will be of the greatest value to the reader. They are grouped in sections of logically related business processes. Each series of programs has been supplied with detailed information/documentation in the following form:

1. A general description of the business process is provided as well as of the computer approach to be used.
2. A description of the system's operation includes flowcharts as well as procedures for recovering from inadvertent errors whenever such procedures are appropriate.

1

3. All files used by the system are explained, and a detailed layout is provided.
4. All major variable names (symbols) appearing in the programs are explained. In addition, all features of a program that may differ slightly in other versions of BASIC are specified. A detailed explanation of these features may be found in the Appendix.
5. A complete listing of individual programs is provided with remarks and data necessary for initialization. All line numbers are incremented by ten (10) to insure ease of entry and extension or modification. A functional description of each program is also provided.
6. Examples of outputs from the programs enable you to follow them in detail from their initialization, to the final result.

Entering and Interpreting Programs

The programming approach taken in this book is meant to facilitate your ease of program interpretation and extension or modification. It does not take advantage of many language facilities that minimize program length or processing speed. Concise, highly efficient routines have been avoided as a rule because they too often result in a lack of clarity and the modularity needed to facilitate modification and change. Indentation and comments have been used liberally to assist you in interpreting each program's operation.

Initially, all programs should be entered and tested exactly as they are given. As you gain familiarity with your machine, you may wish to take advantage of various memory and time-saving features, such as (1) eliminating extraneous spaces in the instructions, (2) variable dimensioning of arrays, and (3) placing multiple statements on a line (so long as clarity is not affected). In addition, you may wish to modify various programs by combining several into one or to build new programs from the processing modules already supplied.

Program Compatibility

Each program within a single application area has been designed to be consistent both in the use of variable names (symbols) and in processing methodology. The Appendix discusses the language features used in the programs both as an aid in surmounting difficulties and to facilitate customization of the programs' functions.

Understanding System Operation

Flowcharts are used to facilitate understanding of the operation of the systems. The flowcharting symbols are the standard ones and remain consistent throughout the book. Figure 1-1 illustrates the symbols used to portray the operations of a system, and Fig. 1-2 exemplifies their use. Note that whenever a symbol is drawn with dashed lines, the process (or function) represented is optional.

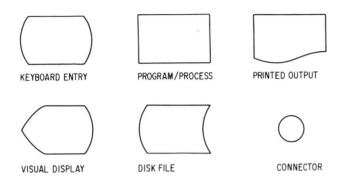

Fig. 1-1 Flowchart symbols used

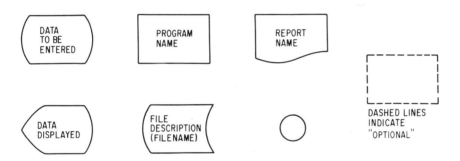

Fig. 1-2 Use of flowchart symbols

I
Financial Control and Analysis

2 Simple Bookkeeping System

This series of programs is designed to provide the processing required to automate a simple bookkeeping system. The necessary accounting reports include (1) a trial balance, (2) an income statement, (3) a balance sheet, and (4) a post closing trial balance. Facilities to initiate, update, and correct files are presented. Additional programs are provided to help you operate the system and to prepare comparative income and expense analyses.

The programs have been designed to work from (accept data in the format of) a typical general-purpose journal. This journal should provide the following information:

1. Date
2. Journal entry number
3. Account to be debited
4. Debit amount
5. Account to be credited
6. Credit amount

With the exception of the date, the items shown constitute the minimum necessary for data entry to the system. The entries in the files are referenced by the journal entry number, which must be entered for each transaction. A zero entry number will cause the transaction to be ignored by the program. It is recommended that journal numbers be entered consecutively to allow ease of reference and comparison to the manual journal. The numbering system should begin with the number 2 since 1 is used by the system to indicate starting balances for the accounting period.

The programs can be used to process several independent accounting systems simultaneously. To do so, it is necessary to create (initialize) a separate file for each system. Since each program requests the filename for processing, different files can be used to separate the accounting systems. If only one system of accounts is to be maintained, the programs can be easily modified to eliminate the need for operator entry

6

of the filename; the PRINT and INPUT statement for the filename is merely replaced with F$=xxxxxx, where "xxxxxx" is the name of the accounts file.

Since this system relies upon random file handling, some differences will occur in other versions of BASIC. The "Functions Used" table indicates the special functions employed. (The Appendix explains the purpose and operation of all functions.) The file handling procedures have been isolated as much as possible in order to facilitate their modification.

Since the security of accounting information is critical to the operation of most businesses, you should institute a procedure that will copy your accounts file whenever a significant number of transactions have been entered. If necessary, of course, recovery can be assured by the reentry of all journal entries.

Operation of the System

The operation of this computer bookkeeping system is similar to the operation of a manual system, with the exception of the assistance the computer offers in each of the steps. The sequence of actions listed in Fig. 2-1 illustrates the operation of the system.

Time	Action	Program or Manual
Initialization at start of year	1) Determine required accounts 2) Initialize files	Manual BCREATE
Throughout accounting period	1) Gather transactions and post journal 2) Post entries to file	Manual BPOST
End of accounting period	1) Prepare trial balance 2) Prepare income statement 3) Post net income/loss to capital accounts 4) Prepare balance sheet 5) Enter closing journal entries 6) Close accounts	BTRIAL BINCOME BPOST BSHEET BPOST and Manual BCLOSE
As required	1) List account file contents 2) Recreate journal entries 3) Correct account information 4) Display accounts	BFLIST BJOURNAL BPRINT BPRINT

Fig. 2-1 Operation of the system

Initialization of files occurs at the beginning of the accounting year. This creation of the files sets up the accounts for the bookkeeping operation.

Normal operation of the system throughout the accounting year involves (1) the posting of journal transactions (using BPOST) for each accounting period (month), (2) producing the necessary reports at the

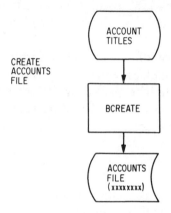

Fig 2-2 Initialization of the accounts file (xxxxxxxx)

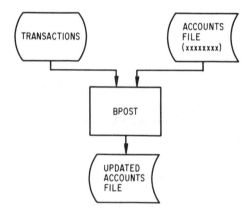

Fig. 2-3 Posting journal transactions

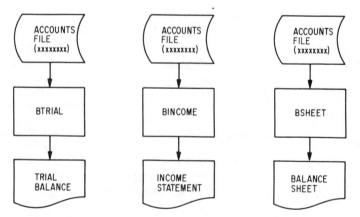

Fig. 2-4 End-of-month reports

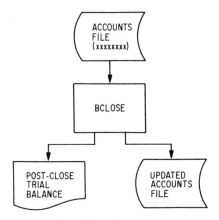

Fig. 2-5 Closing accounts

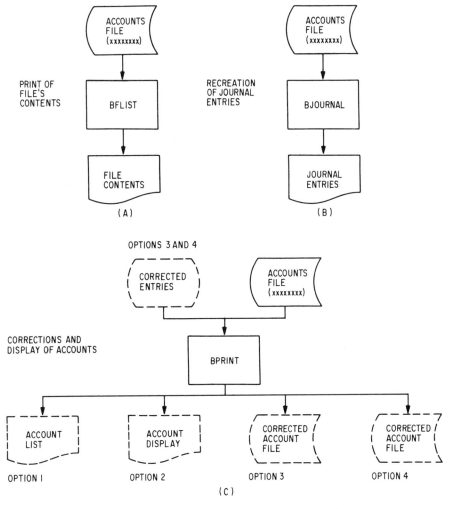

Fig. 2-6 Programs to be executed as required: (a) print of file contents, (b) recreation of journal entries, and (c) corrections and display of accounts

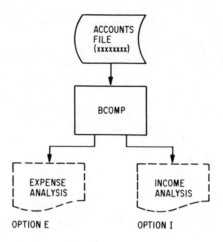

OPTION E   OPTION I

Fig. 2-7 Income and expense analysis

end of each month, and (3) closing out the accounts to prepare for the next month.

The programs BPRINT, BFLIST, BJOURNAL, and BCOMP can be executed at any time they are needed.

The flowcharts in Figs. 2-2 through 2-7 illustrate the processing accomplished at each step of the various programs.

Files Used by the Bookkeeping System

The bookkeeping system requires one file for its operation. The accounts file—created by program BCREATE—is a random access file. All records are identical in format, but the first X records contain system information (X must be greater than 6). The format of the records is shown in Fig. 2-8.

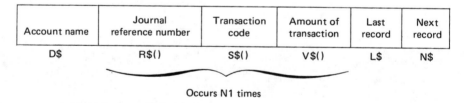

Account name	Journal reference number	Transaction code	Amount of transaction	Last record	Next record
D$	R$( )	S$( )	V$( )	L$	N$

Occurs N1 times

Fig. 2-8 Record format

System records

Records numbered 1 to X are used by the system to maintain file contents information and to provide growth storage locations that will not be affected by the system's operation.

Record No. 1 contains the date of the file's last update (D$), the number of system records [R$(1)], the number of account types [R$(2)], and the last record number used [R$(3)].

Record Nos. 2 to N2 contain the title of each account type (D$) and the number of that type [R$(1)].

Record No. X is the Income/Expense Summary account that is used as an ordinary account for bookkeeping operations.

Account records

Record Nos. X+1 to N3+X+1 are individual records for each account requested. Every account contains a description (D$) and N1 occurrences of the journal entries. Each journal entry contains a reference number (R$), a transaction code (S$), and the amount of the transaction (V$). The last two entries of each record are pointers to preceding or succeeding records. When the number of entries against an account exceeds N1, an extension record is initiated. This record, which is located in the area of the file beyond the account records, is accessed through the use of the next record pointer contained in the basic account record (N$). The last record pointer (L$) is used in the extension record to point back to the basic account record.

The programs that have been provided for maintaining and operating the bookkeeping system are listed in Fig. 2-9.

Program name	Function	Remarks
BCREATE	Creates and initializes files	
BPOST	Enters journal transactions	BPRINT corrects errors, and BJOURNAL recreates journal entries
BTRIAL	Produces a trial balance	
BINCOME	Produces an income statement	
BSHEET	Produces a balance sheet	Requires a journal entry for net income or loss before running
BCLOSE	Closes accounts at month's end	Adjusting journal entries should be completed before running
BFLIST	Prints account file	
BJOURNAL	Recreates and prints the journal entries	
BPRINT	Corrects and displays account contents	Four options: 1) Lists accounts 2) Displays an account 3) Corrects an account 4) Corrects account names
BCOMP	Provides a comparison of income or expenses for several periods	E—Compares expenses I—Compares income

Fig. 2-9 Programs for the bookkeeping system

```
MAJOR SYMBOL TABLE - BOOKKEEPING                                      FUNCTIONS USED
I-----------------------------------------------------------------I   I-----------------------I
I NAME    .. DESCRIPTION                                          I   I  NAME                 I
I-----------------------------------------------------------------I   I-----------------------I
I  A$     .. ANSWER VARIABLE (TEMP)                               I   I  DIM                  I
I  A0     .. ACCOUNT TOTAL ACCUMULATOR                            I   I  TAB                  I
I  A1     .. ACCUMULATOR                                          I   I  GOSUB                I
I  A2()   .. ACCUMULATOR ARRAY                                    I   I  RETURN               I
I  C      .. ACCOUNT NUMBER COUNTER                               I   I  ABS                  I
I  C0     .. TOTAL DEBITS                                         I   I  OPEN                 I
I  C1     .. TOTAL DEBITS                                         I   I  GET                  I
I  D$     .. ACCOUNT DESCRIPTION                                  I   I  PUT                  I
I  D0     .. TOTAL DEBITS                                         I   I  FIELD                I
I  D1     .. TOTAL DEBITS                                         I   I  CVI                  I
I  D1$    .. CURRENT DATE                                         I   I  CVS                  I
I  D2$    .. ACCOUNT DESCRIPTION (TEMP)                           I   I  MKI$                 I
I  D3$    .. AS OF DATE                                           I   I  MKS$                 I
I  D4$    .. PERIOD OF REPORT                                     I   I  LSET                 I
I  E()    .. JOURNAL ENTRY ARRAY                                  I   I-----------------------I
I  F$     .. NAME OF ACCOUNT FILE                                 I
I  I      .. ARRAY AND INDEX POINTER                              I
I  I0     .. ITEM TO BE CORRECTED                                 I
I  I1     .. ARRAY AND INDEX POINTER                              I
I  I2     .. ARRAY AND INDEX POINTER                              I
I  J      .. ARRAY AND INDEX POINTER                              I
I  J1     .. ARRAY AND INDEX POINTER                              I
I  J2     .. ARRAY AND INDEX POINTER                              I
I  K      .. RECORD KEY FOR READS AND WRITES                      I
I  K1     .. INDEX POINTER (TEMP)                                 I
I  K9     .. LAST RECORD NUMBER USED                              I
I  L      .. NUMERIC OF L$                                        I
I  L$     .. POINTER TO LAST RECORD                               I
I  M1     .. MINIMUM REFERENCE NUMBER                             I
I  M2     .. MAXIMUM REFERENCE NUMBER                             I
I  N      .. NUMERIC OF N$                                        I
I  N$     .. POINTER TO NEXT RECORD                               I
I  N0()   .. NUMBER OF EACH ACCOUNT TYPES                         I
I  N1     .. NUMBER OF JOURNAL ENTRIES PER RECORD                 I
I  N2     .. NUMBER OF DIFFERENT ACCOUNT TYPES                    I
I  N3     .. TOTAL NUMBER OF ACCOUNTS                             I
I  N4     .. MAXIMUM NUMBER OF REFERENCES                         I
I  N5     .. MAX NUMBER OF ENTRIES PER REFERENCE                  I
I  N6     .. CONVERSION FACTOR FOR ARRAY POSITION                 I
I  N7     .. NUMBER OF RECORDS TO SKIP                            I
I  N9     .. NUMBER OF PERIODS TO COMPARE                         I
I  O      .. OPTION NUMBER                                        I
I  R$()   .. REFERENCE ARRAY OF JOURNAL NUMBERS                   I
I  R()    .. NUMERIC OF R$()                                      I
I  R1     .. NUMERIC REFERENCE NUMBER                             I
I  S$()   .. DEBIT OR CREDIT INDICATOR                            I
I  S1$    .. INPUT OF DEBIT/CREDIT INDICATOR                      I
I  T      .. SPACES TO TAB                                        I
I  T$()   .. NAME OF ACCOUNT TYPES                                I
I  V$()   .. VALUES APPLIED TO THE ACCOUNT                        I
I  V()    .. NUMERIC OF V$()                                      I
I  X      .. NUMBER OF RESERVED RECORDS                           I
I  X$     .. DUMMY (TEMP) VARIABLE                                I
I-----------------------------------------------------------------I
```

Creating and Initializing Files

Program Name: BCREATE

This program creates and initializes files for the bookkeeping system. It produces one file that is given the name specified during the program's operation. The program passes through the file twice, the first time to initialize the records and the second time to verify their creation and allow the entry of specific account names for each record.

Files Affected: Account file (created)

```
10 REM            SAVED AT BCREATE
20 REM    FILE CREATION PROGRAM FOR BOOKKEEPING
30 REM ****************************************************************
40 N1=15
50 X=9
60 C=X
70 N2=5
80 DIM R$(N1),V$(N1),T$(N2),NO(N2),S$(N1)
90 PRINT "BOOKKEEPING FILE CREATION PROGRAM"
100 PRINT
110 PRINT
120 PRINT "ENTER THE FILE NAME FOR THE FILE OF ACCOUNTS ";
130 INPUT F$
140 PRINT "ENTER TODAY'S DATE";
150 INPUT D1$
160 PRINT
170 FOR I=1 TO N2
180    READ T$(I)
190 NEXT I
200 DATA ASSETS,LIABILITIES,CAPITAL,INCOME,EXPENSES
210 PRINT "ENTER THE MAXIMUM NUMBER OF ACCOUNTS FOR EACH OF THE"
220 PRINT "FOLLOWING TYPES OF ACCOUNT CATEGORIES:"
230 PRINT
240 FOR I=1 TO N2
250    PRINT T$(I);".....";TAB(15);
260    INPUT NO(I)
270 NEXT I
280 GOSUB 710                     'FILE OPEN & DEFINE
290 REM  ****************** RECORD PROCESSING  ******************
300 FOR I=1 TO N2
310    FOR J=1 TO NO(I)
320       C=C+1
330       K=C
340       GOSUB 830                     'FILE WRITE
350    NEXT J
360 NEXT I
370 K9=K
380 GOSUB 900                     'ENTER NAME AND WRITE
390 REM ************* PROGRAM TERMINATION POINT  ***************
400 PRINT
410 FOR I= 1 TO N2
420    LSET R$(1)=MKI$(NO(I))
430    K=I+1
440    GOSUB 830                     'RECORD WRITE
450    LSET R$(1)=MKI$(0)
460 NEXT I
```

14   BASIC Computer Programs for Business

```
470 FOR I = N2+1 TO X-1
480    K=K+1
490    LSET D$="UNUSED"
500    GOSUB 850                    'RECORD WRITE
510 NEXT I
520 K=X
530 LSET D$="INCOME/EXPENSE SUM."
540 GOSUB 850                    'RECORD WRITE
550 FOR I=1 TO N2
560    LSET R$(3+I)=MKI$(NO(I))
570 NEXT I
580 K=1
590 LSET D$=D1$
600 LSET R$(1)=MKI$(X)
610 LSET R$(2)=MKI$(N2)
620 LSET R$(3)=MKI$(K9)
630 GOSUB 850                    'RECORD WRITE
640 PRINT "THE ACCOUNTS FILE - ";F$;" HAS BEEN CREATED"
650 PRINT
660 STOP


670 REM ***********************************************************
680 REM                    SUBROUTINES FOLLOW
690 REM ***********************************************************
700 REM *********** FILE OPEN AND DEFINITION ROUTINE  ***********
710 OPEN "R",1,F$,0
720 FIELD#1,19 AS D$
730 FOR I= 1 TO N1
740    FIELD#1,19+(I-1)*7AS X$,2 AS R$(I),1 AS S$(I),4 AS V$(I)
750    LSET R$(I)=MKI$(0)
760    LSET V$(I)=MKS$(0)
770    LSET S$(I)="X"
780 NEXT I
790 FIELD#1,124 AS X$,2 AS L$,2 AS N$
800 LSET L$=MKI$(0)
810 LSET N$=MKI$(0)
820 RETURN


830 REM *****************  FILE WRITE  RECORD#K  ******************
840 LSET D$=T$(I)
850 PUT#1,K
860 RETURN


870 REM ********************* FILE READ  RECORD#K  ***************
880 GET#1,K
890 RETURN


900 REM ***********  ENTER ACCOUNT DESCRIPTIONS  ****************
910 FOR K=X+1 TO K9
920    GOSUB 870                    'FILE WRITE
930    PRINT "ACCOUNT DESCRIPTION IS: ";D$
940    PRINT "ENTER ACCOUNT NAME";
950    INPUT D2$
960    LSET D$=D2$
970    GOSUB 850                    'FILE WRITE
980 NEXT K
990 RETURN
```

```
RUN "BCREATE"
BOOKKEEPING FILE CREATION PROGRAM


ENTER THE FILE NAME FOR THE FILE OF ACCOUNTS ? MY-BOOKS
ENTER TODAY'S DATE? JANUARY 1 1981

ENTER THE MAXIMUM NUMBER OF ACCOUNTS FOR EACH OF THE
FOLLOWING TYPES OF ACCOUNT CATEGORIES:

ASSETS.....     ? 3
LIABILITIES.....? 2
CAPITAL.....    ? 2
INCOME.....     ? 1
EXPENSES.....   ? 3
ACCOUNT DESCRIPTION IS: ASSETS
ENTER ACCOUNT NAME? CASH
ACCOUNT DESCRIPTION IS: ASSETS
ENTER ACCOUNT NAME? SUPPLIES
ACCOUNT DESCRIPTION IS: ASSETS
ENTER ACCOUNT NAME? EQUIPMENT
ACCOUNT DESCRIPTION IS: LIABILITIES
ENTER ACCOUNT NAME? ACCOUNTS PAYABLE
ACCOUNT DESCRIPTION IS: LIABILITIES
ENTER ACCOUNT NAME? NOTES PAYABLE
ACCOUNT DESCRIPTION IS: CAPITAL
ENTER ACCOUNT NAME? CAPITAL
ACCOUNT DESCRIPTION IS: CAPITAL
ENTER ACCOUNT NAME? DRAWING
ACCOUNT DESCRIPTION IS: INCOME
ENTER ACCOUNT NAME? FEE INCOME
ACCOUNT DESCRIPTION IS: EXPENSES
ENTER ACCOUNT NAME? RENT
ACCOUNT DESCRIPTION IS: EXPENSES
ENTER ACCOUNT NAME? SUPPLIES EXPENSE
ACCOUNT DESCRIPTION IS: EXPENSES
ENTER ACCOUNT NAME? TELEPHONE EXPENSE

THE ACCOUNTS FILE - MY-BOOKS HAS BEEN CREATED

BREAK IN 660
OK
```

Posting Journal Entries

Program Name: BPOST

This program allows the entry of journal transactions in the account file. Transactions can be entered from the journal in batches to increase operator efficiency. Multiple runs will not cause difficulties with the system's operation. Errors made during data entry can be corrected with program BPRINT.

Files Affected: Account file

```
10 REM              SAVED AT BPOST
20 REM      JOURNAL POSTING PROGRAM FOR BOOKKEEPING
30 REM ***********************************************************
40 N1=15
50 DIM R$(N1),V$(N1),S$(N1)
60 DIM R(N1),V(N1)
70 DIM T$(5),NO(5)
80 PRINT "ENTER THE FILE NAME OF THE ACCOUNTS FILE";
90 INPUT F$
100 GOSUB 660                    'OPEN FILES AND DEFINE
110 K=1
120 GOSUB 770                   'FILE READ
130 X=CVI(R$(1))
140 N2=CVI(R$(2))
150 K9=CVI(R$(3))
160 N3=X
170 PRINT
180 PRINT "DATE OF LAST FILE UPDATE WAS: ";D$
190 FOR K=2 TO N2+1
200    GOSUB 770                'FILE READ
210    NO(K-1)=CVI(R$(1))
220    N3=N3+NO(K-1)
230    T$(K-1)=D$
240 NEXT K
250 PRINT
260 PRINT "WOULD YOU LIKE AN ACCOUNTS LIST (Y OR N)";
270 INPUT A$
280 IF   A$="Y" THEN GOSUB 800           'ACCOUNT LIST
290 PRINT
300 PRINT "ENTER JOURNAL TRANSACTIONS IN THE FOLLOWING FORM:"
310 PRINT "JOURNAL NUMBER,D OR C (FOR DEBIT OR CREDIT),ACCOUNT NBR,AMOUNT"
320 PRINT
330 PRINT "      I.E.,     111,D,10,199.99"
340 PRINT "TO POST JOURNAL ENTRY 111 AS A DEBIT OF 199.99 AGAINST ACCOUNT 10"
350 PRINT
360 PRINT "A 0,0,0,0 ENTRY WILL TERMINATE THIS PROGRAM"
370 PRINT
380 PRINT "ENTER YOUR JOURNAL TRANSACTIONS NOW"
390 R1=0
400 INPUT R1,S1$,K,V1
410 IF R1=0 THEN 500
420 IF K>=X AND K<=N3 THEN 450
430 PRINT "INVALID ACCOUNT NUMBER  --  TRY AGAIN"
440 GOTO 390
450 IF S1$="D" OR S1$="C" THEN 480
460 PRINT "ENTER D FOR DEBIT  - OR- C FOR CREDIT     TRY AGAIN"
470 GOTO 390
480 GOSUB 990                    'POST THE TRANSACTION
```

```
490 GOTO 390
500 REM *************** PROGRAM TERMINATION POINT ***************
510 PRINT "ENTER TODAY'S DATE";
520 INPUT D1$
530 K=1
540 GOSUB 770                    'FILE READ
550 LSET D$=D1$
560 LSET R$(3)=MKI$(K9)
570 GOSUB 740                    'FILE WRITE
580 PRINT
590 PRINT
600 PRINT "PROCESSING COMPLETE"
610 PRINT
620 STOP


630 REM ***********************************************************
640 REM                 SUBROUTINES FOLLOW
650 REM ***********************************************************
660 REM *********** FILE OPEN AND DEFINITION ROUTINE  ***********
670 OPEN "R",1,F$,0
680 FIELD#1,19 AS D$
690 FOR I= 1 TO N1
700    FIELD#1,19+(I-1)*7 AS X$,2 AS R$(I),1 AS S$(I),4 AS V$(I)
710 NEXT I
720 FIELD#1,124 AS X$,2 AS L$,2 AS N$
730 RETURN


740 REM **************** FILE WRITE - RECORD#K   ****************
750 PUT#1,K
760 RETURN


770 REM ****************** FILE READ - RECORD#K  ***************
780 GET#1,K
790 RETURN


800 REM ****************** ACCOUNT LIST AREA    ******************
810 PRINT
820 PRINT TAB(4);"ACC #";TAB(12);"DESCRIPTION"
830 PRINT TAB(4);"-----";TAB(12);"-----------"
840 PRINT
850 K=X
860 GOSUB 770                    'FILE READ
870 PRINT TAB(5);K;TAB(12);D$
880 K=X+1
890 FOR I=1 TO N2
900    PRINT T$(I)
910    FOR J=1 TO NO(I)
920      GOSUB 770                'FILE READ
930      PRINT TAB(5);K;TAB(12);D$
940      K=K+1
950    NEXT J
960    PRINT
970 NEXT I
980 RETURN


990 REM ********************** POSTING AREA    ****************
1000 GOSUB 770                    'FILE READ
1010 FOR I=1 TO N1
1020    R(I)=CVI(R$(I))
1030    IF R(I)=0 THEN 1070
1040    V(I)=CVS(V$(I))
1050 NEXT I
1060 GOTO 1120
```

18   BASIC Computer Programs for Business

```
1070 LSET R$(I)=MKI$(R1)
1080 LSET S$(I)=S1$
1090 LSET V$(I)=MKS$(V1)
1100 N=0
1110 IF I<=N1 THEN 1170
1120 N=CVI(N$)
1130 IF N>0 THEN K=N
1140 IF N>0 THEN 1000
1150 K9=K9+1
1160 GOSUB 1230                    'INITIATE EXTENSION RECORD
1170 GOSUB 740                     'FILE WRITE
1180 IF N<=0 THEN 1220
1190 K=N
1200 GOSUB 770                     'READ FILE
1210 GOTO 1000
1220 RETURN

1230 REM ***************** INITIATE EXTENSION RECORD   *************
1240 GET#1,K9
1250 LSET L$=MKI$(K)
1260 LSET N$=MKI$(0)
1270 LSET D$="EXTENSION RECORD"
1280 FOR I=2 TO N1
1290    LSET R$(I)=MKI$(0)
1300    LSET V$(I)=MKS$(0)
1310 NEXT I
1320 LSET R$(1)=MKI$(R1)
1330 LSET S$(1)=S1$
1340 LSET V$(1)=MKS$(V1)
1350 PUT#1,K9
1360 GET#1,K
1370 LSET N$=MKI$(K9)
1380 RETURN
```

```
RUN "BPOST"
ENTER THE FILE NAME OF THE ACCOUNTS FILE? MY-BOOKS

DATE OF LAST FILE UPDATE WAS: JANUARY 1 1981

WOULD YOU LIKE AN ACCOUNTS LIST (Y OR N)? N

ENTER JOURNAL TRANSACTIONS IN THE FOLLOWING FORM:
JOURNAL NUMBER,D OR C (FOR DEBIT OR CREDIT),ACCOUNT NBR,AMOUNT

      I.E.,    111,D,10,199.99
TO POST JOURNAL ENTRY 111 AS A DEBIT OF 199.99 AGAINST ACCOUNT 10

A 0,0,0,0 ENTRY WILL TERMINATE THIS PROGRAM

ENTER YOUR JOURNAL TRANSACTIONS NOW
? 2,D,10,2000
? 2,C,15,2000
? 3,C,10,150
? 3,D,11,150
? 4,D,12,1000
? 4,C,13,1000
? 5,D,10,1250
? 5,C,17,1250
? 6,C,10,250
? 6,D,18,250
? 7,C,10,100
? 7,D,20,100
```

Simple Bookkeeping System   19

```
? 8,C,10,600
? 8,D,13,600
? 9,C,11,100
? 9,D,19,100
? 10,D,16,200
? 10,C,10,200
? 0,0,0,0
ENTER TODAY'S DATE? JANUARY 30 1981


PROCESSING COMPLETE

BREAK IN 620
OK
```

Trial Balance

Program Name: BTRIAL

This program produces a trial balance that allows you to reconcile accounts at month's end. Out-of-balance conditions, or other problems, can be diagnosed and corrected through the use of program BJOURNAL, which recreates all journal entries, or BPRINT, which displays and corrects individual accounts.

Files Affected: None

```
10 REM           SAVED AT BTRIAL
20 REM           PRODUCES TRIAL BALANCE
30 REM **************************************************************
40 N1=15
50 N5=5
60 DIM R$(N1),V$(N1),S$(N1)
70 DIM R(N1),V(N1)
80 DIM T$(5),NO(5)
90 PRINT "ENTER THE NAME OF THE ACCOUNTS FILE";
100 INPUT F$
110 GOSUB 360                    'OPEN FILES AND DEFINE
120 K=1
130 GOSUB 440                    'FILE READ
140 X=CVI(R$(1))
150 N2=CVI(R$(2))
160 N3=X
170 PRINT
180 PRINT "DATE OF FILES LAST UPDATE WAS ";D$
190 FOR K=2 TO N2+1
200    GOSUB 440                 'FILE READ
210    NO(K-1)=CVI(R$(1))
220    N3=N3+NO(K-1)
230    T$(K-1)=D$
240 NEXT K
250 PRINT
260 GOSUB 470                    'PREPARE TRIAL BALANCE
```

```
270 REM ********** PROGRAM TERMINATION POINT ********************
280 PRINT
290 PRINT
300 PRINT "PROCESSING COMPLETE"
310 PRINT
320 STOP


330 REM **************************************************************
340 REM            SUBROUTINES FOLLOW
350 REM **************************************************************
360 REM *********** FILE OPEN AND DEFINITION ROUTINE  ***********
370 OPEN "R",1,F$,0
380 FIELD#1,19 AS D$
390 FOR I= 1 TO N1
400    FIELD#1,19+(I-1)*7 AS X$,2 AS R$(I),1 AS S$(I),4 AS V$(I)
410 NEXT I
420 FIELD#1,124 AS X$,2 AS L$,2 AS N$
430 RETURN


440 REM ****************** FILE READ - RECORD#K  ***************
450 GET#1,K
460 RETURN


470 REM ********************* TRIAL BALANCE  ********************
480 PRINT "ENTER THE AS OF DATE FOR THE REPORT";
490 INPUT D3$
500 PRINT
510 PRINT "POSITION PAPER NOW - PRESS RETURN WHEN READY";
520 INPUT A$
530 PRINT
540 PRINT TAB(30);F$
550 PRINT TAB(30);"TRIAL BALANCE"
560 PRINT TAB(30);D3$
570 PRINT
580 PRINT
590 PRINT TAB(43);"D";TAB(53);"C"
600 PRINT
610 FOR I=X+1 TO N3
620    K=I
630    GOSUB 440               'FILE READ
640    IF K>N3 THEN LSET D$=D2$
650    FOR J=1 TO N1
660      R1=CVI(R$(J))
670      IF R1=0 THEN 720
680      V(0)=CVS(V$(J))
690      IF S$(J)="C" THEN CO=CO+V(0)
700      IF S$(J)="D" THEN DO=DO+V(0)
710    NEXT J
720    N=CVI(N$)
730    IF N<=0 THEN 770
740    D2$=D$
750    K=N
760    GOTO 630
770    AO=DO-CO
780    PRINT TAB(5);I;TAB(10);"- ";D$;
790    T=0
800    IF AO<=0 THEN T=10
810    A1=ABS(AO)
820    IF AO<0 THEN C1=C1+A1
830    IF AO>0 THEN D1=D1+A1
840    PRINT TAB(40+T);A1
850    CO=0
860    DO=0
870 NEXT I
880 PRINT TAB(38);"----------";TAB(48);"----------"
```

```
890 PRINT TAB(39);D1;TAB(49);C1
900 PRINT TAB(38);"=========";TAB(48);"========="
910 RETURN
```

```
RUN "BTRIAL"
ENTER THE NAME OF THE ACCOUNTS FILE? MY-BOOKS

DATE OF FILES LAST UPDATE WAS JANUARY 30 1981

ENTER THE AS OF DATE FOR THE REPORT? JANUARY 31 1981

POSITION PAPER NOW - PRESS RETURN WHEN READY?
```

```
                                   MY-BOOKS
                                   TRIAL BALANCE
                                   JANUARY 31 1981


                                           D          C

          10  - CASH                      1950
          11  - SUPPLIES                    50
          12  - EQUIPMENT                 1000
          13  - ACCOUNTS PAYABLE                      400
          14  - NOTES PAYABLE                           0
          15  - CAPITAL                              2000
          16  - DRAWING                    200
          17  - FEE INCOME                           1250
          18  - RENT                       250
          19  - SUPPLIES EXPENSE           100
          20  - TELEPHONE EXPENSE          100
                                       ---------- ----------
                                          3650       3650
                                       ========== ==========
```

```
PROCESSING COMPLETE

BREAK IN 290
OK
```

Income Statement

Program Name: BINCOME

This program produces an income statement of profit or loss for the accounting period. It queries income and expense accounts only. The results of this report are used as the basis for a journal entry that adjusts capital accounts for the revenue received, prior to the execution of program BSHEET.

Files Affected: None

```
10 REM           SAVED AT BINCOME
20 REM           PRODUCES INCOME STATEMENT
30 REM *******************************************************
40 N1=15
50 N5=5
60 DIM R$(N1),V$(N1),S$(N1)
70 DIM R(N1),V(N1)
80 DIM NO(5),T$(5)
90 PRINT "ENTER THE NAME OF THE ACCOUNTS FILE";
100 INPUT F$
110 GOSUB 360               'OPEN FILES AND DEFINE
120 K=1
130 GOSUB 440               'FILE READ
140 X=CVI(R$(1))
150 N2=CVI(R$(2))
160 N3=X
170 PRINT
180 PRINT "DATE OF FILES LAST UPDATE WAS ";D$
190 FOR K=2 TO N2+1
200    GOSUB 440            'FILE READ
210    NO(K-1)=CVI(R$(1))
220    N3=N3+NO(K-1)
230    T$(K-1)=D$
240 NEXT K
250 PRINT
260 GOSUB 470                      'PERFORM PROCESSING
270 REM *********** PROGRAM TERMINATION POINT ********************
280 PRINT
290 PRINT
300 PRINT "PROCESSING COMPLETE"
310 PRINT
320 STOP


330 REM *******************************************************
340 REM               SUBROUTINES FOLLOW
350 REM *******************************************************
360 REM *********** FILE OPEN AND DEFINITION ROUTINE  ***********
370 OPEN "R",1,F$,0
380 FIELD#1,19 AS D$
390 FOR I= 1 TO N1
400    FIELD#1,19+(I-1)*7 AS X$,2 AS R$(I),1 AS S$(I),4 AS V$(I)
410 NEXT I
420 FIELD#1,124 AS X$,2 AS L$,2 AS N$
430 RETURN
```

```
440 REM ****************** FILE READ - RECORD#K   ****************
450 GET#1,K
460 RETURN


470 REM ********************** INCOME STATEMENT   *****************
480 PRINT "ENTER THE REPORT PERIOD ";
490 INPUT D4$
500 PRINT
510 PRINT "POSITION PAPER NOW - PRESS RETURN WHEN READY";
520 INPUT A$
530 PRINT
540 PRINT TAB(30);F$
550 PRINT TAB(30);"INCOME STATEMENT"
560 PRINT TAB(30);D4$
570 PRINT
580 PRINT
590 N7=NO(1)+NO(2)+NO(3)
600 FOR J=4 TO 5
610   PRINT TAB(5);T$(J)
620   K1=X+1+N7
630   N7=N7+NO(J)
640   FOR I=K1 TO K1+NO(J)-1
650     K=I
660     GOSUB 440                          'FILE READ
670     IF K>N3 THEN LSET D$=D2$
680     FOR J1=1 TO N1
690       R1=CVI(R$(J1))
700       IF R1=0 THEN 750
710       V(0)=CVS(V$(J1))
720       IF S$(J1)="D" THEN A0=A0-V(0)
730       IF S$(J1)="C" THEN A0=A0+V(0)
740     NEXT J1
750     N=CVI(N$)
760     IF N<=0 THEN 800
770     D2$=D$
780     K=N
790     GOTO 660
800     PRINT TAB(10);I;"- ";D$;TAB(40);
810     IF J=5 THEN PRINT A0*(-1)
820     IF J<>5 THEN PRINT A0
830     A1=A1+A0
840     A0=0
850   NEXT I
860   PRINT TAB(38);"-------------"
870   PRINT TAB(5);"TOTAL ";T$(J);;TAB(50);
880   IF J=5 THEN PRINT A1*(-1)
890   IF J<>5 THEN PRINT A1
900   PRINT
910   A2=A2+A1
920   A1=0
930 NEXT J
940 PRINT TAB(48);"----------------"
950 PRINT TAB(5);"NET INCOME(LOSS)";TAB(50);
960 IF A2>0 THEN PRINT A2
970 IF A2<0 THEN PRINT "(";A2;")"
980 PRINT TAB(48);"================"
990 RETURN


RUN "BINCOME"
ENTER THE NAME OF THE ACCOUNTS FILE? MY-BOOKS

DATE OF FILES LAST UPDATE WAS JANUARY 30 1981

ENTER THE REPORT PERIOD ? JANUARY 1981

POSITION PAPER NOW - PRESS RETURN WHEN READY?
```

24   BASIC Computer Programs for Business

```
                              MY-BOOKS
                          INCOME STATEMENT
                          JANUARY 1981


       INCOME
             17 - FEE INCOME              1250
                                     -------------
       TOTAL INCOME                                  1250

       EXPENSES
             18 - RENT                     250
             19 - SUPPLIES EXPENSE         100
             20 - TELEPHONE EXPENSE        100
                                     -------------
       TOTAL EXPENSES                               450


                                     ----------------
       NET INCOME(LOSS)                            800
                                     ================


PROCESSING COMPLETE

BREAK IN 320
OK
```

Balance Sheet

Program Name: BSHEET

This program produces a balance sheet at the end of each accounting period. A journal entry that updates capital accounts for net profit or loss is required to insure proper balancing of assets, liabilities, and capital accounts.

Files Affected: None

```
10 REM            SAVED AT BSHEET
20 REM            PRODUCES BALANCE SHEET
30 REM ********************************************************
40 N1=15
50 N5=5
60 DIM R$(N1),V$(N1),S$(N1)
70 DIM R(N1),V(N1)
80 DIM T$(5),NO(5)
90 PRINT "ENTER THE NAME OF THE ACCOUNTS FILE";
100 INPUT F$
110 GOSUB 350               'OPEN FILES AND DEFINE
120 K=1
130 GOSUB 430               'FILE READ
140 X=CVI(R$(1))
150 N2=CVI(R$(2))
```

```
 160 N3=X
 170 PRINT
 180 PRINT "DATE OF FILES LAST UPDATE WAS ";D$
 190 FOR K=2 TO N2+1
 200    GOSUB 430                      'FILE READ
 210    N0(K-1)=CVI(R$(1))
 220    N3=N3+N0(K-1)
 230    T$(K-1)=D$
 240 NEXT K
 250 PRINT
 260 GOSUB 460                         'PREPARE BALANCE SHEET
 270 PRINT
 280 PRINT
 290 PRINT "PROCESSING COMPLETE"
 300 PRINT
 310 STOP


 320 REM ***********************************************************
 330 REM                    SUBROUTINES FOLLOW
 340 REM ***********************************************************
 350 REM *********** FILE OPEN AND DEFINITION ROUTINE  ************
 360 OPEN "R",1,F$,0
 370 FIELD#1,19 AS D$
 380 FOR I= 1 TO N1
 390    FIELD#1,19+(I-1)*7 AS X$,2 AS R$(I),1 AS S$(I),4 AS V$(I)
 400 NEXT I
 410 FIELD#1,124 AS X$,2 AS L$,2 AS N$
 420 RETURN


 430 REM ****************** FILE READ - RECORD#K  ****************
 440 GET#1,K
 450 RETURN


 460 REM *************** BALANCE SHEET  *************************
 470 PRINT "ENTER THE REPORT DATE ";
 480 INPUT D4$
 490 PRINT
 500 PRINT "POSITION PAPER NOW - PRESS RETURN WHEN READY";
 510 INPUT A$
 520 PRINT
 530 PRINT TAB(30);F$
 540 PRINT TAB(30);"BALANCE SHEET"
 550 PRINT TAB(30);D4$
 560 PRINT
 570 PRINT
 580 T=50
 590 FOR J=1 TO 3
 600    IF J=1 THEN PRINT TAB(30);T$(1)
 610    IFJ<>2 THEN 650
 620    T=40
 630    PRINT TAB(25);"LIABILITIES AND CAPITAL"
 640    A2=0
 650    PRINT
 660    PRINT TAB(5);T$(J)
 670    K1=X+1+N7
 680    N7=N7+N0(J)
 690    FOR I=K1 TO K1+N0(J)-1
 700      K=I
 710      GOSUB 430
 720      IF K>N3 THEN LSET D$=D2$
 730      FOR J1=1 TO N1
 740        R1=CVI(R$(J1))
 750        IF R1=0 THEN 800
 760        V(0)=CVS(V$(J1))
 770        IF S$(J1)="C" THEN A0=A0-V(0)
```

```
780      IF S$(J1)="D" THEN A0=A0+V(0)
790    NEXT J1
800    N=CVI(N$)
810    IF N<=0 THEN 850
820    D2$=D$
830    K=N
840    GOTO 710
850    IF J>1 THEN A0=A0*(-1)
860    PRINT TAB(10);I;"- ";D$;TAB(T);A0
870    A1=A1+A0
880    A0=0
890    NEXT I
900    PRINT TAB(T-2);"----------------"
910    PRINT TAB(5);"TOTAL ";T$(J);;TAB(50);A1
920    IF J=1 THEN PRINT TAB(48);"================"
930    PRINT
940    A2=A2+A1
950    A1=0
960  NEXT J
970  PRINT TAB(48);"----------------"
980  PRINT TAB(5);"TOTAL LIABILITIES AND CAPITAL";TAB(50);A2
990  PRINT TAB(48);"================"
1000 RETURN
```

```
RUN "BPOST"
ENTER THE FILE NAME OF THE ACCOUNTS FILE? MY-BOOKS

DATE OF LAST FILE UPDATE WAS: JANUARY 30 1981

WOULD YOU LIKE AN ACCOUNTS LIST (Y OR N)? N

ENTER JOURNAL TRANSACTIONS IN THE FOLLOWING FORM:
JOURNAL NUMBER,D OR C (FOR DEBIT OR CREDIT),ACCOUNT NBR,AMOUNT

        I.E.,     111,D,10,199.99
TO POST JOURNAL ENTRY 111 AS A DEBIT OF 199.99 AGAINST ACCOUNT 10

A 0,0,0,0 ENTRY WILL TERMINATE THIS PROGRAM

ENTER YOUR JOURNAL TRANSACTIONS NOW
? 11,D,9,800
? 11,C,15,800
? 0,0,0,0
ENTER TODAY'S DATE? JANUARY 31 1981


PROCESSING COMPLETE

BREAK IN 620
OK




RUN "BSHEET"
ENTER THE NAME OF THE ACCOUNTS FILE? MY-BOOKS

DATE OF FILES LAST UPDATE WAS JANUARY 31 1981

ENTER THE REPORT DATE ? JANUARY 31 1981

POSITION PAPER NOW - PRESS RETURN WHEN READY?
```

```
                              MY-BOOKS
                              BALANCE SHEET
                              JANUARY 31 1981


                                   ASSETS

          ASSETS
                  10 - CASH                              1950
                  11 - SUPPLIES                          50
                  12 - EQUIPMENT                         1000
                                                    ------------------
          TOTAL ASSETS                                   3000
                                                    ==================

                        LIABILITIES AND CAPITAL

          LIABILITIES
                  13 - ACCOUNTS PAYABLE         400
                  14 - NOTES PAYABLE            0
                                           ------------------
          TOTAL LIABILITIES                            400


          CAPITAL
                  15 - CAPITAL                  2800
                  16 - DRAWING                  -200
                                           ------------------
          TOTAL CAPITAL                                2600


                                                   ------------------
          TOTAL LIABILITIES AND CAPITAL            3000
                                                   ==================


     PROCESSING COMPLETE

     BREAK IN 310
     OK
```

Closing Accounts

Program Name: BCLOSE

  This program closes accounts at the end of the accounting period and provides a "post closing trial balance." It does *not* provide closing entries for the adjustment of accounts. It totals each asset, liability, and capital account and enters a journal reference entry of 1 that contains the balance of the account at the beginning of the next accounting period. Income and expense accounts are totaled, and a journal reference 1 entry is provided that has a transaction type of "*". These entries are preserved in the record for later use in BCOMP for the comparison of different accounting periods. The "*" entries are ignored for normal bookkeeping operations but continue to be maintained throughout the life of the accounts file.

Files Affected: Account file

```
10 REM           SAVED AT BCLOSE
20 REM           CLOSES MONTHLY ACCOUNTS
30 REM ****************************************************
40 N1=15
50 N5=5
60 DIM R$(N1),V$(N1),S$(N1)
70 DIM R(N1),V(N1)
80 DIM T$(5),NO(5)
90 PRINT "ENTER THE NAME OF THE ACCOUNTS FILE";
100 INPUT F$
110 GOSUB 410                  'OPEN FILES AND DEFINE
120 K=1
130 GOSUB 520                  'FILE READ
140 X=CVI(R$(1))
150 N2=CVI(R$(2))
160 N3=X
170 PRINT
180 PRINT "DATE OF FILES LAST UPDATE WAS ";D$
190 FOR K=2 TO N2+1
200    GOSUB 520               'FILE READ
210    NO(K-1)=CVI(R$(1))
220    N3=N3+NO(K-1)
230    T$(K-1)=D$
240 NEXT K
250 PRINT
260 GOSUB 550
270 PRINT                      'CLOSE OUT
280 K=1
290 GOSUB 520                  'READ FILE
300 LSET R$(3)=MKI$(N3)
310 LSET D$=D3$
320 GOSUB 490                  'FILE   WRITE
330 REM ********** PROGRAM TERMINATION POINT **********************
340 PRINT
350 PRINT "PROCESSING COMPLETE"
360 PRINT
370 STOP
```

```
380 REM ***********************************************************
390 REM                    SUBROUTINES FOLLOW
400 REM ***********************************************************
410 REM *********** FILE OPEN AND DEFINITION ROUTINE  ************
420 OPEN "R",1,F$,0
430 FIELD#1,19 AS D$
440 FOR I= 1 TO N1
450    FIELD#1,19+(I-1)*7 AS X$,2 AS R$(I),1 AS S$(I),4 AS V$(I)
460 NEXT I
470 FIELD#1,124 AS X$,2 AS L$,2 AS N$
480 RETURN


490 REM *************** FILE WRITE - RECORD#K   ****************
500 PUT#1,K
510 RETURN


520 REM ****************** FILE READ - RECORD#K   ***************
530 GET#1,K
540 RETURN


550 REM *************** CLOSE OUT MONTHLY FILES  ****************
560 PRINT "ENTER TODAYS DATE"
570 INPUT D3$
580 PRINT
590 PRINT "POSITION PAPER NOW - PRESS RETURN WHEN READY";
600 INPUT A$
610 PRINT
620 PRINT TAB(30);F$
630 PRINT TAB(25);"POST CLOSING TRIAL BALANCE"
640 PRINT TAB(30);D3$
650 PRINT
660 PRINT
670 PRINT TAB(43);"D";TAB(53);"C"
680 PRINT
690 N7=N0(1)+N0(2)+N0(3)+X+1
700 FOR I=X+1 TO N3
710    K=I
720    GOSUB 520                    'FILE READ
730    IF K>N3 THEN LSET D$=D2$
740    FOR J=1 TO N1
750      R1=CVI(R$(J))
760      IF R1=0 THEN 810
770      V(0)=CVS(V$(J))
780      IF S$(J)="C" THEN CO=CO+V(0)
790      IF S$(J)="D" THEN DO=DO+V(0)
800    NEXT J
810    N=CVI(N$)
820    IF N<=0 THEN 860
830    D2$=D$
840    K=N
850    GOTO 720
860    AO=DO-CO
870    T=0
880    IF AO<=0 THEN T=10
890    A1=ABS(AO)
900    IF AO<0 THEN C1=C1+A1
910    IF AO>0 THEN D1=D1+A1
920    IF I<N7 THEN GOSUB 1010        'RESET RECORDS
930    IF I=N7 THEN GOSUB 1150        'HEADINGS AND E/I SUMMARY
940    IF I>N7 THEN GOSUB 1200        'EXP/INC SUMMARY
950    PRINT TAB(5);I;TAB(10);"- ";D$;
960    PRINT TAB(40+T);A1
970    CO=0
980    DO=0
990 NEXT I
1000 RETURN
```

```
1010 REM ************************* RESET RECORD   *****************
1020 LSET S$(1)="D"
1030 IF A0<0 THEN LSET S$(1)="C"
1040 LSET R$(1)=MKI$(1)
1050 LSET V$(1)=MKS$(A1)
1060 FOR I1=2 TO N1
1070   LSET R$(I1)=MKI$(0)
1080   LSET V$(I1)=MKS$(0)
1090   LSET S$(I1)=" "
1100 NEXT I1
1110 LSET N$=MKI$(0)
1120 LSET L$=MKI$(0)
1130 GOSUB 490               'FILE WRITE
1140 RETURN


1150 REM *************    PRINT HEADING   ************************
1160 PRINT
1170 PRINT TAB(25);"EXPENSE AND INCOME SUMMARY  "
1180 PRINT TAB(30);"LAST PERIOD"
1190 PRINT


1200 REM *************  RESET EXPENSE AND INCOME RECORDS *********
1210 FOR I1=1 TO N1
1220   IF S$(I1)="*" THEN GOTO 1350
1230   LSET S$(I1)="*"
1240   LSET R$(I1)=MKI$(1)
1250   LSET V$(I1)=MKS$(A0)
1260   IF I1=N1 THEN 1320
1270   FOR I2=I1+1 TO N1
1280     LSET S$(I2)=" "
1290     LSET R$(I2)=MKI$(0)
1300     LSET V$(I2)=MKS$(0)
1310   NEXT I2
1320   LSET N$=MKI$(0)
1330   LSET L$=MKI$(0)
1340   GOTO 1360
1350 NEXT I1
1360 GOSUB 490               'FILE WRITE
1370 RETURN
```

```
RUN "BCLOSE"
ENTER THE NAME OF THE ACCOUNTS FILE? MY-BOOKS

DATE OF FILES LAST UPDATE WAS JANUARY 31 1981

ENTER TODAYS DATE
? FEBRUARY 1 1981

POSITION PAPER NOW - PRESS RETURN WHEN READY?


                    MY-BOOKS
             POST CLOSING TRIAL BALANCE
                 FEBRUARY 1 1981


                              D          C

    10  - CASH              1950
    11  - SUPPLIES            50
    12  - EQUIPMENT         1000
```

Simple Bookkeeping System   31

```
     13  -  ACCOUNTS PAYABLE                              400
     14  -  NOTES PAYABLE                                 0
     15  -  CAPITAL                                       2800
     16  -  DRAWING                           200
```

```
                    EXPENSE AND INCOME SUMMARY
                          LAST PERIOD

     17  -  FEE INCOME                                    1250
     18  -  RENT                              250
     19  -  SUPPLIES EXPENSE                  100
     20  -  TELEPHONE EXPENSE                 100


PROCESSING COMPLETE

BREAK IN 370
OK
```

Account File Print

Program Name: BFLIST

   This program provides a list of the current file's contents. It is an unformatted list that can be used to diagnose unexpected data entry difficulties occurring during the system's operation. "X" transaction codes indicate that the entry area does not contain current data.

Files Affected: None

```
10 REM           SAVED AT BFLIST
20 REM           LISTS ACCOUNT FILE
30 REM ***********************************************************
40 N1=15
50 N5=5
60 DIM R$(N1),V$(N1),S$(N1)
70 DIM R(N1),V(N1)
80 DIM T$(5),NO(5)
90 PRINT "ENTER THE NAME OF THE ACCOUNTS FILE";
100 INPUT F$
110 GOSUB 490                       'OPEN FILES AND DEFINE
120 K=1
130 GOSUB 570                       'FILE READ
140 X=CVI(R$(1))
150 N2=CVI(R$(2))
160 N3=X
170 PRINT
180 PRINT "DATE OF FILES LAST UPDATE WAS ";D$
190 FOR K=2 TO N2+1
200    GOSUB 570                    'FILE READ
210    NO(K-1)=CVI(R$(1))
220    N3=N3+NO(K-1)
230    T$(K-1)=D$
240 NEXT K
```

```
250 PRINT
260 FOR J=1 TO N3
270    K=J
280    GOSUB 570                    'FILE READ
290    PRINT
300    PRINT "********************  RECORD";K;"********************"
310    PRINT D$;
320    FOR I=1 TO N1
330      R(I)=CVI(R$(I))
340      V(I)=CVS(V$(I))
350      PRINT R(I);S$(I);V(I);
360    NEXT I
370    L=CVI(L$)
380    N=CVI(N$)
390    PRINT L;R
400    IF N<=0 THEN 430
410    K=N
420    GOTO 280
430 NEXT J
440 REM ********** PROGRAM TERMINATION POINT *********************
450 PRINT
460 PRINT "PROCESSING COMPLETE"
470 PRINT
480 STOP


490 REM ************ FILE OPEN AND DEFINITION ROUTINE  ************
500 OPEN "R",1,F$,0
510 FIELD#1,19 AS D$
520 FOR I= 1 TO N1
530   FIELD#1,19+(I-1)*7 AS X$,2 AS R$(I),1 AS S$(I),4 AS V$(I)
540 NEXT I
550 FIELD#1,124 AS X$,2 AS L$,2 AS N$
560 RETURN


570 REM ******************  FILE READ - RECORD#K  ****************
580 GET#1,K
590 RETURN




RUN "BFLIST"
ENTER THE NAME OF THE ACCOUNTS FILE? MY-BOOKS

DATE OF FILES LAST UPDATE WAS FEBRUARY 1 1981


********************  RECORD 1 ************************
FEBRUARY 1 1981     9 X 0  5 X 0  20 X 0  3 X 0  2 X 0  2 X 0  1 X 0  3 X 0  0 X
 0   0 X 0  0 X 0  0 X 0  0 X 0  0 X 0  0 X 0  0  0

********************  RECORD 2 ************************
ASSETS              3 X 0  0 X 0  0 X 0  0 X 0  0 X 0  0 X 0  0 X 0  0 X 0  0 X
 0   0 X 0  0 X 0  0 X 0  0 X 0  0 X 0  0 X 0  0  0

********************  RECORD 3 ************************
LIABILITIES         2 X 0  0 X 0  0 X 0  0 X 0  0 X 0  0 X 0  0 X 0  0 X 0  0 X
 0   0 X 0  0 X 0  0 X 0  0 X 0  0 X 0  0 X 0  0  0

********************  RECORD 4 ************************
CAPITAL             2 X 0  0 X 0  0 X 0  0 X 0  0 X 0  0 X 0  0 X 0  0 X 0  0 X
 0   0 X 0  0 X 0  0 X 0  0 X 0  0 X 0  0 X 0  0  0

********************  RECORD 5 ************************
INCOME              1 X 0  0 X 0  0 X 0  0 X 0  0 X 0  0 X 0  0 X 0  0 X 0  0 X
 0   0 X 0  0 X 0  0 X 0  0 X 0  0 X 0  0 X 0  0  0
```

Simple Bookkeeping System   33

```
******************** RECORD 6 ************************
EXPENSES              3 X 0  0 X 0  0 X 0  0 X 0  0 X 0  0 X 0  0 X 0  0 X 0  0 X
 0  0 X 0  0 X 0  0 X 0  0 X 0  0 X 0  0 X 0  0 0

******************** RECORD 7 ************************
UNUSED                  0 X 0  0 X 0  0 X 0  0 X 0  0 X 0  0 X 0  0 X 0  0 X 0  0 X
 0  0 X 0  0 X 0  0 X 0  0 X 0  0 X 0  0 X 0  0 0

******************** RECORD 8 ************************
UNUSED                  0 X 0  0 X 0  0 X 0  0 X 0  0 X 0  0 X 0  0 X 0  0 X 0  0 X
 0  0 X 0  0 X 0  0 X 0  0 X 0  0 X 0  0 X 0  0 0

******************** RECORD 9 ************************
INCOME/EXPENSE SUM. 11 D 800  0 X 0  0 X 0  0 X 0  0 X 0  0 X 0  0 X 0  0 X 0
 0 X 0  0 X 0  0 X 0  0 X 0  0 X 0  0 X 0  0 X 0  0 0

******************** RECORD 10 ************************
CASH                  1 D 1950  0    0 0  0 0  0 0   0 0   0 0   0 0   0 0   0
 0    0    0 0   0 0    0 0   0 0   0 0   0 0 0

******************** RECORD 11 ************************
SUPPLIES              1 D 50   0    0 0  0 0   0 0   0 0   0 0   0 0   0 0   0  0
 0    0    0 0   0 0   0 0   0 0   0 0 0

******************** RECORD 12 ************************
EQUIPMENT             1 D 1000  0    0 0   0 0   0 0   0 0   0 0   0 0   0 0   0
 0    0    0 0   0 0   0 0   0 0   0 0 0

******************** RECORD 13 ************************
ACCOUNTS PAYABLE      1 C 400  0    0 0   0 0   0 0   0 0   0 0   0 0   0 0   0 0
 0    0    0 0   0 0   0 0   0 0   0 0 0

******************** RECORD 14 ************************
NOTES PAYABLE         1 D 0    0 0   0 0   0 0   0 0   0 0   0 0   0 0   0 0   0 0
 0    0    0 0   0 0   0 0   0 0   0 0 0

******************** RECORD 15 ************************
CAPITAL               1 C 2800  0    0 0   0 0   0 0   0 0   0 0   0 0   0 0   0
 0    0    0 0   0 0   0 0   0 0   0 0 0

******************** RECORD 16 ************************
DRAWING               1 D 200  0    0 0   0 0   0 0   0 0   0 0   0 0   0 0   0 0
 0    0    0 0   0 0   0 0   0 0   0 0 0

******************** RECORD 17 ************************
FEE INCOME            1 *-1250  0    0 0   0 0   0 0   0 0   0 0   0 0   0 0   0 0
 0    0    0 0   0 0   0 0   0 0   0 0 0

******************** RECORD 18 ************************
RENT                  1 * 250  0    0 0   0 0   0 0   0 0   0 0   0 0   0 0   0 0
 0    0    0 0   0 0   0 0   0 0   0 0 0

******************** RECORD 19 ************************
SUPPLIES EXPENSE      1 * 100  0    0 0   0 0   0 0   0 0   0 0   0 0   0 0   0 0
 0    0    0 0   0 0   0 0   0 0   0 0 0

******************** RECORD 20 ************************
TELEPHONE EXPENSE     1 * 100  0    0 0   0 0   0 0   0 0   0 0   0 0   0 0   0 0
 0    0    0 0   0 0   0 0   0 0   0 0 0

PROCESSING COMPLETE

BREAK IN 480
OK
```

Account Displaying and Correcting

Program Name: BPRINT

This program has four options useful to the bookkeeper:

Option 1 produces a formatted list of account numbers and associated names.

Option 2 produces a display of a specific account in the form of a "T account." Each journal entry is printed on the appropriate (debit or credit) side of the account with its journal reference number.

Option 3 prints a list of all journal entries for the account in a report format (with headings). The individual entries can be changed selectively by the operator. Note that a reference number of 0 will cause the entry to be deleted. If there are extension records for the account, they will also be displayed and can be corrected.

Option 4 allows the operator to change the account name of specified accounts.

Files Affected: Account file

```
10 REM            SAVED AT BPRINT
20 REM            DISPLAYS AND CORRECTS RECORDS
30 REM **************************************************************
40 N1=15
50 DIM R$(N1),V$(N1),S$(N1)
60 DIM R(N1),V(N1)
70 DIM T$(5),NO(5)
80 PRINT "ENTER THE FILE NAME OF THE ACCOUNTS FILE";
90 INPUT F$
100 GOSUB 460                    'OPEN FILES AND DEFINE
110 K=1
120 GOSUB 570                    'FILE READ
130 X=CVI(R$(1))
140 N2=CVI(R$(2))
150 PRINT
160 PRINT "DATE OF FILES LAST UPDATE WAS ";D$
170 FOR K=2 TO N2+1
180    GOSUB 570                 'FILE READ
190    NO(K-1)=CVI(R$(1))
200    T$(K-1)=D$
210 NEXT K
220 PRINT
230 REM **************** CHOICE OF PROCESSING OPTIONS  ***********
240 PRINT "THE FOLLOWING OPTIONS ARE AVAILABLE:"
250 PRINT
260 REM *********** PROGRAM TERMINATION POINT ********************
270 PRINT TAB(5);1;".....ACCOUNT NUMBER/DESCRIPTION LIST"
280 PRINT TAB(5);2;".....ACCOUNT DISPLAY"
290 PRINT TAB(5);3;".....CORRECT ACCOUNT"
300 PRINT TAB(5);4;".....ENTER ACCOUNT DESCRIPTIONS"
310 PRINT
320 PRINT "ENTER THE OPTION DESIRED";
330 INPUT O
340 IF O=1 THEN GOSUB 600        'ACCOUNT LIST
350 IF O=2 THEN GOSUB 790        'ACCOUNT DISPLAY
360 IF O=3 THEN GOSUB 1000       'DISPLAY ACCOUNT
```

```
370 IF O=4 THEN GOSUB 1370            'ENTER ACCOUNT DESC
380 PRINT
390 PRINT
400 PRINT "PROCESSING COMPLETE"
410 PRINT
420 STOP


430 REM ****************************************************************
440 REM                 SUBROUTINES FOLLOW
450 REM ****************************************************************
460 REM ******** FILE OPEN AND DEFINITION ROUTINE  ************
470 OPEN "R",1,F$,0
480 FIELD#1,19 AS D$
490 FOR I= 1 TO N1
500   FIELD#1,19+(I-1)*7 AS X$,2 AS R$(I),1 AS S$(I),4 AS V$(I)
510 NEXT I
520 FIELD#1,124 AS X$,2 AS L$,2 AS N$
530 RETURN


540 REM **************** FILE WRITE - RECORD#K   ****************
550 PUT#1,K
560 RETURN


570 REM ****************** FILE READ - RECORD#K  ****************
580 GET#1,K
590 RETURN


600 REM ****************** ACCOUNT LIST AREA   ******************
610 PRINT
620 PRINT TAB(4);"ACC #";TAB(12);"DESCRIPTION"
630 PRINT TAB(4);"-----";TAB(12);"-----------"
640 PRINT
650 K=X
660 GOSUB 570                    'FILE READ
670 PRINT TAB(5);K;TAB(12);D$
680 K=X+1
690 FOR I=1 TO N2
700   PRINT T$(I)
710   FOR J=1 TO NO(I)
720     GOSUB 570                'FILE READ
730     PRINT TAB(5);K;TAB(12);D$
740     K=K+1
750   NEXT J
760   PRINT
770 NEXT I
780 RETURN


790 REM ********************** ACCOUNT DISPLAY  ******************
800 PRINT "ENTER THE ACCOUNT NUMBER TO BE DISPLAYED";
810 INPUT K
820 PRINT
830 GOSUB 570                    'FILE READ
840 PRINT TAB(30);D$
850 PRINT "----------------------------I---------------------"
860 PRINT TAB(10);"REF";TAB(23);"AMT";TAB(33);"I";TAB(38);"REF";TAB(51);"AMT"
870 FOR  I=1 TO N1
880   R(I)=CVI(R$(I))
890   IF R(I)=0 THEN 930
900   V(I)=CVS(V$(I))
910   IF S$(I)="D" THEN PRINT  TAB(10);R(I);TAB(20);V(I);TAB(33);"I"
920   IF S$(I)="C" THEN PRINT TAB(33);"I";TAB(38);R(I);TAB(48);V(I)
930 NEXT I
940 N=CVI(N$)
```

```
950 IF N<=0 THEN 990
960 K=N
970 GOSUB 570                    'READ FILE
980 GOTO 870
990 RETURN


1000 REM ********************** CORRECT ACCOUNT   ********************
1010 PRINT "ENTER THE ACCOUNT NUMBER TO BE CORRECTED";
1020 INPUT K
1030 GOSUB 570                    'FILE READ
1040 PRINT
1050 PRINT "ACCOUNT NAME: ";D$
1060 PRINT
1070 PRINT "ITEM";TAB(6);"REF";TAB(11);"D/C";TAB(16);"AMT"
1080 PRINT "----";TAB(6);"----";TAB(11);"---";TAB(16);"-------"
1090 FOR I=1 TO N1
1100   R(I)=CVI(R$(I))
1110   IF R(I)=0 THEN 1140
1120   V(I)=CVS(V$(I))
1130   PRINT I;TAB(5);R(I);TAB(12);S$(I);TAB(15);V(I)
1140 NEXT I
1150 N=CVI(N$)
1160 IF N>0 THEN PRINT "**** CONTINUED ****"
1170 PRINT
1180 PRINT "DO YOU WISH TO CORRECT ANY ENTRIES (Y OR N)";
1190 INPUT A$
1200 IF A$<>"Y" THEN 1320
1210 PRINT "ENTER THE ITEM NUMBER TO CORRECT";
1220 INPUT IO
1230 PRINT "ENTER THE REFERENCE NUMBER, D OR C, AND AMOUNT";
1240 INPUT R(IO),SO$(IO),V(IO)
1250 LSET R$(IO)=MKI$(R(IO))
1260 LSET S$(IO)=SO$(IO)
1270 LSET V$(IO)=MKS$(V(IO))
1280 PRINT "ANY OTHER CORRECTIONS (Y OR N)";
1290 INPUT A$
1300 IF A$="Y" THEN 1210
1310 GOSUB 540                    'FILE WRITE
1320 IF N<=0 THEN 1360
1330 K=N
1340 GOSUB 570                    'READ FILE
1350 GOTO  1060
1360 RETURN


1370 REM **********  ENTER ACCOUNT DESCRIPTIONS   *****************
1380 PRINT
1390 PRINT "ENTER ACCOUNT NUMBER ";
1400 INPUT K
1410 GOSUB  570                   'FILE READ
1420 PRINT "ACCOUNT DESCRIPTION IS: ";D$
1430 PRINT "ENTER NEW ACCOUNT NAME";
1440 INPUT D2$
1450 LSET D$=D2$
1460 GOSUB 540                    'FILE WRITE
1470 PRINT "ANY MORE ENTRIES (Y OR N)";
1480 INPUT A$
1490 IF A$="Y" THEN 1380
1500 RETURN
```

```
RUN 'BPRINT'
ENTER THE FILE NAME OF THE ACCOUNTS FILE? MY-BOOKS

DATE OF FILES LAST UPDATE WAS JANUARY 30 1981

THE FOLLOWING OPTIONS ARE AVAILABLE:

        1 .....ACCOUNT NUMBER/DESCRIPTION LIST
        2 .....ACCOUNT DISPLAY
        3 .....CORRECT ACCOUNT
        4 .....ENTER ACCOUNT DESCRIPTIONS

ENTER THE OPTION DESIRED? 2
ENTER THE ACCOUNT NUMBER TO BE DISPLAYED? 10
                              CASH
    -------------------------------I-------------------------------
        REF         AMT        I    REF            AMT
         2         2000        I
                               I     3            150
         5         1250        I
                               I     6            250
                               I     7            100
                               I     8            600
                               I    10            200


PROCESSING COMPLETE

BREAK IN 420
OK
```

```
RUN 'BPRINT'
ENTER THE FILE NAME OF THE ACCOUNTS FILE? MY-BOOKS

DATE OF FILES LAST UPDATE WAS FEBRUARY 1 1981

THE FOLLOWING OPTIONS ARE AVAILABLE:

        1 .....ACCOUNT NUMBER/DESCRIPTION LIST
        2 .....ACCOUNT DISPLAY
        3 .....CORRECT ACCOUNT
        4 .....ENTER ACCOUNT DESCRIPTIONS

ENTER THE OPTION DESIRED? 1

    ACC #    DESCRIPTION
    -----    -----------

      9      INCOME/EXPENSE SUM.
ASSETS
     10      CASH
     11      SUPPLIES
     12      EQUIPMENT

LIABILITIES
     13      ACCOUNTS PAYABLE
     14      NOTES PAYABLE

CAPITAL
     15      CAPITAL
     16      DRAWING
```

```
INCOME
      17    FEE INCOME

EXPENSES
      18    RENT
      19    SUPPLIES EXPENSE
      20    TELEPHONE EXPENSE


PROCESSING COMPLETE

BREAK IN 420
OK
```

```
RUN 'BPRINT'
ENTER THE FILE NAME OF THE ACCOUNTS FILE? MY-BOOKS

DATE OF FILES LAST UPDATE WAS FEBRUARY 1 1981

THE FOLLOWING OPTIONS ARE AVAILABLE:

      1 .....ACCOUNT NUMBER/DESCRIPTION LIST
      2 .....ACCOUNT DISPLAY
      3 .....CORRECT ACCOUNT
      4 .....ENTER ACCOUNT DESCRIPTIONS

ENTER THE OPTION DESIRED? 2
ENTER THE ACCOUNT NUMBER TO BE DISPLAYED? 10

                             CASH
-----------------------------------I-----------------------------
      REF          AMT       I    REF          AMT
       1          1950       I
                             I


PROCESSING COMPLETE

BREAK IN 420
OK
```

Journal Print

Program Name: BJOURNAL

This program recreates the journal entries that were entered in the accounts file. The entries are printed in a formatted way that facilitates comparison with the actual journal. There are two options available to the user:

Option 1 produces a report indicating the starting and ending journal reference numbers that have been entered.

Option 2 produces the output of option 1 plus the journal reference listing.

Files Affected: None

```
10 REM            SAVED AT BJOURNAL
20 REM            PRINTS JOURNAL ENTRIES
30 REM ***********************************************************************
40 N1=15
50 M1=999999
60 M2=0
70 N5=5
80 DIM R$(N1),V$(N1),S$(N1)
90 DIM R(N1),V(N1)
100 DIM T$(5),NO(5)
110 PRINT "ENTER THE FILE NAME OF THE ACCOUNTS FILE";
120 INPUT F$
130 GOSUB 510                    'OPEN FILES AND DEFINE
140 K=1
150 GOSUB 590                    'FILE READ
160 X=CVI(R$(1))
170 N2=CVI(R$(2))
180 N3=X
190 PRINT
200 PRINT "DATE OF FILES LAST UPDATE WAS ";D$
210 FOR K=2 TO N2+1
220    GOSUB 590                 'FILE READ
230    NO(K-1)=CVI(R$(1))
240    N3=N3+NO(K-1)
250    T$(K-1)=D$
260 NEXT K
270 PRINT
280 REM ***************** CHOICE OF PROCESSING OPTIONS   ***********
290 PRINT "THE FOLLOWING OPTIONS ARE AVAILABLE:"
300 PRINT
310 PRINT TAB(5);1;".....STARTING AND ENDING REFERENCE NUMBERS"
320 PRINT TAB(5);2;".....JOURNAL ENTRIES IN REFERENCE NUMBER ORDER"
330 PRINT
340 PRINT "ENTER THE OPTION DESIRED";
350 INPUT O
360 PRINT
370 PRINT
380 IF O=1 THEN GOSUB 620                'START AND END REF
390 IF O<>2 THEN 430
400 GOSUB 620                    'FIND ARRAY SIZE
410 GOSUB 780                    'REFERENCE ORDER
420 REM ********* PROGRAM TERMINATION POINT ***********************
430 PRINT
440 PRINT
```

```
450 PRINT "PROCESSING COMPLETE"
460 PRINT
470 STOP


480 REM ***********************************************************
490 REM                    SUBROUTINES FOLLOW
500 REM ***********************************************************
510 REM *********** FILE OPEN AND DEFINITION ROUTINE  ***********
520 OPEN "R",1,F$,0
530 FIELD#1,19 AS D$
540 FOR I= 1 TO N1
550   FIELD#1,19+(I-1)*7 AS X$,2 AS R$(I),1 AS S$(I),4 AS V$(I)
560 NEXT I
570 FIELD#1,124 AS X$,2 AS L$,2 AS N$
580 RETURN


590 REM ******************  FILE READ - RECORD#K  ****************
600 GET#1,K
610 RETURN


620 REM **********  FIND STARTING AND ENDING REFERENCES **********
630 FOR K=X+1 TO N3
640   GOSUB 590          'READ FILE
650   FOR I=1 TO N1
660     R1=CVI(R$(I))
670     IF R1<=1 THEN 700
680     IF R1<M1 THEN M1=R1
690     IF R1>M2 THEN M2=R1
700   NEXT I
710   N=CVI(N$)
720   IF N<=0 THEN 750
730   GET#1,N
740   GOTO 650
750 NEXT K
760 PRINT "JOURNAL REFERENCES WERE ENTERED ";M1;"TO";M2;"INCLUSIVE."
770 RETURN


780 REM ****************** REFERENCE NUMBER ORDER   ***************
790 REM ***************** CREATE REFERENCE NUMBER ARRAY  ********
800 N4=M2-M1+1
810 N6=M1-1
820 DIM E(N4,N5)
830 FOR K=X TO N3
840   GOSUB  590                    'READ FILE
850   FOR I=1 TO N1
860     R1=CVI(R$(I))
870     IF R1=0 THEN 940
880     J1=R1-N6
890     FOR J2=1 TO N5
900       IF E(J1,J2)<>0 THEN 930
910       E(J1,J2)=K
920       GOTO 940
930     NEXT J2
940   NEXT I
950   N=CVI(N$)
960   IF N<=0 THEN 990
970   GET#1,N
980   GOTO 850
990 NEXT K
1000 REM ***************** PRINTING JOURNAL  ****************
1010 PRINT
1020 PRINT
1030 PRINT TAB(20);"JOURNAL REFERENCE LISTING"
1040 PRINT
```

```
1050 PRINT
1060 PRINT "REF";TAB(15);"ACCOUNT";TAB(40);"DEBIT";TAB(50);"CREDIT"
1070 PRINT
1080 FOR J1=1 TO N4
1090   PRINT J1+N6;
1100   FOR J2=1 TO N5
1110     IF E(J1,J2)=0 THEN 1300
1120     K=E(J1,J2)
1130     GOSUB 590              'READ FILE
1140     IF K<=N3 THEN 1170
1150     K=CVI(L$)
1160     LSET D$=D2$
1170     FOR I=1 TO N1
1180       R1=CVI(R$(I))
1190       IF R1=0 THEN 1260
1200       IF R1<>J1+N6 THEN 1260
1210       V(0)=CVS(V$(I))
1220       T=0
1230       IF S$(I)="C" THEN T=10
1240       PRINT TAB(10+T);K;TAB(15+T);"- ";D$;TAB(40+T);V(0)
1250       GOTO 1330
1260     NEXT I
1270     D2$=D$
1280     K=CVI(N$)
1290     GOTO 1130
1300     IF E(J1,1)<>0 THEN 1330
1310     PRINT "***** NOT RECORDED *****"
1320     GOTO 1350
1330   NEXT J2
1340   PRINT
1350 NEXT J1
1360 RETURN
```

```
RUN "BJOURNAL"
ENTER THE FILE NAME OF THE ACCOUNTS FILE? MY-BOOKS

DATE OF FILES LAST UPDATE WAS JANUARY 30 1981

THE FOLLOWING OPTIONS ARE AVAILABLE:

        1 ......STARTING AND ENDING REFERENCE NUMBERS
        2 ......JOURNAL ENTRIES IN REFERENCE NUMBER ORDER

ENTER THE OPTION DESIRED? 2


JOURNAL REFERENCES WERE ENTERED  2 TO 10 INCLUSIVE.


                    JOURNAL REFERENCE LISTING
```

REF	ACCOUNT	DEBIT	CREDIT
2	10 - CASH	2000	
	15 - CAPITAL		2000
3	10 - CASH		150
	11 - SUPPLIES	150	
4	12 - EQUIPMENT	1000	
	13 - ACCOUNTS PAYABLE		1000
5	10 - CASH	1250	
	17 - FEE INCOME		1250

```
6               10  - CASH                        250
        18  - RENT                250

7               10  - CASH                        100
        20  - TELEPHONE EXPENSE    100

8               10  - CASH                        600
        13  - ACCOUNTS PAYABLE     600

9               11  - SUPPLIES                     100
        19  - SUPPLIES EXPENSE     100

10              10  - CASH                        200
        16  - DRAWING             200


PROCESSING COMPLETE

BREAK IN 470
OK
```

Income and Expense Comparison

Program Name: BCOMP

This program produces a comparison of expenses (option E) or of income (option I) for several previous periods. The formatted output includes detailed data and totals for each period and totals and averages for each account and period. Note that the records with the transaction code "*" are used as input to this program. The number of periods to be compared is specified in response to program prompting.

Files Affected: None

```
10 REM              SAVED AT BCOMP
20 REM              INCOME AND EXPENSE ANALYSIS
30 REM ***********************************************************
40 N1=15
50 T=10
60 N5=5
70 DIM R$(N1),V$(N1),S$(N1)
80 DIM R(N1),V(N1)
90 DIM T$(5),NO(5)
100 PRINT "ENTER THE NAME OF THE ACCOUNTS FILE";
110 INPUT F$
120 GOSUB 370                    'OPEN FILES AND DEFINE
130 K=1
140 GOSUB 450                    'FILE READ
150 X=CVI(R$(1))
160 N2=CVI(R$(2))
170 N3=X
180 PRINT
```

```
190 PRINT "DATE OF FILES LAST UPDATE WAS ";D$
200 FOR K=2 TO N2+1
210    GOSUB 450                    'FILE READ
220    NO(K-1)=CVI(R$(1))
230    N3=N3+NO(K-1)
240    T$(K-1)=D$
250 NEXT K
260 PRINT
270 GOSUB 480                       'PERFORM ANALYSIS
280 REM ******************************************************************
290 PRINT
300 PRINT
310 PRINT "PROCESSING COMPLETE"
320 PRINT
330 STOP


340 REM ******************************************************************
350 REM                    SUBROUTINES FOLLOW
360 REM ******************************************************************
370 REM ************* FILE OPEN AND DEFINITION ROUTINE   ************
380 OPEN "R",1,F$,0
390 FIELD#1,19 AS D$
400 FOR I= 1 TO N1
410    FIELD#1,19+(I-1)*7 AS X$,2 AS R$(I),1 AS S$(I),4 AS V$(I)
420 NEXT I
430 FIELD#1,124 AS X$,2 AS L$,2 AS N$
440 RETURN


450 REM ****************** FILE READ - RECORD#K   ****************
460 GET#1,K
470 RETURN


480 REM ****************INCOME AND EXPENSE ANALYSIS ****************
490 PRINT "HOW MANY ACCOUNTING PERIODS SHALL I INCLUDE";
500 INPUT N9
510 PRINT "DO YOU WISH TO COMPARE INCOME OR EXPENSES (I OR E)";
520 INPUT A$
530 J=4
540 IF A$="E" THEN J=5
550 DIM A2(N9+1)
560 PRINT
570 PRINT "POSITION PAPER NOW - PRESS RETURN WHEN READY";
580 INPUT A$
590 PRINT
600 PRINT TAB(30);F$
610 PRINT TAB(25);"COMPARISON OF ";T$(J)
620 PRINT TAB(30);D4$
630 PRINT
640 FOR I1=1 TO  N9
650    PRINT TAB(T*(I1-1)+20);"PER";I1;
660 NEXT I1
670 PRINT "     TOTAL     AVERAGE"
680 PRINT
690 N7=NO(1)+NO(2)+NO(3)
700 IF J=5 THEN N7=N7+NO(4)
710 K1=X+1+N7
720 N7=N7+NO(J)
730 FOR I=K1 TO K1+NO(J)-1
740    I1=N9
750    K=I
760    GOSUB 450                    'FILE READ
770    IF K>N3 THEN LSET D$=D2$
780    FOR J1=N1 TO 1 STEP -1
790       V(0)=CVS(V$(J1))
800       IF S$(J1)<>"*" THEN 850
```

```
810     V(I1)=V(0)
820     IF J=4 THEN V(I1)=V(I1)*(-1)
830     I1=I1-1
840     IF I1=0 THEN 860
850   NEXT J1
860   PRINT D$;
870   FOR I1=1 TO N9+1
880     IF I1<=N9 THEN   V(N9+1)=V(N9+1)+V(I1)
890     A2(I1)=A2(I1)+V(I1)
900     PRINT TAB(T*(I1-1)+20);V(I1);
910   NEXT I1
920   PRINT TAB(T*(I1-1)+20);V(N9+1)/N9
930   V(N9+1)=0
940 NEXT I
950 PRINT TAB(20);"------------------------------------------------------"
960 PRINT TAB(5);"TOTAL ";
970 FOR I1=1 TO N9+1
980    PRINT TAB(T*(I1-1)+20);A2(I1);
990 NEXT I1
1000 PRINT TAB(T*(I1-1)+20);A2(I1-1)/N9
1010 PRINT
1020 RETURN
```

```
RUN "BCOMP"
ENTER THE NAME OF THE ACCOUNTS FILE? MY-BOOKS

DATE OF FILES LAST UPDATE WAS FEBRUARY 1 1981

HOW MANY ACCOUNTING PERIODS SHALL I INCLUDE? 2
DO YOU WISH TO COMPARE INCOME OR EXPENSES (I OR E)? I

POSITION PAPER NOW - PRESS RETURN WHEN READY?


                    MY-BOOKS
              COMPARISON OF INCOME


              PER 1     PER 2     TOTAL     AVERAGE

FEE INCOME      0        1250      1250       625
            -----------------------------------------------------
    TOTAL       0        1250      1250       625



PROCESSING COMPLETE

BREAK IN 330
OK




RUN "BCOMP"
ENTER THE NAME OF THE ACCOUNTS FILE? MY-BOOKS

DATE OF FILES LAST UPDATE WAS FEBRUARY 1 1981

HOW MANY ACCOUNTING PERIODS SHALL I INCLUDE? 1
DO YOU WISH TO COMPARE INCOME OR EXPENSES (I OR E)? E

POSITION PAPER NOW - PRESS RETURN WHEN READY?
```

Simple Bookkeeping System   45

```
                        MY-BOOKS
                COMPARISON OF EXPENSES


                    PER 1        TOTAL        AVERAGE

RENT                250          250          250
SUPPLIES EXPENSE    100          100          100
TELEPHONE EXPENSE   100          100          100
                    -----------------------------------------------------------
        TOTAL       450          450          450


PROCESSING COMPLETE

BREAK IN 330
OK
```

3 Accounts Receivable System

The two programs in this chapter perform all functions necessary for the processing of a computerized accounts receivable system, including the closing of accounts at month's-end and the preparation of customer statements. They have been designed to accept transaction information throughout the month and record these transactions in each account. In their present form, the only information needed to update the file with "charge" transactions is the following: account number, payment (P) or charge (C) code, and amount. These transactions can be accumulated and then entered in the file at the end of day, or as time permits.

The programs can be used to process several independent accounts receivable systems simultaneously, provided that a separate accounts receivable file is created for each system. If multiple files are maintained, care must be taken to insure that accounts are not inadvertently entered in the wrong file. This potential difficulty can be eliminated by using unique customer numbers in each file.

Since the security of accounts receivable information is critical to the continued operation of most businesses, a procedure must be instituted to recover the data in case of system (or file) failure. It is recommended that the file be copied after a significant number of transactions have been entered and that a record of transactions entered be maintained to insure your ability to update the file. It almost goes without saying that an adequate audit trail must be maintained for these types of financial transactions.

Operation of the System

The operation of the computerized accounts receivable system is very similar to the operation of a manual system. The two programs provided perform the following functions:

1. Accounts receivable processing (program name: ACCTSREC)—
   This program allows for the addition of new accounts, correcting

existing accounts, the display (printing) of specific accounts, and entering charge/payment transactions for recording in the file.

2. Accounts receivable printing (program name: ACCTPRNT)— This program produces monthly statements, closes out the accounts at the end of each month, and copies the file for recovery purposes.

Initialization of files occurs as a normal part of the system's operation (whenever a new file name is entered) and does not require that a specific procedure be followed.

Normal operation of the system during the month involves the execution of ACCTSREC to initialize accounts and process transactions against them. At the end of each month, ACCTPRNT must be executed to produce statements and then close the accounts prior to entering the next period's transactions. Note that the monthly statements must be prepared before closing the accounts. As a minimum requirement, the recovery (file copy) protection feature should be executed prior to closing out the files for each period. These files can then be maintained to provide a snapshot of the account status at the end of each period. Furthermore, they will provide the basis for both file recovery and subsequent analysis of account activity.

The flowcharts in Figs. 3-1 and 3-2 illustrate the processing of the accounts receivable system.

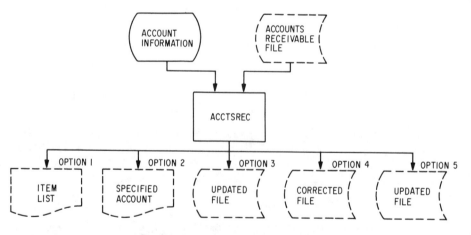

Fig. 3-1 Accounts receivable processing

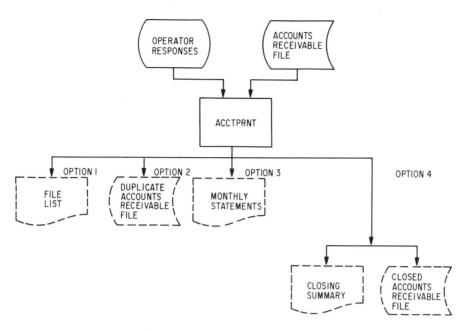

Fig. 3-2 Accounts receivable printing

Files Used by the Accounts Receivable System

The accounts receivable system requires only one file for its operation—a random-access file that contains two record types. The first record for each account is a master record containing the customer name and address, account number, credit limit, date of last closing, the balance at the start of the period, and the payment amount scheduled. The second type of record maintains a duplicate of the account information but replaces the customer name and address data with the actual transactions that occur throughout the month. Both record types contain a pointer to the next record number that applies to the account. When the number of transactions exceeds the space allowed in a single transaction record, additional records are linked to the earlier record by means of the next record pointer. The format of the records is shown in Fig. 3-3.

Master record

Code	Account number	Date of close	Credit limit	Previous balance	Pay due	Name	Address information	Next record no.
P$	A$	U$	L$	B$	D$	C$(1)	C$(2)–C$(4)	N$

Transaction record

Previous record no.	Account number	Date of close	Credit limit	Previous balance	Pay due	Transaction type	Transaction amount . . .	Next record no.
P$	A$	U$	L$	B$	D$	T$()	T1S()	N$

Occurs M times

Fig. 3-3 Record formats

```
     MAJOR SYMBOL TABLE - ACCOUNTS RECEIVABLE SYSTEM         FUNCTIONS USED
I--------------------------------------------------------I  I---------------I
I NAME   .. DESCRIPTION                                  I  I NAME          I
I--------------------------------------------------------I  I---------------I
I A$     .. ACCOUNT NUMBER - IN FILE                     I  I DIM           I
I A1$    .. TEMP ANSWER VARIABLE                         I  I CVI           I
I A2$()  .. ACCOUNT NUMBER ARRAY                         I  I MKI$          I
I A9$    .. INPUT ACCOUNT NUMBER                         I  I CVS           I
I B$     .. PREVIOUS BALANCE - IN FILE                   I  I MKS$          I
I C      .. LINE COUNTER                                 I  I GOSUB         I
I C$()   .. CUSTOMER NAME AND ADDRESS - IN FILE          I  I RETURN        I
I C0     .. TOTAL CHARGES                                I  I TAB           I
I C1     .. RECORD COUNTER                               I  I LSET          I
I C1$()  .. INPUT CUSTOMER NAME/ADDRESS                  I  I OPEN          I
I C2     .. PAYMENT STATUS INDICATOR                     I  I CLOSE         I
I C3     .. MAXIMUM LINES PER ACCOUNT                    I  I GET           I
I D      .. NEXT PAYMENT AMOUNT                          I  I PUT           I
I D$     .. PAYMENT DUE - IN FILE                        I  I LEN           I
I D1     .. NUMERIC OF LAST PAYMENT AMOUNT               I  I SPACE$        I
I D1$    .. NEXT PAYMENT DUE DATE                        I  I INT           I
I D9$    .. DATE OF PROCESSING                           I  I LOF(1)        I
I F$     .. FILE   NAME                                  I  I---------------I
I F1$    .. FILE NAME TO COPY TO                         I
I I      .. INDEX AND ARRAY POINTER                      I
I J      .. INDEX AND ARRAY POINTER                      I
I J1     .. RECORD'S FOUND COUNTER                       I
I K      .. RECORD NUMBER TO READ AND WRITE              I
I K1()   .. RECORD #'S FOR ADDITIONS                     I
I L$     .. CREDIT LIMIT - IN FILE                       I
I L1     .. LAST RECORD NUMBER USED IN FILE              I
I L9$    .. INPUT CREDIT LIMIT                           I
I M      .. MAX NUMBER OF TRANSACTION PER RECORD         I
I M$     .. MESSAGE TO ALL ACCOUNTS                      I
I M1     .. MAXIMUM ACCOUNTS                             I
I M1$    .. MESSAGE TO ACCOUNTS IN ARREARS               I
I M2$    .. MESSAGE TO ACCOUNTS EXCEEDING LIMIT          I
I M3     .. NUMBER OF ACCOUNTS                           I
I N      .. NUMERIC OF NEXT RECORD #                     I
I N$     .. NEXT RECORD NUMBER - IN FILE                 I
I O      .. OPTION NUMBER                                I
I P      .. NUMERIC OF PREVIOUS RECORD #                 I
I P$     .. PREVIOUS RECORD # - IN FILE                  I
I P0     .. TOTAL PAYMENTS                               I
```

```
I  R()    .. RECORD POINTER ARRAY                       I
I  T      .. TAB VARIABLE                               I
I  T$()   .. TRANSACTION TYPE - IN FILE                 I
I  T0     .. TOTAL BALANCE OF ACCOUNT                   I
I  T1     .. NUMERIC OF T1$                             I
I  T1$()  .. TRANSACTION AMOUNT - IN FILE               I
I  T9     .. INPUT TRANSACTION AMOUNT                   I
I  T9$    .. INPUT TRANSACTION TYPE                     I
I  U$     .. DATE OF PREVIOUS CLOSE OUT - IN FILE       I
I  X$     .. LINE OF ASTERISKS                          I
I  X1$    .. DUMMY VARIABLE                             I
I  X2$    .. LINE OF HYPHENS                            I
I  X3$    .. OUTPUT ATTENTION INDICATOR                 I
I  Z1$    .. INPUT COPY RECORD                          I
I  Z2$    .. OUTPUT COPY RECORD                         I
I----------------------------------------------------------I
```

Accounts Receivable Processing

Program Name: ACCTSREC

This program performs all functions necessary to add, change, and update accounts with payment and charge transactions. The following five options are available to the operator through keyboard responses to program messages:

Option 1 lists all current account numbers and indicates the record number at which they are stored in the file.

Option 2 prints a specified account in statement format.

Option 3 adds new accounts to the file. Program messages request all necessary information from the operator.

Option 4 corrects information in the master record for each account. The operator is allowed to change name, address, account number, and credit limit. For security reasons, changes to recorded transactions are not allowed.

Option 5 allows for the entry of payments and charges against customer accounts. The present form of the program allows entry of payment (P) and charge (C) transactions only. The allowable transaction codes can easily be extended to meet your specific needs.

```
10 REM          SAVED AT ACCTSREC
20 REM          ACCOUNTS RECEIVABLE SYSTEM
30 REM *******************************************************************
40 X$="*******************************************************************"
50 X2$="---------------------------------------------------------------"
60 M=20
70 M3=50
80 M1=200
```

```
90 DIM T$(M),T1$(M),R(M1),A2$(M1),C$(4),C1$(4),K1(2)
100 PRINT "ENTER ACCOUNTS RECEIVABLE FILE NAME";
110 INPUT F$
120 GOSUB 440                        'FILE OPEN AND DEFINE
130 GOSUB 1380                       'BUILD ACCOUNT TABLE
140 PRINT
150 PRINT X$
160 PRINT
170 PRINT "THE FOLLOWING OPTIONS ARE AVAILABLE:"
180 PRINT
190 PRINT TAB(5);"1..ACCOUNT LIST (WITH RECORD NUMBERS)"
200 PRINT TAB(5);"2..PRINT OF SPECIFIED ACCOUNTS"
210 PRINT TAB(5);"3..ADDING NEW ACCOUNTS"
220 PRINT TAB(5);"4..CORRECTING ACCOUNT INFORMATION"
230 PRINT TAB(5);"5..ENTERING CHARGE/PAYMENT TRANSACTIONS"
240 PRINT
250 PRINT "ENTER OPTION DESIRED";
260 INPUT O
270 IF O=1 THEN GOSUB 2580           'ACCOUNT LIST
280 IF O=2 THEN GOSUB 2080           'RECORD PRINT
290 IF O=3 THEN GOSUB 650            'ADD NEW ACCOUNTS
300 IF O=4 THEN GOSUB 2710           'CORRECT ACCOUNT INFO
310 IF O=5 THEN GOSUB 1680           'ADD TRANSACTIONS
320 PRINT
330 PRINT "DO YOU WISH TO CONTINUE (Y OR N)";
340 INPUT A1$
350 IF A1$="Y" THEN 250
360 REM **********************************************************
370 REM             PROGRAM TERMINATION POINT
380 REM **********************************************************
390 PRINT
400 PRINT
410 PRINT "PROCESSING COMPLETE"
420 PRINT
430 STOP


440 REM **********************************************************
450 REM             OPEN AND DEFINE FILE
460 REM **********************************************************
470 OPEN "R",1,F$,0
480 FIELD#1,2 AS P$,8 AS A$,8 AS U$,2 AS L$,4 AS B$,2 AS D$
490 FOR I=1 TO M
500     FIELD#1,26 +(I-1)*5 AS X1$,1 AS T$(I),4 AS T1$(I)
510 NEXT I
520 FIELD#1,26 AS X1$,25 AS C$(1),25 AS C$(2),25 AS C$(3),25 AS C$(4)
530 FIELD#1,126 AS X1$,2 AS N$
540 GET#1,1
550 L1=CVI(P$)
560 IF L1<1 THEN L1=1
570 RETURN


580 REM **********************************************************
590 REM                 FILE READ
600 REM **********************************************************
610 GET#1,K
620 F=CVI(P$)
630 N=CVI(N$)
640 RETURN


650 REM **********************************************************
660 REM                 ADD NEW ACCOUNTS
670 REM **********************************************************
680 PRINT "***** ADD NEW ACCOUNTS *****"
690 PRINT
700 PRINT "ENTER THE ACCOUNT NUMBER";
710 A9$=""
720 INPUT A9$
```

```
730 IF A9$="" THEN 940
740 M3=M3+1
750 IF LEN(A9$)<8 THEN A9$=A9$+SPACE$(8-LEN(A9$))
760 A2$(M3)=A9$
770 PRINT "ENTER THE CREDIT LIMIT";
780 L9=0
790 INPUT L9
800 PRINT "ENTER THE CUSTOMER'S NAME";
810 C1$(1)=""
820 INPUT C1$(1)
830 PRINT "ENTER THEIR ADDRESS - 3 LINES MAX"
840 FOR I=2 TO 4
850    C1$(I)=""
860    IF C1$(I-1)<>"" THEN INPUT C1$(I)
870 NEXT I
880 GOSUB 950                     'FIND RECORD #
890 R(M3)=K1(1)
900 K=1
910 LSET P$=MKI$(L1)
920 GOSUB 1330                    'FILE WRITE
930 GOTO 700
940 RETURN


950 REM ************************************************************
960 REM                  FIND RECORD NUMBERS
970 REM ************************************************************
980 I=2
990 J=1
1000 IF I<=L1 THEN 1040
1010 L1=L1+1
1020 I=L1+1
1030 GOTO 1080
1040 K=I
1050 GOSUB 580                     'FILE READ
1060 I=I+1
1070 IF A$<>"          "THEN 1000
1080 K1(J)=I-1
1090 J=J+1
1100 IF J<=2 THEN 1000
1110 REM *************** SETUP AND WRITE RECORDS   ****************
1120 LSET P$=MKI$(0)
1130 LSET L$=MKI$(L9)
1140 LSET B$=MKS$(0)
1150 LSET U$="NEW ACCT"
1160 LSET N$=MKI$(K1(2))
1170 LSET C$(1)=C1$(1)
1180 LSET C$(2)=C1$(2)
1190 LSET C$(3)=C1$(3)
1200 LSET C$(4)=C1$(4)
1210 LSET A$=A9$
1220 K=K1(1)
1230 GOSUB 1330                    'WRITE ADDED RECORD-MASTER
1240 LSET P$=MKI$(K1(1))
1250 LSET N$=MKI$(0)
1260 LSET A$=A9$
1270 FOR I=1 TO M
1280    LSET T$(I)=" "
1290 NEXT I
1300 K=K1(2)
1310 GOSUB 1330                    'WRITE ADDED RECORD-TRANSACTION
1320 RETURN


1330 REM ************************************************************
1340 REM                     FILE WRITE
1350 REM ************************************************************
1360 PUT#1,K
1370 RETURN
```

```
1380 REM ****************************************************************
1390 REM                    BUILD ACCT TABLE
1400 REM ****************************************************************
1410 I=1
1420 K=2
1430 GOSUB 580                     'FILE READ
1440 IF P<>0 THEN 1480
1450 R(I)=K
1460 A2$(I)=A$
1470 I=I+1
1480 K=K+1
1490 IF K<L1 THEN 1430
1500 M3=I-1
1510 RETURN

1520 REM ****************************************************************
1530 REM                    SEARCH TABLE
1540 REM ****************************************************************
1550 PRINT "ENTER ACCT NBR";
1560 A9$=""
1570 INPUT A9$
1580 IF A9$="" THEN 1660
1590 IF LEN(A9$)<8 THEN A9$=A9$+SPACE$(8-LEN(A9$))
1600 FOR I=1 TO M3
1610    IF A9$=A2$(I) THEN 1650
1620 NEXT I
1630 PRINT "ACCOUNT NOT FOUND"
1640 GOTO 1550
1650 K=R(I)
1660 RETURN

1670 REM ****************************************************************
1680 REM                    ADD TRANSACTIONS
1690 REM ****************************************************************
1700 PRINT "***** ENTERING TRANSACTIONS *****"
1710 PRINT
1720 K=0
1730 J1=0
1740 GOSUB 1520                    'SEARCH TABLE
1750 IF K=0 THEN 2070
1760 PRINT "ENTER TRANSACTION CODE (P OR C),AMOUNT";
1770 INPUT T9$,T9
1780 IF T9$="C" OR T9$="P" THEN 1810
1790 PRINT "ERRONEOUS TRANSACTION CODE - TRY AGAIN"
1800 GOTO 1760
1810 GOSUB 580                     'FILE READ-MASTER
1820 K=N
1830 GOSUB 580                     'FILE READ-TRANSACTIONS
1840 IF N>0 THEN 1820
1850 FOR J=1 TO M
1860    IF T$(J)=" " THEN 1990
1870 NEXT J
1880 L1=L1+1
1890 LSET N$=MKI$(L1)
1900 GOSUB 1330                    'FILE WRITE
1910 J1=1
1920 LSET P$=MKI$(K)
1930 K=L1
1940 LSET N$=MKI$(0)
1950 FOR I=1 TO M
1960    LSET T$(I)=" "
1970 NEXT I
1980 J=1
1990 LSET T$(J)=T9$
2000 LSET T1$(J)=MKS$(T9)
2010 GOSUB 1330                    'FILE WRITE
2020 IF J1<>1 THEN 1720
2030 LSET P$=MKI$(L1)
```

```
2040 K=1
2050 GOSUB 1330              'FILE WRITE
2060 GOTO 1720
2070 RETURN

2080 REM ********************************************************************
2090 REM                    RECORD PRINT
2100 REM ********************************************************************
2110 PRINT "***** ACCOUNT PRINT *****"
2120 PRINT
2130 K=0
2140 GOSUB 1520             'SEARCH TABLE
2150 IF A9$="" THEN 2560
2160 IF K=0 THEN 2560
2170 GOSUB 580                'FILE READ
2180 PRINT
2190 PRINT X$
2200 PRINT
2210 PRINT TAB(5);C$(1);TAB(35);"ACCOUNT #:";A$
2220 PRINT TAB(5);C$(2)
2230 PRINT TAB(5);C$(3)
2240 PRINT TAB(5);C$(4)
2250 L=CVI(L$)
2260 B=CVS(B$)
2270 TO=B
2280 PRINT
2290 PRINT X2$
2300 PRINT "PREVIOUS BALANCE:";B;TAB(35);"AS OF: ";U$
2310 PRINT X2$
2320 PRINT TAB(35);"CHARGES";TAB(45);"PAYMENTS"
2330 K=N
2340 GOSUB 580                 'FILE READ
2350 FOR J=1 TO M
2360   IF T$(J)=" " THEN 2460
2370   T1=CVS(T1$(J))
2380   T=35
2390   IF T$(J)="C" THEN 2430
2400   T=45
2410   TO=TO-T1
2420   GOTO 2440
2430   TO=TO+T1
2440   PRINT TAB(T);T1
2450 NEXT J
2460 IF N>0 THEN 2330
2470 PRINT X2$
2480 D=.1*TO                'COMPUTES PAYMENT AMOUNT AT 10% BALANCE
2490 D=(INT(D*100))/100
2500 IF D<0 THEN D=0
2510 PRINT   "CREDIT LIMIT:";L
2520 PRINT "NEW BALANCE:";TO;TAB(25);"MONTHLY PAYMENT:";D
2530 PRINT
2540 PRINT X$
2550 GOTO 2130
2560 RETURN

2570 REM ********************************************************************
2580 REM                  PRINT ACCOUNT NUMBERS
2590 REM ********************************************************************
2600 PRINT "***** ACCOUNT LIST *****"
2610 PRINT
2620 PRINT
2630 PRINT X$
2640 PRINT
2650 PRINT "NBR";TAB(10);"ACCOUNT";TAB(20);"REC #"
2660 PRINT
2670 FOR I=1 TO M3
2680   PRINT I;TAB(10);A2$(I);TAB(20);R(I)
2690 NEXT I
2700 RETURN
```

```
2710 REM ****************************************************************
2720 REM                     CORRECT ACCOUNT INFORMATION
2730 REM ****************************************************************
2740 PRINT "***** CORRECTIONS *****"
2750 PRINT
2760 GOSUB 1520                          'SEARCH TABLE
2770 IF A9$="" THEN 3190
2780 PRINT "ENTER THE INFORMATION TO BE CHANGED"
2790 PRINT "NAME..(N)  ADDRESS..(A)  ACCT NBR..(AN)  LIMIT..(L)"
2800 A1$=""
2810 INPUT A1$
2820 IF A1$="" THEN 2760
2830 GOSUB 580                           'FILE READ
2840 IF A1$<>"N" THEN 2900
2850 REM ***************    CHANGE NAME    ***********************
2860 PRINT  "ENTER NEW NAME";
2870 INPUT C1$(1)
2880 LSET C$(1)=C1$(1)
2890 GOTO 3130
2900 IF A1$<>"A" THEN 3000
2910 REM ***************    CHANGE ADDRESS   **********************
2920 PRINT "ENTER NEW ADDRESS -3 LINES MAX"
2930 C1$(1)="*"
2940 FOR I=2 TO 4
2950    C1$(I)=""
2960    IF C1$(I-1)<>"" THEN INPUT C1$(I)
2970    LSET C$(I)=C1$(I)
2980 NEXT I
2990 GOTO 3130
3000 IF A1$<>"L" THEN 3060
3010 REM ***************   CHANGE CREDIT LIMIT   ******************
3020 PRINT "ENTER NEW CREDIT LIMIT";
3030 INPUT L9
3040 LSET L$=MKI$(L9)
3050 GOTO 3130
3060 IF A1$<>"AN" THEN 3190
3070 REM ***************   CHANGE ACCOUNT NUMBER   ****************
3080 PRINT "ENTER NEW ACCOUNT NUMBER";
3090 INPUT A9$
3100 IF LEN(A9$)<8 THEN A9$=A9$+SPACE$(8-LEN(A9$))
3110 A2$(I)=A9$
3120 LSET A$=A9$
3130 GOSUB 1330                          'FILE WRITE
3140 IF A1$<>"AN" THEN 2760
3150 K=N
3160 IF K<=0 THEN 2760
3170 GOSUB 580                           'FILE READ
3180 GOTO 3120
3190 RETURN




RUN "ACCTSREC"
ENTER ACCOUNTS RECEIVABLE FILE NAME? ACCOUNTS

******************************************************************

THE FOLLOWING OPTIONS ARE AVAILABLE:

     1..ACCOUNT LIST (WITH RECORD NUMBERS)
     2..PRINT OF SPECIFIED ACCOUNTS
     3..ADDING NEW ACCOUNTS
     4..CORRECTING ACCOUNT INFORMATION
     5..ENTERING CHARGE/PAYMENT TRANSACTIONS
```

```
ENTER OPTION DESIRED? 3
***** ADD NEW ACCOUNTS *****

ENTER THE ACCOUNT NUMBER? 11111
ENTER THE CREDIT LIMIT? 1000
ENTER THE CUSTOMER'S NAME? JOHN D. JONES
ENTER THEIR ADDRESS - 3 LINES MAX
? 9415 TOLLHOUSE ROAD
? SYRACUSE NY 13203
?
ENTER THE ACCOUNT NUMBER? 22222
ENTER THE CREDIT LIMIT? 1500
ENTER THE CUSTOMER'S NAME? JANE E. DOE
ENTER THEIR ADDRESS - 3 LINES MAX
? 113 HARRISON WAY APT 4
? MERCED CA 95340
?
ENTER THE ACCOUNT NUMBER?

DO YOU WISH TO CONTINUE (Y OR N)? N


PROCESSING COMPLETE

BREAK IN 430
OK




RUN "ACCTSREC"
ENTER ACCOUNTS RECEIVABLE FILE NAME? ACCOUNTS

***************************************************************

THE FOLLOWING OPTIONS ARE AVAILABLE:

        1..ACCOUNT LIST (WITH RECORD NUMBERS)
        2..PRINT OF SPECIFIED ACCOUNTS
        3..ADDING NEW ACCOUNTS
        4..CORRECTING ACCOUNT INFORMATION
        5..ENTERING CHARGE/PAYMENT TRANSACTIONS

ENTER OPTION DESIRED? 1
***** ACCOUNT LIST *****


***************************************************************

NBR        ACCOUNT    REC #

 1         11111       2
 2         22222       4

DO YOU WISH TO CONTINUE (Y OR N)? Y
ENTER OPTION DESIRED? 2
***** ACCOUNT PRINT *****

ENTER ACCT NBR? 11111
```

```
***********************************************************
        JOHN D. JONES                ACCOUNT #:11111
        9415  TOLLHOUSE ROAD
        SYRACUSE NY 13203


-----------------------------------------------------------
PREVIOUS BALANCE: 0                    AS OF: NEW ACCT
-----------------------------------------------------------
                                       CHARGES    PAYMENTS
-----------------------------------------------------------
CREDIT LIMIT: 1000
NEW BALANCE: 0             MONTHLY PAYMENT: 0

***********************************************************
ENTER ACCT NBR?

DO YOU WISH TO CONTINUE (Y OR N)? N


PROCESSING COMPLETE

BREAK IN 430
OK




RUN 'ACCTSREC
ENTER ACCOUNTS RECEIVABLE FILE NAME? ACCOUNTS

***********************************************************

THE FOLLOWING OPTIONS ARE AVAILABLE:

        1..ACCOUNT LIST (WITH RECORD NUMBERS)
        2..PRINT OF SPECIFIED ACCOUNTS
        3..ADDING NEW ACCOUNTS
        4..CORRECTING ACCOUNT INFORMATION
        5..ENTERING CHARGE/PAYMENT TRANSACTIONS

ENTER OPTION DESIRED? 4
***** CORRECTIONS *****

ENTER ACCT NBR? 11111
ENTER THE INFORMATION TO BE CHANGED
NAME..(N)  ADDRESS..(A)  ACCT NBR..(AN)  LIMIT..(L)
? L
ENTER NEW CREDIT LIMIT? 1200
ENTER ACCT NBR?

DO YOU WISH TO CONTINUE (Y OR N)? Y
ENTER OPTION DESIRED? 5
***** ENTERING TRANSACTIONS *****

ENTER ACCT NBR? 11111
ENTER TRANSACTION CODE (P OR C),AMOUNT? C
?? 15.89
ENTER ACCT NBR? 22222
ENTER TRANSACTION CODE (P OR C),AMOUNT? P,14.43
ENTER ACCT NBR? 11111
ENTER TRANSACTION CODE (P OR C),AMOUNT? C,12.34
ENTER ACCT NBR? 22222
ENTER TRANSACTION CODE (P OR C),AMOUNT? C,30.12
ENTER ACCT NBR?
```

```
DO YOU WISH TO CONTINUE (Y OR N)? Y
ENTER OPTION DESIRED? 2
***** ACCOUNT PRINT *****

ENTER ACCT NBR? 11111

**************************************************************

     JOHN D. JONES              ACCOUNT #:11111
     9415  TOLLHOUSE ROAD
     SYRACUSE NY 13203
-------------------------------------------------------------
PREVIOUS BALANCE: 0             AS OF: NEW ACCT
-------------------------------------------------------------
                                CHARGES    PAYMENTS
                                15.89
                                12.34
-------------------------------------------------------------
CREDIT LIMIT: 1200
NEW BALANCE: 28.23      MONTHLY PAYMENT: 2.82

**************************************************************
ENTER ACCT NBR?

DO YOU WISH TO CONTINUE (Y OR N)? N


PROCESSING COMPLETE

BREAK IN 430
OK
```

Accounts Receivable—Reports

Program Name: ACCTPRNT

This program performs all functions necessary to process the accounts receivable reports at the end of the month. In addition, it offers an option that copies the files for recovery purposes. The following four options are available to the operator through keyboard responses to program messages:

Option 1 lists all current account numbers and indicates the record number at which they are stored in the file.

Option 2 allows the operator to create a duplicate of the accounts receivable file. At a minimum, this option should be executed monthly, prior to closing the accounts.

Option 3 prepares monthly statements for the customers. By changing variable C3 to an appropriate value, a single statement can be prepared on preprinted forms. Minor modifications to the "Monthly Statements" subroutine may be necessary to match preprinted forms. The operator can indicate the messages that are to be printed when specific account conditions are identified. In the program's present form, three messages are available: the first can be printed on all accounts, the second on overdue accounts, and the third on accounts that have exceeded their credit limitation.

Option 4 closes the accounts receivable file at the end of the accounting period and produces a summary report to indicate the status of each account.

```
10 REM            SAVED AT ACCTPRNT
20 REM         ACCOUNTS RECEIVABLE SYSTEM - REPORTS
30 REM ***********************************************************
40 X$="***********************************************************"
50 X2$="------------------------------------------------------------"
60 C3=35
70 M=20
80 M3=50
90 M1=200
100 DIM T$(M),T1$(M),R(M1),A2$(M1),C$(4),C1$(4),K1(2)
110 PRINT "ENTER TODAY'S DATE";
120 INPUT D9$
130 PRINT "ENTER ACCOUNTS RECEIVABLE FILE NAME";
140 INPUT F$
150 GOSUB 450                    'FILE OPEN AND DEFINE
160 GOSUB 710                    'BUILD ACCOUNT TABLE
170 PRINT
180 PRINT X$
190 PRINT
200 PRINT "THE FOLLOWING OPTIONS ARE AVAILABLE:"
210 PRINT
220 PRINT TAB(5);"1..ACCOUNT LIST (WITH RECORD NUMBERS)"
230 PRINT TAB(5);"2..COPY FILE"
240 PRINT TAB(5);"3..MONTHLY STATEMENT PREPARATION"
250 PRINT TAB(5);"4..MONTHLY  CLOSE-OUT OF ACCOUNTS"
260 PRINT
270 PRINT "ENTER THE OPTION DESIRED";
280 INPUT O
290 PRINT
300 IF O=1 THEN GOSUB 1660           'ACCOUNT LIST
310 IF O=2 THEN GOSUB 1800           'COPY FILE
320 IF O=3 THEN GOSUB 860            'MONTHLY STATEMENTS
330 IF O=4 THEN GOSUB 1970           'CLOSE ACCOUNTS
340 PRINT "DO YOU WISH TO CONTINUE (Y OR N)";
```

```
350 INPUT A1$
360 IF A1$="Y" THEN 270
370 REM ************************************************************
380 REM                   PROGRAM TERMINATION POINT
390 REM ************************************************************
400 PRINT
410 PRINT
420 PRINT "PROCESSING COMPLETE"
430 PRINT
440 STOP


450 REM ************************************************************
460 REM                   OPEN AND DEFINE FILE
470 REM ************************************************************
480 OPEN "R",1,F$,0
490 FIELD#1,2 AS P$,8 AS A$,8 AS U$,2 AS L$,4 AS B$,2 AS D$
500 FOR I=1 TO M
510     FIELD#1,26 +(I-1)*5 AS X1$,1 AS T$(I),4 AS T1$(I)
520 NEXT I
530 FIELD#1,26 AS X1$,25 AS C$(1),25 AS C$(2),25 AS C$(3),25 AS C$(4)
540 FIELD#1,126 AS X1$,2 AS N$
550 GET#1,1
560 L1=CVI(P$)
570 IF L1<1 THEN L1=1
580 RETURN

590 REM ************************************************************
600 REM                   FILE READ
610 REM ************************************************************
620 GET#1,K
630 P=CVI(P$)
640 N=CVI(N$)
650 RETURN

660 REM ************************************************************
670 REM                   FILE WRITE
680 REM ************************************************************
690 PUT#1,K
700 RETURN

710 REM ************************************************************
720 REM                   BUILD ACCT TABLE
730 REM ************************************************************
740 I=1
750 K=2
760 GOSUB 590                   'FILE READ
770 IF P<>0 THEN 810
780 R(I)=K
790 A2$(I)=A$
800 I=I+1
810 K=K+1
820 IF K<L1 THEN 760
830 M3=I-1
840 RETURN

850 REM ************************************************************
860 REM                   MONTHLY STATEMENTS
870 REM ************************************************************
880 PRINT "***** ACCOUNT PRINT *****"
890 PRINT "ENTER THE DUE DATE FOR PAYMENTS";
900 INPUT D1$
910 PRINT "ENTER MESSAGE FOR ALL ACCOUNTS"
920 INPUT M$
930 PRINT "ENTER MESSAGE FOR OVERDUE ACCOUNTS"
940 INPUT M1$
950 PRINT "ENTER MESSAGE FOR ACCOUNTS OVER THEIR CREDIT LIMIT"
960 INPUT M2$
```

```
970 PRINT "POSITION PAPER NOW
980 INPUT A1$
990 PRINT
1000 FOR I=1 TO M3
1010    K=R(I)
1020    GOSUB 590                              'FILE READ
1030    PRINT
1040    REM ************* PRINT HEADINGS **************************
1050    PRINT X$
1060    PRINT
1070    PRINT TAB(35);"ACCOUNT #:";A$
1080    PRINT TAB(5);C$(1)
1090    PRINT TAB(5);C$(2)
1100    PRINT TAB(5);C$(3)
1110    PRINT TAB(5);C$(4)
1120    L=CVI(L$)
1130    B=CVS(B$)
1140    D1=CVI(D$)
1150    TO=B
1160    PRINT
1170    PRINT TAB(15);"STATEMENT DATE: ";D9$
1180    PRINT X2$
1190    PRINT "PREVIOUS BALANCE:";B;TAB(35);"AS OF: ";U$
1200    PRINT X2$
1210    PRINT TAB(35);"CHARGES";TAB(45);"PAYMENTS"
1220    C=C+13
1230    K=N
1240    REM ************* PRINT TRANSACTIONS ******************
1250    GOSUB 590                              'FILE READ
1260    FOR J=1 TO M
1270      IF T$(J)=" " THEN 1390
1280      T1=CVS(T1$(J))
1290      T=35
1300      IF T$(J)="C" THEN 1350
1310      T=45
1320      PO=PO+T1
1330      TO=TO-T1
1340      GOTO 1360
1350      TO=TO+T1
1360      PRINT TAB(T);T1
1370      C=C+1
1380    NEXT J
1390    IF N>0 THEN 1230
1400    PRINT X2$
1410    GOSUB 2560                             'COMPUTE PAYMENT
1420    PRINT "CREDIT LIMIT:";L
1430    PRINT "NEW BALANCE:";TO;TAB(25);"PAYMENT DUE:";D;"  ";D1$
1440    PRINT
1450    PRINT X$
1460    C=C+5
1470    PO=0
1480    REM ************* PRINT MESSAGES **************************
1490    PRINT M$
1500    PRINT
1510    C=C+2
1520    IF C2=0 THEN 1550
1530    PRINT M1$
1540    C=C+1
1550    IF TO<=L THEN 1580
1560    PRINT M2$
1570    C=C+1
1580    FOR J=C TO C3
1590      PRINT
1600    NEXT J
1610    C=0
1620    TO=0
1630 NEXT I
1640 RETURN
```

62   BASIC Computer Programs for Business

```
1650 REM ******************************************************
1660 REM                    PRINT ACCOUNT NUMBERS
1670 REM ******************************************************
1680 PRINT "***** ACCOUNT LIST *****"
1690 PRINT
1700 PRINT
1710 PRINT X$
1720 PRINT
1730 PRINT "NBR";TAB(10);"ACCOUNT";TAB(20);"REC #"
1740 PRINT
1750 FOR I=1 TO M3
1760   PRINT I;TAB(10);A2$(I);TAB(20);R(I)
1770 NEXT I
1780 RETURN

1790 REM ******************************************************
1800 REM                    COPY FILE
1810 REM ******************************************************
1820 CLOSE 1
1830 OPEN "R",1,F$,0
1840 PRINT "ENTER THE NAME OF THE FILE TO BE COPIED TO";
1850 INPUT F1$
1860 OPEN "R",2,F1$,0
1870 FIELD#1,128 AS Z1$
1880 FIELD#2,128 AS Z2$
1890 FOR K=1 TO LOF(1)
1900   GET#1,K
1910   LSET Z2$=Z1$
1920   PUT#2,K
1930 NEXT K
1940 CLOSE 1,2
1950 GOSUB 460                     'FILE OPEN AND DEFINE
1960 RETURN

1970 REM ******************************************************
1980 REM                    CLOSE OUT ACCOUNTS
1990 REM ******************************************************
2000 PRINT "***** CLOSE OUT ACCOUNTS *****
2010 PRINT "ARE YOU CERTAIN THAT YOU WANT TO CLOSE THE ACCOUNTS (Y OR N)";
2020 INPUT A1$
2030 IF A1$<>"Y" THEN 2540
2040 PRINT "POSITION PAPER NOW";
2050 INPUT A1$
2060 PRINT
2070 PRINT
2080 PRINT X$
2090 PRINT
2100 PRINT TAB(5);"ACCOUNTS CLOSED ";D9$
2110 PRINT
2120 PRINT "ACCOUNT";TAB(12);"NAME";TAB(38);"LIMIT";TAB(46);"BALANCE";
2130 PRINT TAB(55);"PAYMENT"
2140 PRINT
2150 FOR I=1 TO M3
2160   C1=1
2170   K=R(I)
2180   GOSUB 590                   'FILE READ-MASTER RECORD
2190   K=N
2200   GOSUB 590                   'FILE READ-TRANSACTION RECORD
2210   FOR J=1 TO M
2220     IF T$(J)=" " THEN 2280
2230     IF T$(J)="P" THEN P0=P0+CVS(T1$(J))
2240     IF T$(J)="C" THEN C0=C0+CVS(T1$(J))
2250     LSET T$(J)=" "
2260     LSET T1$(J)=MKS$(0)
2270   NEXT J
2280   C1=C1+1
2290   IF C1>=2 THEN LSET N$=MKI$(0)
2300   IF C1>2 THEN LSET P$=MKI$(0)
```

Accounts Receivable System   63

```
2310    GOSUB 670                       'FILE WRITE-BLANK TRANS RECORD
2320    IF N>0 THEN 2190
2330    K=R(I)
2340    GOSUB 590                       'FILE READ-MASTER RECORD TO UPDATE
2350    TO=CO-PO+CVS(B$)
2360    GOSUB 2560                      'COMPUTE PAYMENT
2370    L=CVI(L$)
2380    PRINT A$;TAB(10);C$(1);TAB(37);L;TAB(45);CVS(B$);TAB(55);CVI(D$)
2390    PRINT TAB(5);"CHARGES ";CO;TAB(25);"PAYMENTS ";PO;
2400    PRINT TAB(45);TO;TAB(55);D;TAB(65);
2410    CO=0
2420    PO=0
2430    LSET B$=MKS$(TO)
2440    LSET U$=D9$
2450    LSET D$=MKI$(D)
2460    GOSUB 670                       'FILE WRITE-MASTER RECORD
2470    X3$=""
2480    IF C2=1 OR TO>L THEN X3$="****"
2490    PRINT X3$
2500    PRINT
2510    TO=0
2520    L=CVI(L$)
2530 NEXT I
2540 RETURN
2550 REM ***************************************************************
2560 REM                     COMPUTE PAYMENT
2570 REM ***************************************************************
2580 REM         INTEREST COMPUTATIONS CAN GO HERE
2590 D=.1*TO
2600 D=(INT(D*100))/100
2610 D=D+D1-PO
2620 IF D<0 THEN D=0
2630 C2=0
2640 IF PO<D1 THEN C2=1
2650 RETURN




RUN "ACCTPRNT
ENTER TODAY'S DATE? 02/28/80
ENTER ACCOUNTS RECEIVABLE FILE NAME? ACCOUNTS

****************************************************************

THE FOLLOWING OPTIONS ARE AVAILABLE:

        1..ACCOUNT LIST (WITH RECORD NUMBERS)
        2..COPY FILE
        3..MONTHLY STATEMENT PREPARATION
        4..MONTHLY  CLOSE-OUT OF ACCOUNTS

ENTER THE OPTION DESIRED? 1

***** ACCOUNT LIST *****


****************************************************************

NBR         ACCOUNT    REC #

1           11111        2
2           22222        4
DO YOU WISH TO CONTINUE (Y OR N)? Y
ENTER THE OPTION DESIRED? 2

ENTER THE NAME OF THE FILE TO BE COPIED TO? ACCTSAVE
DO YOU WISH TO CONTINUE (Y OR N)? N
```

```
PROCESSING COMPLETE

BREAK IN 440
OK




RUN "ACCTPRNT"
ENTER TODAY'S DATE? 02/28/80
ENTER ACCOUNTS RECEIVABLE FILE NAME? ACCOUNTS

***************************************************************

THE FOLLOWING OPTIONS ARE AVAILABLE:

     1..ACCOUNT LIST (WITH RECORD NUMBERS)
     2..COPY FILE
     3..MONTHLY STATEMENT PREPARATION
     4..MONTHLY  CLOSE-OUT OF ACCOUNTS

ENTER THE OPTION DESIRED? 3

***** ACCOUNT PRINT *****
ENTER THE DUE DATE FOR PAYMENTS? 03/31/80
ENTER MESSAGE FOR ALL ACCOUNTS
? STOP IN TO SEE OUTFITS FOR THE ENTIRE FAMILY - MONTH END SALE!
ENTER MESSAGE FOR OVERDUE ACCOUNTS
? PERHAPS YOU HAVE OVERLOOKED YOUR FEBRUARY PAYMENT - IT'S OVERDUE
ENTER MESSAGE FOR ACCOUNTS OVER THEIR CREDIT LIMIT
? YOUR ACCOUNT IS NOW OVER ITS LIMIT - PLEASE CALL OUR CREDIT MANAGER
POSITION PAPER NOW
?




***************************************************************

                              ACCOUNT #:11111

     JOHN D. JONES
     9415  TOLLHOUSE ROAD
     SYRACUSE NY 13203


          STATEMENT DATE: 02/28/80
----------------------------------------------------------------
PREVIOUS BALANCE: 0                AS OF: NEW ACCT
----------------------------------------------------------------
                         CHARGES    PAYMENTS
                         15.89
                         12.34
----------------------------------------------------------------
CREDIT LIMIT: 1200
NEW BALANCE: 28.23      PAYMENT DUE: 2.82    03/31/80

***************************************************************
STOP IN TO SEE OUTFITS FOR THE ENTIRE FAMILY - MONTH END SALE!
***************************************************************
                              ACCOUNT #:22222

     JANE E. DOE
     113 HARRISON WAY APT 4
     MERCED CA 95340


          STATEMENT DATE: 02/28/80
```

```
-------------------------------------------------------------------
PREVIOUS BALANCE: 0                      AS OF: NEW ACCT
-------------------------------------------------------------------
                                CHARGES      PAYMENTS
                                               14.43
                                  30.12
-------------------------------------------------------------------
CREDIT LIMIT: 1500
NEW BALANCE: 15.69        PAYMENT DUE: 0    03/31/80

*****************************************************************
STOP IN TO SEE OUTFITS FOR THE ENTIRE FAMILY - MONTH END SALE!


DO YOU WISH TO CONTINUE (Y OR N)? N

PROCESSING COMPLETE

BREAK IN 440
OK




RUN "ACCTPRNT"
ENTER TODAY'S DATE? 02/28/80
ENTER ACCOUNTS RECEIVABLE FILE NAME? ACCOUNTS

*****************************************************************

THE FOLLOWING OPTIONS ARE AVAILABLE:

     1..ACCOUNT LIST (WITH RECORD NUMBERS)
     2..COPY FILE
     3..MONTHLY STATEMENT PREPARATION
     4..MONTHLY  CLOSE-OUT OF ACCOUNTS

ENTER THE OPTION DESIRED? 4

***** CLOSE OUT ACCOUNTS *****
ARE YOU CERTAIN THAT YOU WANT TO CLOSE THE ACCOUNTS (Y OR N)? Y
POSITION PAPER NOW?


*****************************************************************

     ACCOUNTS CLOSED 02/28/80

ACCOUNT      NAME                      LIMIT   BALANCE  PAYMENT

11111    JOHN D. JONES                1200      0        0
     CHARGES  28.23     PAYMENTS  0            28.23     2.82

22222    JANE E. DOE                  1500      0        0
     CHARGES  30.12     PAYMENTS  14.43        15.69     0

DO YOU WISH TO CONTINUE (Y OR N)? N

PROCESSING COMPLETE

BREAK IN 440
OK
```

4 Financial Programs (General)

Breakeven Analysis—Basic

Program Name: BREAK-1

This program accepts cost and price information from the operator and produces a table describing a product's breakeven point and the cost breakdown for that level of production.

Files Affected: None

```
10 REM           SAVED AT BREAK-1
20 REM ****************** PROCESSING AREA  **********************
30 PRINT
40 PRINT "COMPUTES  BREAKEVEN POINT"
50 PRINT
60 PRINT "ENTER FIXED COSTS ";
70 INPUT F
80 PRINT "ENTER VARIABLE COSTS PER UNIT ";
90 INPUT V
100 PRINT "ENTER UNIT PRICE";
110 INPUT P
120 REM **************** CALCULATE COSTS  ********************
130 Q=F/(P-V)
140 V1=V*Q
150 R=P*Q
160 C=F+(V*Q)
170 U=C/Q
180 PRINT
190 PRINT "*******************************"
200 PRINT "     BREAKEVEN POINT"
210 PRINT
220 PRINT "BREAKEVEN QUANTITY ";TAB(25);Q
230 PRINT "BREAKEVEN REVENUES";TAB(24);"$";R
240 PRINT
250 PRINT "FIXED COSTS";TAB(15);"$";F
260 PRINT "VARIABLE COSTS";TAB(15);"$";V1
270 PRINT "------------------------"
280 PRINT "TOTAL COSTS";TAB(15);"$";C
290 PRINT
300 PRINT "UNIT COST";TAB(15);"$";U;"EACH"
310 PRINT "*******************************"
320 PRINT
330 REM ****************** TERMINATION POINT  ******************
340 STOP
```

```
RUN "BREAK-1"

COMPUTES  BREAKEVEN POINT

ENTER FIXED COSTS ? 10000
ENTER VARIABLE COSTS PER UNIT ? .4
ENTER UNIT PRICE? .6

********************************
     BREAKEVEN POINT

BREAKEVEN QUANTITY        50000
BREAKEVEN REVENUES    $  30000

FIXED COSTS    $ 10000
VARIABLE COSTS $ 20000
------------------------
TOTAL COSTS    $ 30000

UNIT COST      $ .6 EACH
********************************

BREAK IN 340
OK
```

```
    MAJOR SYMBOL TABLE - BREAK-1              FUNCTIONS USED
I---------------------------------------I   I---------------I
I NAME    .. DESCRIPTION                I   I  NAME         I
I---------------------------------------I   I---------------I
I  C      .. TOTAL COSTS                I   I TAB           I
I  F      .. FIXED COSTS                I   I---------------I
I  P      .. PRICE PER UNIT             I
I  Q      .. BREAKEVEN QUANTITY         I
I  R      .. TOTAL REVENUES             I
I  U      .. COST PER UNIT              I
I  V      .. VARIABLE COSTS PER UNIT    I
I  V1     .. TOTAL VARIABLE COSTS       I
I---------------------------------------I
```

Breakeven Analysis—Extended

Program Name: BREAK-2

This program produces a cost/revenue schedule that includes information relating to a product's breakeven point. The cost/revenue schedule is produced over the range of values specified during program initialization, including cost, revenue, profit and loss, and unit cost information for each of the production quantity levels specified.

Files Affected: None

```
10 REM          SAVED AT BREAK-2
20 REM ****************** PROCESSING AREA  ***********************
30 PRINT
40 PRINT "PRODUCES COSTS/REVENUES SCHEDULE"
50 PRINT
60 PRINT "ENTER FIXED COSTS ";
70 INPUT F
80 PRINT "ENTER VARIABLE COSTS PER UNIT ";
90 INPUT V
100 PRINT "ENTER UNIT PRICE";
110 INPUT P
120 PRINT "ENTER BEGINNING QUANTITY FOR COMPUTATIONS";
130 INPUT Q1
140 PRINT "ENTER ENDING QUANTITY FOR COMPUTATIONS";
150 INPUT Q2
160 PRINT "ENTER STEP INCREMENTS TO BE PRINTED";
170 INPUT S
180 PRINT
190 PRINT
200 PRINT "*************************************************"
210 PRINT
220 PRINT "          COST/PRICE SCHEDULE"
230 PRINT
240 PRINT "QUANTITY";TAB(11);"COST";TAB(20);"REVENUE";
250 PRINT TAB(30);"PROF/LOSS";TAB(40);"UNIT COST"
260 PRINT
270 REM ***************** CALCULATE BREAKEVEN   *****************
280 Q0=F/(P-V)
290 R0=P*Q0
300 C0=F+(V*Q0)
310 REM ***************** CALCULATION AND PRINTING LOOP  *********
320 FOR Q=Q1 TO Q2 STEP S
330    V1=V*Q
340    R=P*Q
350    C=F+(V*Q)
360    U=C/Q
370    A=R-C
380    IF Q<Q0 THEN 430           'SKIPPING BREAKEVEN PRINT
390      PRINT "--------------------------------------------------"
400      PRINT Q0;TAB(10);C0;TAB(20);R0;TAB(30);"BREAKEVEN"
410      PRINT "--------------------------------------------------"
420      Q0=999999999999
430    PRINT Q;TAB(10);C;TAB(20);R;TAB(30);A;TAB(40);U
440 NEXT Q
450 PRINT "*************************************************"
460 PRINT
470 REM ****************** TERMINATION POINT   ******************
480 STOP
```

```
RUN "BREAK-2"

PRODUCES COSTS/REVENUES SCHEDULE

ENTER FIXED COSTS ? 1000
ENTER VARIABLE COSTS PER UNIT ? .40
ENTER UNIT PRICE? 1.60
ENTER BEGINNING QUANTITY FOR COMPUTATIONS? 100
ENTER ENDING QUANTITY FOR COMPUTATIONS? 1000
ENTER STEP INCREMENTS TO BE PRINTED? 100
```

```
************************************************************
           COST/PRICE SCHEDULE

QUANTITY    COST      REVENUE    PROF/LOSS UNIT COST

   100      1040        160       -880      10.4
   200      1080        320       -760      5.4
   300      1120        480       -640      3.73333
   400      1160        640       -520      2.9
   500      1200        800       -400      2.4
   600      1240        960       -280      2.06667
   700      1280       1120       -160      1.82857
   800      1320       1280        -40      1.65
  ---------------------------------------------------------
  833.333  1333.33    1333.33    BREAKEVEN
  ---------------------------------------------------------
   900      1360       1440        80       1.51111
  1000      1400       1600        200      1.4
************************************************************

BREAK IN 480
OK
```

```
     MAJOR SYMBOL TABLE - BREAK-2                    FUNCTIONS USED
I------------------------------------------------I   I----------------I
I NAME    .. DESCRIPTION                         I   I  NAME          I
I------------------------------------------------I   I----------------I
I  A      .. PROFIT OR LOSS                      I   I TAB            I
I  C      .. TOTAL COSTS                         I   I----------------I
I  CO     .. BREAKEVEN COSTS                     I
I  F      .. FIXED COSTS                         I
I  P      .. UNIT PRICE                          I
I  QO     .. BREAKEVEN POINT                     I
I  Q1     .. BEGINNING QUANTITY                  I
I  Q2     .. ENDING QUANTITY                     I
I  R      .. TOTAL REVENUES                      I
I  RO     .. BREAKEVEN REVENUE                   I
I  S      .. STEP INCREMENT FOR PRINTING         I
I  U      .. UNIT COST                           I
I  V      .. VARIABLE COSTS                      I
I  V1     .. TOTAL VARIABLE COSTS                I
I------------------------------------------------I
```

Financial Support Programs

The following two programs (RECORD and AMTS) are utility programs designed to assist in the creation and maintenance of the formatted files necessary to support the other programs in this section. The latter programs are designed to provide simplified financial analysis and reporting, as follows:

1. Program INCOME produces an income statement.
2. Program BALANCE produces a balance sheet.
3. Program FCOMP analyzes income and expenses.
4. Program BUDGET produces a cash flow analysis and budgets.

Program Name: RECORD

This program produces a sequential data file containing the name of each type of account necessary for financial recording. Account names are output to the file (in sorted order) with a type code that indicates the account's status as asset, liability, capital, income, or expense account. These account categories and names should be set up to correspond with your bookkeeping accounts so that comparable financial statements may be prepared. The file name that contains the account information is specified in response to program prompting. Multiple files can be maintained for special purposes.

Files Affected: File xxxxxx (created)

```
10 REM           SAVED AT RECORD
20 REM     SIMPLIFIED FINANCIAL RECORDING PROGRAM
30 REM **************************************************************
40 M=25
50 DIM T$(M),N$(M),T1$(5)
60 T1$(1)="A"
70 T1$(2)="L"
80 T1$(3)="C"
90 T1$(4)="I"
100 T1$(5)="E"
110 PRINT
120 PRINT
130 PRINT "WILL THE ACCOUNT NAME INPUT BE FROM A FILE (Y OR N)";
140 INPUT A$
150 IF A$<>"Y" THEN 180
160 GOSUB 720                    'OPEN AND READ FILE
170 GOTO 330
180 REM **************** ENTER ACCOUNTS FROM KEYBOARD  *********
190 PRINT "ENTER THE ACCOUNTS IN THE FOLLOWING FORM:"
200 PRINT "ACCOUNT TYPE,ACCOUNT NAME"
210 PRINT
220 PRINT "TYPES  A=ASSETS, L=LIABILITIES,C=CAPITAL,I=INCOME,E=EXPENSE"
230 PRINT "EXAMPLE INPUTS:   A,CASH         OR      L,ACCOUNTS PAYABLE"
240 PRINT
250 PRINT "ENTER INFORMATION NOW - RETURN ONLY WILL TERMINATE INPUT"
260 I=1
270    T$(I)=" "
280    INPUT T$(I),N$(I)
290    IF T$(I)=" " THEN 320
300    I=I+1
310 GOTO 270
320 N=I-1
330 REM **************** PRINT ACCOUNT NAMES ********************
340 PRINT
350 PRINT " #   TYPE     NAME"
360 FOR I=1 TO N
370    PRINT I;TAB(6);T$(I);TAB(12);N$(I)
380 NEXT I
390 REM **************** ADDING NEW ACCOUNTS  ******************
400 PRINT
410 PRINT "ARE THERE OTHER ACCOUNTS TO BE ADDED (Y OR N)";
420 INPUT A$
430 IF A$<>"Y" THEN 520
440 PRINT "ENTER NEW ACCOUNTS - JUST RETURN WHEN FINISHED"
450 N=N+1
460    T$(N)=" "
```

```
470    INPUT T$(N),N$(N)
480     IF T$(N)=" " THEN 500
490 GOTO 450
500 N=N-1
510 GOTO 330
520 REM **************** CHANGING EXISTING ACCOUNTS  **************
530 PRINT "ARE THERE ANY ITEMS TO CHANGE (Y OR N)";
540 INPUT A$
550 IF A$<>"Y" THEN 590
560 PRINT "ENTER THE # TO BE CHANGED FOLLOWED BY, THE NEW TYPE, NAME"
570 INPUT K,T$(K),N$(K)
580 GOTO 530
590 REM **************** SAVING ARRAY IN FILE ******************
600 PRINT "ENTER FILE NAME FOR STORING NAMES";
610 INPUT F$
620 GOSUB 830                       'OPEN AND WRITE FILE
630 REM ******************** PROGRAM TERMINATION  ****************
640 PRINT
650 PRINT
660 PRINT "PROCESSING COMPLETE"
670 PRINT
680 STOP


690 REM **************************************************************
700 REM                    SUBROUTINES FOLLOW
710 REM **************************************************************
720 REM *************** OPEN AND INPUT NAME FILE  *****************
730 PRINT "ENTER THE INPUT FILE NAME";
740 INPUT F$
750 OPEN "I",1,F$
760 INPUT#1,N
770 FOR I=1 TO N
780    INPUT#1,T$(I),N$(I)
790 NEXT I
800 F$=""
810 CLOSE 1
820 RETURN


830 REM  ************** OPEN AND WRITE TO FILE   ****************
840 OPEN "O",2,F$
850 PRINT#2,N
860 FOR J=1 TO 5
870    FOR I=1 TO N
880       IF T1$(J)=T$(I) THEN PRINT#2,T$(I);",";N$(I)
890    NEXT I
900 NEXT J
910 CLOSE 2
920 RETURN




RUN "RECORD"


WILL THE ACCOUNT NAME INPUT BE FROM A FILE (Y OR N)? N
ENTER THE ACCOUNTS IN THE FOLLOWING FORM:
ACCOUNT TYPE,ACCOUNT NAME

TYPES  A=ASSETS, L=LIABILITIES,C=CAPITAL,I=INCOME,E=EXPENSE
EXAMPLE INPUTS:   A,CASH          OR      L,ACCOUNTS PAYABLE

ENTER INFORMATION NOW - RETURN ONLY WILL TERMINATE INPUT
? A,CASH
? A,SUPPLIES
```

```
? A,EQUIPPMENT
? L,ACCOUNTS PAYABLE
? C,CAPITAL
? I,INCOME
? E,RENT EXPENSE
? E,SUPPLIES EXPENSE
? E,TELEPHONE EXPENSE
?

 #      TYPE      NAME
 1       A        CASH
 2       A        SUPPLIES
 3       A        EQUIPPMENT
 4       L        ACCOUNTS PAYABLE
 5       C        CAPITAL
 6       I        INCOME
 7       E        RENT EXPENSE
 8       E        SUPPLIES EXPENSE
 9       E        TELEPHONE EXPENSE

ARE THERE OTHER ACCOUNTS TO BE ADDED (Y OR N)? N
ARE THERE ANY ITEMS TO CHANGE (Y OR N)? Y
ENTER THE # TO BE CHANGED FOLLOWED BY, THE NEW TYPE, NAME
? 3,A,EQUIPMENT
ARE THERE ANY ITEMS TO CHANGE (Y OR N)? N
ENTER FILE NAME FOR STORING NAMES? ACCTS


PROCESSING COMPLETE

BREAK IN 680
OK
```

Program Name: AMTS

This program enters dollar information that reflects the status of accounts. The information is entered in response to program prompting that is based upon entries in the specified account name input file (created by program RECORD). The information can be data suitable for creating current financial statements, historical information for the preparation of comparative analyses, or future projections for the preparation of budgets or cash flow forecasts. The file created to contain the data is specified during program execution.

Files Affected: File xxxxxx (created)


```
10 REM            SAVED AT AMTS
20 REM      SIMPLIFIED FINANCIAL RECORDING PROGRAM - AMOUNTS
30 REM ****************************************************************
40 M=25
50 DIM T$(M),N$(M),A(M)
60 PRINT
70 PRINT
```

```
80 GOSUB 400                         'OPEN AND READ NAMES
90 REM ******************** ENTER AMOUNTS *********************
100 PRINT
110 PRINT "ENTER AMOUNTS FOR THE ACCOUNTS SHOWN"
120 PRINT
130 FOR I=1 TO N
140   PRINT T$(I);"....";N$(I);"....";
150   INPUT A(I)
160 NEXT I
170 REM ********************** PRINT RESULTS *****************
180 PRINT
190 PRINT " #    TYPE      NAME";TAB(35);"AMOUNT"
200 FOR I=1 TO N
210   PRINT I;TAB(6);T$(I);TAB(12);N$(I);TAB(35);A(I)
220 NEXT I
230 REM *************** CHANGING EXISTING ACCOUNTS *************
240 PRINT "ARE THERE ANY ITEMS TO CHANGE (Y OR N)";
250 INPUT A$
260 IF A$<>"Y" THEN 300
270 PRINT "ENTER THE REFERENCE # FOLLOWED BY ,THE NEW AMOUNT"
280 INPUT K,A(K)
290 GOTO 240
300 REM ********************* SAVING ARRAY IN FILE ***********
310 PRINT "ENTER FILE NAME FOR STORING AMOUNTS";
320 INPUT F$
330 GOSUB 510                         'OPEN AND WRITE FILE
340 REM ******************** PROGRAM TERMINATION *************
350 PRINT
360 PRINT
370 PRINT "PROCESSING COMPLETE"
380 PRINT
390 STOP


400 REM ******************** OPEN AND READ NAME FILE ***********
410 PRINT "ENTER THE NAME OF THE INPUT NAME FILE";
420 INPUT F$
430 OPEN "I",1,F$
440 INPUT#1,N
450 FOR I=1 TO N
460   INPUT#1,T$(I),N$(I)
470 NEXT I
480 F$=""
490 CLOSE 1
500 RETURN


510 REM ******************** OPEN AND WRITE TO FILE **********
520 OPEN "O",2,F$
530 PRINT#2,N;
540 FOR I=1 TO N
550   PRINT#2,A(I);
560 NEXT I
570 CLOSE 2
580 RETURN
```

```
RUN "AMTS"

ENTER THE NAME OF THE INPUT NAME FILE? ACCTS

ENTER AMOUNTS FOR THE ACCOUNTS SHOWN

A....CASH....? 1950
A....SUPPLIES....? 50
A....EQUIPMENT....? 1000
L....ACCOUNTS PAYABLE....? 400
C....CAPITAL....? 1800
I....INCOME....? 1250
E....RENT EXPENSE....? 250
E....SUPPLIES EXPENSE....? 100
E....TELEPHONE EXPENSE....? 100

  #    TYPE      NAME              AMOUNT
  1    A         CASH              1950
  2    A         SUPPLIES          50
  3    A         EQUIPMENT         1000
  4    L         ACCOUNTS PAYABLE  400
  5    C         CAPITAL           1800
  6    I         INCOME            1250
  7    E         RENT EXPENSE      250
  8    E         SUPPLIES EXPENSE  100
  9    E         TELEPHONE EXPENSE 100
ARE THERE ANY ITEMS TO CHANGE (Y OR N)? N
ENTER FILE NAME FOR STORING AMOUNTS? JAN81


PROCESSING COMPLETE

BREAK IN 390
OK
```

MAJOR SYMBOL TABLE — RECORD AND AMTS

NAME	DESCRIPTION
A$	TEMP ANSWER VARIABLE
A()	AMOUNT ARRAY
F$	FILE NAME
I	INDEX AND ARRAY POINTER
J	INDEX AND ARRAY POINTER
K	REFERENCE TO THE NUMBER TO CHANGE
M	MAXIMUM NUMBER OF ACCOUNTS
N	NUMBER OF ACCOUNTS
N$()	ACCOUNT NAME ARRAY
T$()	ACCOUNT TYPE ARRAY

FUNCTIONS USED

NAME
TAB
GOSUB
RETURN
OPEN
PRINT#
INPUT#
CLOSE
DIM

Income Statement Preparation

Program Name: INCOME

This program produces an income statement from information entered at the keyboard and from the input files specified during the program's execution. It does *not* require the processing of a computerized bookkeeping system but *does* require that account name and amount information be available in an input file. The programs RECORD and AMTS provide files that are compatible with this program.

Files Affected: None

```
10 REM            SAVED AT INCOME
20 REM            PRODUCES INCOME STATEMENT
30 REM ********************************************************
40 M=25
50 DIM T$(M),N$(M),A(M),T1$(2)
60 T1$(1)="INCOME"
70 T1$(2)="EXPENSES"
80 PRINT "ENTER THE NAME OF THE ACCOUNTS NAME FILE";
90 INPUT F$
100 PRINT "ENTER THE NAME OF THE AMOUNT FILE";
110 INPUT F1$
120 GOSUB 210                    'OPEN AND READ FILES
130 GOSUB 340                    'PERFORM PROCESSING
140 REM *********** PROGRAM TERMINATION POINT ****************
150 PRINT
160 PRINT
170 PRINT "PROCESSING COMPLETE"
180 PRINT
190 CLOSE 1,2
200 STOP


210 REM ****************** OPEN AND READ FILES ***************
220 OPEN"I",1,F$
230 OPEN "I",2,F1$
240 INPUT#1,N
250 INPUT#2,N1
260 IF N=N1 THEN 290
270 PRINT "FILES ARE NOT COMPATIBLE"
280 GOTO 150
290 FOR I=1 TO N
300    INPUT#1,T$(I),N$(I)
310    INPUT#2,A(I)
320 NEXT I
330 RETURN


340 REM ****************** INCOME STATEMENT ****************
350 PRINT "ENTER THE REPORT PERIOD ";
360 INPUT D4$
370 PRINT
380 PRINT "POSITION PAPER NOW - PRESS RETURN WHEN READY";
390 INPUT A$
400 PRINT
410 PRINT TAB(30);F$
420 PRINT TAB(30);"INCOME STATEMENT"
430 PRINT TAB(30);D4$
```

```
440 PRINT
450 PRINT
460 FOR I=1 TO N
470   IF T$(I)="I" THEN 490
480 NEXT I
490 K1=I
500 J=1
510 PRINT TAB(5);T1$(J)
520 FOR I=K1 TO N
530   IF T$(I)="E" AND J=1 THEN GOTO 580
540   PRINT TAB(10);N$(I);TAB(40);
550   PRINT A(I)
560   A1=A1+A(I)
570 NEXT I
580 PRINT TAB(38);"-------------"
590 PRINT TAB(5);"TOTAL ";T1$(J);;TAB(50);A1
600 PRINT
610 IF J=1 THEN A2=A2+A1
620 IF J=2 THEN A2=A2-A1
630 J=J+1
640 A1=0
650 K1=I
660 IF J<=2 THEN 510
670 PRINT TAB(48);"----------------"
680 PRINT TAB(5);"NET INCOME(LOSS)";TAB(50);
690 IF A2>0 THEN PRINT A2
700 IF A2<0 THEN PRINT "(";A2;")"
710 PRINT TAB(48);"================"
720 RETURN
```

```
RUN "INCOME"
ENTER THE NAME OF THE ACCOUNTS NAME FILE? ACCTS
ENTER THE NAME OF THE AMOUNT FILE? JAN81
ENTER THE REPORT PERIOD ? JANUARY 1981

POSITION PAPER NOW - PRESS RETURN WHEN READY?


                         ACCTS
                         INCOME STATEMENT
                         JANUARY 1981


     INCOME
           INCOME                      1250
                                 ---------------
     TOTAL INCOME                              1250


     EXPENSES
           RENT EXPENSE                 250
           SUPPLIES EXPENSE             100
           TELEPHONE EXPENSE            100
                                 ---------------
     TOTAL EXPENSES                             450


                                        ---------------
     NET INCOME(LOSS)                          800
                                        ===============


PROCESSING COMPLETE

BREAK IN 200
OK
```

```
MAJOR SYMBOL TABLE - INCOME                                                  FUNCTIONS USED
I------------------------------------------------------------------I        I------------------I
I NAME    .. DESCRIPTION                                           I        I  NAME            I
I------------------------------------------------------------------I        I------------------I
I  A$     .. TEMP ANSWER VARIABLE                                  I        I DIM              I
I  A()    .. AMOUNT ARRAY                                          I        I CLOSE            I
I  A1     .. TOTAL VARIABLE                                        I        I OPEN             I
I  A2     .. NET INCOME                                            I        I GOSUB            I
I  D4$    .. REPORT PERIOD                                         I        I RETURN           I
I  F$     .. NAME OF ACCOUNT NAME FILE                             I        I INPUT#           I
I  F1$    .. NAME OF AMOUNT FILE                                   I        I TAB              I
I  I      .. INDEX AND ARRAY POINTER                               I        I------------------I
I  J      .. POSITION VARIABLE 1=INCOME 2=EXPENSES                 I
I  K1     .. INDEX START POINT                                     I
I  M      .. MAXIMUM ARRAY SIZE                                    I
I  N      .. NUMBER OF ACCOUNT NAMES                               I
I  N$()   .. ACCOUNT NAME ARRAY                                    I
I  N1     .. NUMBER OF AMOUNTS RECORDED                            I
I  T$()   .. ACCOUNT TYPE ARRAY                                    I
I  T1$()  .. ACCOUNT TYPE NAME ARRAY                               I
I------------------------------------------------------------------I
```

Balance Sheet Preparation

Program Name: BALANCE

This program produces a balance sheet from information entered at the keyboard and from the input files specified during the program's execution. It does *not* require the operation of a fully computerized bookkeeping system but *does* require that an account name file and amount information in an input file be available. The programs RECORD and AMTS provide the files that are necessary for the operation of this program.

Files Affected: None

```
10 REM            SAVED AT BALANCE
20 REM            PRODUCES BALANCE SHEET
30 REM ************************************************************
40 M=25
50 DIM T$(M),N$(M),A(M),T1$(3)
60 T1$(1)="ASSETS"
70 T1$(2)="LIABILITIES"
80 T1$(3)="CAPITAL"
90 PRINT "ENTER THE NAME OF THE ACCOUNTS NAME FILE";
100 INPUT F$
110 PRINT "ENTER THE NAME OF THE AMOUNT FILE";
120 INPUT F1$
130 PRINT
140 PRINT "ENTER THE NET INCOME OR LOSS (-) FOR THE PERIOD";
150 INPUT N9
```

```
160 GOSUB 250                    'OPEN AND READ FILES
170 GOSUB 380                    'PERFORM PROCESSING
180 REM ************* PROGRAM TERMINATION POINT ******************
190 PRINT
200 PRINT
210 PRINT "PROCESSING COMPLETE"
220 PRINT
230 CLOSE 1,2
240 STOP


250 REM ****************** OPEN AND READ FILES ******************
260 OPEN"I",1,F$
270 OPEN "I",2,F1$
280 INPUT#1,N
290 INPUT#2,N1
300 IF N=N1 THEN 330
310 PRINT "FILES ARE NOT COMPATIBLE"
320 GOTO 190
330 FOR I=1 TO N
340   INPUT#1,T$(I),N$(I)
350   INPUT#2,A(I)
360 NEXT I
370 RETURN


380 REM **************** BALANCE SHEET ***********************
390 PRINT "ENTER THE REPORT DATE ";
400 INPUT D4$
410 PRINT
420 PRINT "POSITION PAPER NOW - PRESS RETURN WHEN READY";
430 INPUT A$
440 PRINT
450 PRINT TAB(30);F$
460 PRINT TAB(30);"BALANCE SHEET"
470 PRINT TAB(30);D4$
480 PRINT
490 PRINT
500 T=50
510 K1=1
520 T$(0)=T$(1)
530 FOR J=1 TO 3
540   IF J=1 THEN PRINT TAB(30);T1$(1)
550   IFJ<>2 THEN 590
560   T=40
570   PRINT TAB(25);"LIABILITIES AND CAPITAL"
580   A2=0
590   PRINT
600   PRINT TAB(5);T1$(J)
610   IF J<>3 THEN 640
620   PRINT TAB(10);"NET INCOME/LOSS(-)";TAB(T);N9
630   A1=A1+N9
640   FOR I=K1 TO N
650     IF T$(I)<>T$(0) THEN 710
660     A0=A(I)
670     PRINT TAB(10);N$(I);TAB(40);A0
680     A1=A1+A0
690     A0=0
700   NEXT I
710   PRINT TAB(T-2);"----------------"
720   PRINT TAB(5);"TOTAL ";T1$(J);;TAB(50);A1
730   IF J=1 THEN PRINT TAB(48);"================"
740   K1=I
750   PRINT
760   A2=A2+A1
770   A1=0
780   T$(0)=T$(I)
790 NEXT J
```

```
800 PRINT TAB(48);"----------------"
810 PRINT TAB(5);"TOTAL LIABILITIES AND CAPITAL";TAB(50);A2
820 PRINT TAB(48);"================"
830 RETURN
```

```
RUN "BALANCE"
ENTER THE NAME OF THE ACCOUNTS NAME FILE? ACCTS
ENTER THE NAME OF THE AMOUNT FILE? JAN81

ENTER THE NET INCOME OR LOSS (-) FOR THE PERIOD? 800
ENTER THE REPORT DATE ? JANUARY 31 1981

POSITION PAPER NOW - PRESS RETURN WHEN READY?



                              ACCTS
                              BALANCE SHEET
                              JANUARY 31 1981


                              ASSETS

        ASSETS
              CASH                        1950
              SUPPLIES                    50
              EQUIPMENT                   1000
                                                  ----------------
        TOTAL ASSETS                              3000
                                                  ================

                        LIABILITIES AND CAPITAL

        LIABILITIES
              ACCOUNTS PAYABLE            400
                                          ----------------
        TOTAL LIABILITIES                          400


        CAPITAL
              NET INCOME/LOSS(-)          800
              CAPITAL                     1800
                                                  ----------------
        TOTAL CAPITAL                              2600


                                                  ----------------
        TOTAL LIABILITIES AND CAPITAL             3000
                                                  ================


PROCESSING COMPLETE

BREAK IN 240
OK
```

```
MAJOR SYMBOL TABLE - BALANCE                              FUNCTIONS USED
I----------------------------------------------I          I------------------I
I NAME     .. DESCRIPTION                     I          I  NAME            I
I----------------------------------------------I          I------------------I
I  A$      .. TEMP ANSWER VARIABLE            I          I  DIM             I
I  A()     .. AMOUNT ARRAY                    I          I  CLOSE           I
I  A0      .. AMOUNT FOR PRINTING             I          I  OPEN            I
I  A1      .. TOTAL VARIABLE                  I          I  GOSUB           I
I  A2      .. TOTAL VARIABLE                  I          I  RETURN          I
I  D4$     .. DATE OF REPORT                  I          I  INPUT#          I
I  F$      .. FILE NAME                       I          I  TAB             I
I  F1$     .. NAME OF AMOUNT FILE             I          I------------------I
I  I       .. INDEX AND ARRAY POINTER         I
I  J       .. INDEX AND ARRAY POINTER         I
I  K1      .. INDEX START POINT               I
I  M       .. MAXIMUM ARRAY SIZE              I
I  N       .. NUMBER OF ACCOUNT NAMES         I
I  N$()    .. ACCOUNT NAME ARRAY              I
I  N1      .. NUMBER OF AMOUNTS IN FILE       I
I  N9      .. NET INCOME/LOSS                 I
I  T$()    .. ACCOUNT TYPE ARRAY              I
I  T1$()   .. ACCOUNT TYPE NAME ARRAY         I
I----------------------------------------------I
```

Cash Flow and Budget Analysis

Program Name: BUDGET

This program produces either a cash flow forecast or a budget forecast for future time periods. It does *not* require the operation of a fully
automated bookkeeping system but *does* require that amount information for each account be available in an input file. The programs
RECORD and AMTS produce the files necessary for the operation of
this program. All other information is entered in response to program
prompting.

Files Affected: None

```
10 REM            SAVED AT BUDGET
20 REM    CASH FLOW AND BUDGET ANALYSIS PROGRAM
30 REM *********************************************************
40 T=10
50 M=25
60 PRINT "HOW MANY ACCOUNTING PERIODS (FILES SHALL I INCLUDE";
70 INPUT N9
80 DIM P$(N9)
90 PRINT "ENTER THE 3 CHARACTER ABBREVIATION FOR EACH PERIOD"
100 FOR I=1 TO N9
110    INPUT P$(I)
120 NEXT I
130 PRINT "ENTER THE FILE NAMES"
```

```
140 DIM T$(M),N$(M),A(M,N9+1),T1$(5),F1$(N9),N1(9),A2(N9+1),T2(N9+1)
150 FOR I=1 TO N9
160    INPUT F1$(I)
170 NEXT I
180 T1$(1)="ASSETS"
190 T1$(2)="LIABILITIES"
200 T1$(3)="CAPITAL"
210 T1$(4)="INCOME"
220 T1$(5)="EXPENSES"
230 PRINT "ENTER THE NAME OF THE ACCOUNTS NAME FILE";
240 INPUT F$
250 PRINT
260 GOSUB 350                        'OPEN AND READ FILES
270 GOSUB 520                        'PERFORM PROCESSING
280 REM ****************** PROGRAM TERMINATION POINT  *************
290 PRINT
300 PRINT
310 PRINT "PROCESSING COMPLETE"
320 PRINT
330 CLOSE 1,2
340 STOP


350 REM *****************  OPEN AND READ FILES ********************
360 OPEN"I",1,F$
370 INPUT#1,N
380 FOR I=2 TO N9+1
390    OPEN "I",I,F1$(I-1)
400    INPUT#I,N1(I-1)
410    IF N=N1(I-1) THEN 440
420    PRINT "FILES ARE NOT COMPATIBLE"
430    GOTO 290
440 NEXT I
450 FOR I=1 TO N
460    INPUT#1,T$(I),N$(I)
470    FOR J=1 TO N9
480       INPUT#J+1,A(I,J)
490    NEXT J
500 NEXT I
510 RETURN


520 REM ****************INCOME AND EXPENSE ANALYSIS ****************
530 PRINT "ARE WE ANALYZING CASH FLOWS OR BUDGETS (C OR B)";
540 INPUT A$
550 IF A$<>"C" THEN 580
560 PRINT "ENTER INITIAL CASH POSITION";
570 INPUT C
580 J1=3
590 T$(0)=T$(1)
600 J=1
610 FOR K1=1 TO N
620    IF T$(K1)<>T$(0) THEN J=J+1
630    T$(0)=T$(K1)
640    IF J>J1 THEN GOTO 660
650 NEXT K1
660 PRINT
670 PRINT "POSITION PAPER NOW - PRESS RETURN WHEN READY";
680 INPUT
690 PRINT
700 REM ********************  PRINT HEADINGS *******************
710 PRINT TAB(30);F$
720 PRINT TAB(25);
730 IF A$="C" THEN PRINT "CASH FLOW ANALYSIS"
740 IF A$="B" THEN PRINT "BUDGET ANALYSIS"
750 PRINT
760 IF A$="C" THEN PRINT "INITIAL CASH";C
770 PRINT
```

```
780 FOR I=1 TO  N9
790    PRINT TAB(T*(I-1)+22);P$(I);
800 NEXT I
810 PRINT "     TOTAL      AVERAGE"
820 PRINT
830 REM ********************** PRINTING LOOP *********************
840 FOR I=K1 TO N
850    IF T$(0)<>T$(I) THEN 960
860    PRINT N$(I);
870    FOR I1=1 TO N9+1
880       IF I1<=N9 THEN  A(I,N9+1)=A(I,N9+1)+A(I,I1)
890       A2(I1)=A2(I1)+A(I,I1)
900       PRINT TAB(T*(I1-1)+20);A(I,I1);
910    NEXT I1
920    PRINT TAB(T*(I1-1)+20);A(I,N9+1)/N9
930    A(I,N9+1)=0
940 NEXT I
950 REM ***************** PRINT SUBTOTAL LINES  *******************
960 PRINT TAB(20);"----------------------------------------------------------------"
970 PRINT TAB(5);"SUBTOTAL ";
980 FOR I1=1 TO N9+1
990    PRINT TAB(T*(I1-1)+20);A2(I1);
1000    IF J1=3 THEN T2(I1)=A2(I1)
1010    IF J1=4 THEN T2(I1)=T2(I1)-A2(I1)
1020    IF I1<N9+1 THEN A2(I1)=0
1030 NEXT I1
1040 PRINT TAB(T*(I1-1)+20);A2(I1-1)/N9
1050 A2(I1-1)=0
1060 PRINT
1070 J1=J1+1
1080 K1=I
1090 T$(0)=T$(I)
1100 IF J1<=4 THEN 830
1110 REM ***************** PRINT TOTAL   ***********************
1120 PRINT TAB(20);"================================================================"
1130 PRINT TAB(5);"TOTAL";
1140 FOR  I1=1 TO N9+1
1150    PRINT TAB(T*(I1-1)+20);T2(I1);
1160 NEXT I1
1170 PRINT TAB(T*(I1-1)+20);T2(I1-1)/N9
1180 PRINT
1190 REM ***************** PRINT CASH POSITION *****************
1200 IF A$<>"C" THEN 1260
1210 PRINT "CASH POSITION - END";
1220 FOR I1=1 TO N9
1230    C=C+T2(I1)
1240    PRINT TAB(T*(I1-1)+20);C;
1250 NEXT I1
1260 PRINT
1270 PRINT
1280 PRINT
1290 RETURN




RUN "BUDGET"
HOW MANY ACCOUNTING PERIODS (FILES SHALL I INCLUDE? 1
ENTER THE 3 CHARACTER ABBREVIATION FOR EACH PERIOD
? JAN
ENTER THE FILE NAMES
? JAN81
ENTER THE NAME OF THE ACCOUNTS NAME FILE? ACCTS

ARE WE ANALYZING CASH FLOWS OR BUDGETS (C OR B)? C
ENTER INITIAL CASH POSITION? 2100

POSITION PAPER NOW - PRESS RETURN WHEN READY?
```

```
                            ACCTS
                    CASH FLOW ANALYSIS

INITIAL CASH 2100

                        JAN      TOTAL      AVERAGE

INCOME                 1250      1250       1250
                   ------------------------------------------------------------
        SUBTOTAL       1250      1250       1250

RENT EXPENSE            250       250        250
SUPPLIES EXPENSE        100       100        100
TELEPHONE EXPENSE       100       100        100
                   ------------------------------------------------------------
        SUBTOTAL        450       450        450

                   ============================================================
        TOTAL           800       800        800

CASH POSITION - END    2900



PROCESSING COMPLETE

BREAK IN 340
OK
```

```
    MAJOR SYMBOL TABLE - BUDGET                          FUNCTIONS USED
I------------------------------------------------I   I------------------I
I NAME   .. DESCRIPTION                          I   I  NAME            I
I------------------------------------------------I   I------------------I
I  A$    .. TYPE OF PRINT                        I   I DIM              I
I  A()   .. AMOUNT ARRAY                         I   I OPEN             I
I  A2()  .. SUBTOTAL ARRAY                       I   I CLOSE            I
I  C     .. CASH POSITION                        I   I GOSUB            I
I  F$    .. NAME OF ACCOUNT NAME FILE            I   I RETURN           I
I  F1$() .. ARRAY OF FILE NAMES                  I   I INPUT#           I
I  I     .. INDEX AND ARRAY POINTER              I   I TAB              I
I  I1    .. INDEX AND ARRAY POINTER              I   I------------------I
I  J     .. INDEX AND ARRAY POINTER              I
I  J1    .. POINTER TO STOP POSITION             I
I  K1    .. POINTER TO START POSITION            I
I  M     .. MAXIMUM ARRAY SIZE                   I
I  N     .. NUMBER OF ACCOUNT NAMES              I
I  N$()  .. ACCOUNT NAME ARRAY                   I
I  N1()  .. NUMBER OF AMOUNTS IN THE FILE        I
I  N9    .. NUMBER OF PERIODS TO USE             I
I  P$()  .. NAME OF PERIOD ARRAY                 I
I  T     .. NUMBER OF SPACES TO TAB              I
I  T$()  .. ACCOUNT TYPE ARRAY                   I
I  T1$() .. ACCOUNT TYPE - NAME ARRAY            I
I  T2()  .. TOTAL ARRAY                          I
I------------------------------------------------I
```

Income and Expense Analysis

Program Name: FCOMP

This program produces an income or expense analysis report that may be compared with reports for other periods and account averages. It does *not* require the operation of a fully automated bookkeeping system but *does* require the availability of account name and amount files that are produced by the RECORD and AMTS programs.

Files Affected: None

```
10 REM              SAVED AT FCOMP
20 REM      INCOME AND EXPENSE ANALYSIS PROGRAM
30 REM ***********************************************************
40 T=10
50 M=25
60 PRINT "HOW MANY ACCOUNTING PERIODS (FILES SHALL I INCLUDE";
70 INPUT N9
80 PRINT "ENTER THE FILE NAMES"
90 DIM T$(M),N$(M),A(M,N9+1),T1$(5),F1$(N9),N1(9),A2(N9+1)
100 FOR I=1 TO N9
110    INPUT F1$(I)
120 NEXT I
130 T1$(1)="ASSETS"
140 T1$(2)="LIABILITIES"
150 T1$(3)="CAPITAL"
160 T1$(4)="INCOME"
170 T1$(5)="EXPENSES"
180 PRINT "ENTER THE NAME OF THE ACCOUNTS NAME FILE";
190 INPUT F$
200 PRINT
210 GOSUB 300                    'OPEN AND READ FILES
220 GOSUB 470                    'PERFORM PROCESSING
230 REM ****************** PROGRAM TERMINATION POINT  ***********
240 PRINT
250 PRINT
260 PRINT "PROCESSING COMPLETE"
270 PRINT
280 CLOSE 1,2
290 STOP


300 REM ****************  OPEN AND READ FILES ********************
310 OPEN"I",1,F$
320 INPUT#1,N
330 FOR I=2 TO N9+1
340    OPEN "I",I,F1$(I-1)
350    INPUT#I,N1(I-1)
360    IF N=N1(I-1) THEN 390
370    PRINT "FILES ARE NOT COMPATIBLE"
380    GOTO 240
390 NEXT I
400 FOR I=1 TO N
410    INPUT#1,T$(I),N$(I)
420    FOR J=1 TO N9
430       INPUT#J+1,A(I,J)
440    NEXT J
450 NEXT I
460 RETURN
```

```
470 REM ****************INCOME AND EXPENSE ANALYSIS *****************
480 PRINT "DO YOU WISH TO COMPARE INCOME OR EXPENSES (I OR E)";
490 INPUT A$
500 J1=3
510 IF A$="E" THEN J1=4
520 T$(0)=T$(1)
530 J=1
540 FOR K1=1 TO N
550   IF T$(K1)<>T$(0) THEN J=J+1
560   T$(0)=T$(K1)
570   IF J>J1 THEN GOTO 590
580 NEXT K1
590 PRINT
600 PRINT "POSITION PAPER NOW - PRESS RETURN WHEN READY";
610 INPUT A$
620 PRINT
630 REM ******************** PRINT HEADINGS *********************
640 PRINT TAB(30);F$
650 PRINT TAB(25);"COMPARISON OF ";T1$(J)
660 PRINT TAB(30);D4$
670 PRINT
680 FOR I=1 TO N9
690   PRINT TAB(T*(I-1)+20);"PER";I;
700 NEXT I
710 PRINT "    TOTAL    AVERAGE"
720 PRINT
730 REM ********************** PRINT DETAIL RECORDS ***************
740 FOR I=K1 TO N
750   IF T$(0)<>T$(I) THEN 870
760   I1=N9
770   PRINT N$(I);
780   FOR I1=1 TO N9+1
790     IF I1<=N9 THEN  A(I,N9+1)=A(I,N9+1)+A(I,I1)
800     A2(I1)=A2(I1)+A(I,I1)
810     PRINT TAB(T*(I1-1)+20);A(I,I1);
820   NEXT I1
830   PRINT TAB(T*(I1-1)+20);A(I,N9+1)/N9
840   A(I,N9+1)=0
850 NEXT I
860 REM ********************** PRINT TOTALS *********************
870 PRINT TAB(20);"----------------------------------------------
880 PRINT TAB(5);"TOTAL ";
890 FOR I1=1 TO N9+1
900   PRINT TAB(T*(I1-1)+20);A2(I1);
910 NEXT I1
920 PRINT TAB(T*(I1-1)+20);A2(I1-1)/N9
930 PRINT
940 RETURN



RUN "FCOMP"
HOW MANY ACCOUNTING PERIODS (FILES SHALL I INCLUDE? 2
ENTER THE FILE NAMES
? DEC80
? JAN81
ENTER THE NAME OF THE ACCOUNTS NAME FILE? ACCTS

DO YOU WISH TO COMPARE INCOME OR EXPENSES (I OR E)? I

POSITION PAPER NOW - PRESS RETURN WHEN READY?
```

ACCTS
COMPARISON OF INCOME

	PER 1	PER 2	TOTAL	AVERAGE
INCOME	1500	1250	2750	1375
TOTAL	1500	1250	2750	1375

```
PROCESSING COMPLETE

BREAK IN 290
OK




RUN "FCOMP"
HOW MANY ACCOUNTING PERIODS (FILES SHALL I INCLUDE? 2
ENTER THE FILE NAMES
? DEC80
? JAN81
ENTER THE NAME OF THE ACCOUNTS NAME FILE? ACCTS

DO YOU WISH TO COMPARE INCOME OR EXPENSES (I OR E)? E

POSITION PAPER NOW - PRESS RETURN WHEN READY?

                         ACCTS
                  COMPARISON OF EXPENSES


                  PER 1      PER 2      TOTAL      AVERAGE

RENT EXPENSE       250        250        500        250
SUPPLIES EXPENSE   150        100        250        125
TELEPHONE EXPENSE  60         100        160        80
                  ----------------------------------------------------
     TOTAL         460        450        910        455



PROCESSING COMPLETE

BREAK IN 290
OK
```

```
  MAJOR SYMBOL TABLE - FCOMP                    FUNCTIONS USED
I----------------------------------------------I   I----------------I
I NAME  .. DESCRIPTION                         I   I   NAME         I
I----------------------------------------------I   I----------------I
I  A$    .. TEMP ANSWER VARIABLE               I   I DIM            I
I  A()   .. AMOUNT ARRAY                       I   I OPEN           I
I  A2()  .. TOTAL ARRAY                        I   I CLOSE          I
I  F$    .. NAME OF ACCOUNT NAME FILE          I   I GOSUB          I
I  F1$() .. ARRAY OF FILE NAMES                I   I RETURN         I
I  I     .. INDEX AND ARRAY POINTER            I   I INPUT#         I
I  I1    .. INDEX AND ARRAY POINTER            I   I TAB            I
I  J     .. INDEX AND ARRAY POINTER            I   I----------------I
I  J1    .. POINTER TO STOP POSITION           I
I  K1    .. POINTER TO START POSITION          I
I  M     .. MAXIMUM ARRAY SIZE                 I
I  N     .. NUMBER OF ACCOUNT NAMES            I
I  N$()  .. ACCOUNT NAME ARRAY                 I
I  N1()  .. NUMBER OF AMOUNTS IN THE FILE      I
I  N9    .. NUMBER OF PERIODS TO USE           I
I  T     .. NUMBER OF SPACES TO TAB            I
I  T$()  .. ACCOUNT TYPE ARRAY                 I
I  T1$() .. ACCOUNT TYPE - NAME ARRAY          I
I----------------------------------------------I
```

Forecasting

This series of programs has been provided to assist in the projection of business activity into future time periods. Since no one forecasting methodology is suitable for all circumstances, several different methodologies are represented in these programs. A detailed explanation of the theory and assumptions behind each of the approaches can easily be found in a wide variety of publications. This knowledge is unnecessary, however, for the actual execution of the programs contained in this book. Since these programs do not utilize any files, they are independent of all other systems. All required information is entered in response to program prompting.

Least Squares Regression Forecasting

Program Name: FCAST1

This program provides for the forecasting of business activity by means of the least squares regression methodology. Historical data of sales, demand, utilization, and the like, are entered for each past period in response to program prompting. From this information, the program projects the trend for all future periods specified. This data is plotted as a straight line on a graph. Both of the relevant parameters—A (the Y intercept) and B (the slope of the line)—are provided for those who are mathematically inclined. The program also produces a table providing forecasts for all periods specified.

Files Affected: None

```
10 REM            SAVED AT FCAST1
20 REM   USES LEAST SQUARES REGRESSION METHODOLOGY
30 REM ***********************************************************
40 PRINT "ENTER THE NUMBER OF TIME PERIODS TO BE ENTERED";
50 INPUT N
60 PRINT "ENTER THE NUMBER OF FUTURE PERIODS TO FORECAST";
70 INPUT N1
80 FOR P=1 TO N
90    X0=P
100   PRINT "ENTER VALUE FOR PERIOD ";P;
110   INPUT Y0
120   Y1=Y1+Y0
130   X1=X1+X0
140   Z1=Z1+X0*Y0
150   X2=X2+X0^2
160 NEXT P
170 REM ***************** COMPUTATION OF A AND B ***************
180 A=(X2*Y1-X1*Z1)/(N*X2-X1^2)
190 B=(N*Z1-X1*Y1)/(N*X2-X1^2)
200 PRINT
210 PRINT
```

```
220 REM ******************* FORECAST AREA  ********************
230 PRINT "****************************************"
240 PRINT "LEAST SQUARES REGRESSION FORECAST"
250 PRINT
260 PRINT
270 PRINT "VALUE OF REGRESSION LINE IS:"
280 PRINT "Y=";A;"+";B;"X"
290 PRINT
300 PRINT "PERIOD";TAB(10);"FORECAST"
310 FOR P=1 TO N+N1
320    Y9=A+B*P
330    PRINT P;TAB(10);Y9
340    IF P<>N THEN 380
350    PRINT "*************************"
360    PRINT "FORECASTED FUTURE PERIODS"
370    PRINT
380 NEXT P
390 PRINT
400 PRINT "****************************************"
410 REM ****************** PROGRAM TERMINATION POINT  ***********
420 PRINT
430 STOP
```

```
RUN "FCAST1"
ENTER THE NUMBER OF TIME PERIODS TO BE ENTERED? 5
ENTER THE NUMBER OF FUTURE PERIODS TO FORECAST? 2
ENTER VALUE FOR PERIOD  1 ? 40
ENTER VALUE FOR PERIOD  2 ? 50
ENTER VALUE FOR PERIOD  3 ? 55
ENTER VALUE FOR PERIOD  4 ? 72
ENTER VALUE FOR PERIOD  5 ? 81


****************************************
LEAST SQUARES REGRESSION FORECAST


VALUE OF REGRESSION LINE IS:
Y= 28.4001 + 10.4 X

PERIOD     FORECAST
  1          38.8001
  2          49.2001
  3          59.6002
  4          70.0002
  5          80.4002
*************************
FORECASTED FUTURE PERIODS

  6          90.8002
  7         101.2


****************************************

BREAK IN 430
OK
```

```
MAJOR SYMBOL TABLE - FCAST1                                              FUNCTIONS USED
I-------------------------------------------------------------------I    I-------------------I
I NAME    .. DESCRIPTION                                            I    I NAME            I
I-------------------------------------------------------------------I    I-------------------I
I  A      .. VALUE OF Y INTERCEPT                                   I    I TAB             I
I  B      .. VALUE OF SLOPE                                         I    I-------------------I
I  N      .. NUMBER OF PERIODS TO BE ENTERED                        I
I  N1     .. NUMBER OF FUTURE PERIODS TO FORECAST                   I
I  P      .. PERIOD NUMBER                                          I
I  XO     .. PERIOD NUMBER                                          I
I  X1     .. SUM OF XO                                              I
I  X2     .. SUM OF X SQUARED                                       I
I  YO     .. VALUE FOR PERIOD                                       I
I  Y1     .. SUM OF YO                                              I
I  Y9     .. FORECASTED VALUE OF YO                                 I
I  Z1     .. SUM OF XO TIMES YO                                     I
I-------------------------------------------------------------------I
```

Moving-Average Forecasting

Program Name: FCAST2

This program provides for the forecasting of business activity by means of a simple-moving average technique. The forecast for any given period is determined by averaging the data for a specified number of previous periods. This number is specified during program initialization.

Files Affected: None

```
10 REM            SAVED AT FCAST2
20 REM   USES SIMPLE MOVING AVERAGE FORECASTING
30 REM ****************************************************************
40 PRINT "ENTER THE NUMBER OF TIME PERIODS TO BE ENTERED";
50 INPUT N
60 DIM YO(N+1)
70 PRINT "ENTER THE NUMBER OF PERIODS FOR THE MOVING AVERAGE";
80 INPUT M
90 FOR P=1 TO N
100    PRINT "ENTER VALUE FOR PERIOD ";P;
110    INPUT YO(P)
120 NEXT P
130 PRINT
140 PRINT
150 REM ******************* FORECAST AREA  **********************
160 PRINT "****************************************"
170 PRINT
180 PRINT "SIMPLE MOVING AVERAGE FORECAST"
190 PRINT
200 PRINT "PERIOD";TAB(10);"ACTUAL";TAB(20);"FORECAST";TAB(30);"DIFF"
210 PRINT
220 FOR P=1 TO N+1
230    Y9=0
240    IF P<=M THEN 310
250    FOR I= 1 TO M
260      Y9=Y9+YO(P-I)
270    NEXT I
```

```
280    Y9=Y9/M
290    IF P=N+1 THEN 350
300    D=Y9-Y0(P)
310    PRINT P;TAB(10);Y0(P);TAB(20);Y9;TAB(30);D
320    IF P<>N THEN 340
330    PRINT "---------------------------------------"
340 NEXT P
350 PRINT P;TAB(20);Y9
360 PRINT
370 PRINT "*****************************************"
380 REM ******************* PROGRAM TERMINATION POINT  ***********
390 PRINT
400 STOP
```

```
RUN "FCAST2"
ENTER THE NUMBER OF TIME PERIODS TO BE ENTERED? 9
ENTER THE NUMBER OF PERIODS FOR THE MOVING AVERAGE? 3
ENTER VALUE FOR PERIOD  1 ? 500
ENTER VALUE FOR PERIOD  2 ? 520
ENTER VALUE FOR PERIOD  3 ? 570
ENTER VALUE FOR PERIOD  4 ? 530
ENTER VALUE FOR PERIOD  5 ? 590
ENTER VALUE FOR PERIOD  6 ? 580
ENTER VALUE FOR PERIOD  7 ? 480
ENTER VALUE FOR PERIOD  8 ? 520
ENTER VALUE FOR PERIOD  9 ? 520


*****************************************

SIMPLE MOVING AVERAGE FORECAST

PERIOD    ACTUAL    FORECAST  DIFF

1         500       0         0
2         520       0         0
3         570       0         0
4         530       530       0
5         590       540       -50
6         580       563.333   -16.6667
7         480       566.667   86.6667
8         520       550       30
9         520       526.667   6.66669
-----------------------------------------
10                  506.667

*********************************************

BREAK IN 400
OK
```

```
  MAJOR SYMBOL TABLE - FCAST2                                          FUNCTIONS USED
I----------------------------------------------------------I       I---------------I
I NAME   .. DESCRIPTION                                     I       I NAME          I
I----------------------------------------------------------I       I---------------I
I  D     .. DIFFERENCE BETWEEN FORECASTED AND OBSERVED      I       I TAB           I
I  I     .. TEMPORARY WORK VARIABLE                         I       I DIM           I
I  M     .. NUMBER OF PERIODS TO COMBINE IN THE AVERAGE     I       I---------------I
I  N     .. NUMBER OF HISTORY PERIODS TO BE ENTERED         I
I  P     .. PERIOD NUMBER                                   I
I  Y0()  .. ACTUAL VALUES FOR EACH PERIOD                   I
I  Y9    .. FORECASTED VALUE                                I
I----------------------------------------------------------I
```

Exponential-Smoothing Forecasting

Program Name: FCAST3

This program uses a forecasting methodology known as *exponential smoothing*, in which the forecast for a period is based upon combining a percentage of the forecast for the previous period with the actual figures for that period. This percentage, called the *smoothing constant*, can take any value between 0 and 1, depending upon the weighting you wish to give the two factors. A value of 1 gives full weight to the actual data for the previous period, whereas zero gives full weight to the previous forecast. The constant is specified during the program's initialization phase.

Files Affected: None

```
10 REM             SAVED AT FCAST3
20 REM    USES EXPONENTIAL SMOOTHING METHODOLOGY
30 REM *********************************************************************
40 PRINT "ENTER THE NUMBER OF TIME PERIODS TO BE ENTERED";
50 INPUT N
60 DIM Y0(N),Y9(N+1)
70 PRINT "ENTER THE VALUE OF THE SMOOTHING CONSTANT (0-1)";
80 INPUT A
90 FOR P=1 TO N
100    PRINT "ENTER VALUE FOR PERIOD ";P;
110    INPUT Y0(P)
120 NEXT P
130 PRINT
140 PRINT
150 REM ******************** FORECAST AREA  ************************
160 PRINT "****************************************"
170 PRINT
180 PRINT "EXPONENTIAL SMOOTHING FORECAST"
190 PRINT
200 PRINT "PERIOD";TAB(10);"ACTUAL";TAB(20);"FORECAST";TAB(30);"DIFF"
210 PRINT
220 Y9(1)=Y0(1)
230 FOR P=1 TO N+1
240    IF P=1 THEN 270
250    Y9(P)=A*Y0(P-1)+(1-A)*Y9(P-1)
260    IF P>N THEN GOTO 320
270    D=Y9(P)-Y0(P)
280    PRINT P;TAB(10);Y0(P);TAB(20);Y9(P);TAB(30);D
290    IF P<>N THEN 310
300    PRINT "------------------------------------------"
310 NEXT P
320 PRINT P;TAB(20);Y9(P)
330 PRINT
340 PRINT "****************************************"
350 REM ******************** PROGRAM TERMINATION POINT  ***********
360 PRINT
370 STOP
```

```
RUN "FCAST3"
ENTER THE NUMBER OF TIME PERIODS TO BE ENTERED? 12
ENTER THE VALUE OF THE SMOOTHING CONSTANT (0-1)? .5
ENTER VALUE FOR PERIOD   1 ? 490
ENTER VALUE FOR PERIOD   2 ? 500
ENTER VALUE FOR PERIOD   3 ? 550
ENTER VALUE FOR PERIOD   4 ? 400
ENTER VALUE FOR PERIOD   5 ? 450
ENTER VALUE FOR PERIOD   6 ? 540
ENTER VALUE FOR PERIOD   7 ? 560
ENTER VALUE FOR PERIOD   8 ? 580
ENTER VALUE FOR PERIOD   9 ? 560
ENTER VALUE FOR PERIOD  10 ? 590
ENTER VALUE FOR PERIOD  11 ? 610
ENTER VALUE FOR PERIOD  12 ? 600
```

```
******************************************

EXPONENTIAL SMOOTHING FORECAST

PERIOD    ACTUAL    FORECAST   DIFF

1         490       490        0
2         500       490        -10
3         550       495        -55
4         400       522.5      122.5
5         450       461.25     11.25
6         540       455.625    -84.375
7         560       497.813    -62.1875
8         580       528.906    -51.0938
9         560       554.453    -5.54688
10        590       557.227    -32.7734
11        610       573.613    -36.3867
12        600       591.807    -8.19336
------------------------------------------------
13                  595.903

******************************************

BREAK IN 370
OK
```

```
   MAJOR SYMBOL TABLE - FCAST3                              FUNCTIONS USED
I------------------------------------------------------I    I----------------I
I NAME   .. DESCRIPTION                                I    I NAME           I
I------------------------------------------------------I    I----------------I
I A      .. VALUE OF SMOOTHING CONSTANT                I    I TAB            I
I D      .. DIFFERENCE FORECAST VS ACTUAL              I    I DIM            I
I N      .. NUMBER OF HISTORY PERIODS TO BE ENTERED    I    I----------------I
I P      .. PERIOD BEING CONSIDERED                    I
I Y0()   .. INPUT VALUE ARRAY                          I
I Y9()   .. FORECAST ARRAY                             I
I------------------------------------------------------I
```

Ratio Analysis

Program Name: RATIO

    This program calculates and prints a number of ratios that have been found to be useful in business, namely: the current ratio, the acid test ratio, the net profit on sales ratio, the investment turnover ratio, the return on investment ratio, and the inventory turnover ratio. The terminal operator chooses the ratio desired, and the program produces the appropriate result.

    Since the definition of the ratios often differs from text to text, the formula for each is printed by the program at the outset. The program is structured to maintain the independence of all the ratios. Thus, individual computations can be changed without affecting the accuracy of the rest. Moreover, still other ratios can easily be added by incorporating the relevant subroutines and specifying the appropriate GOSUB for the option number specified.

Files Affected: None

```
10 REM              SAVED AT RATIO
20 REM   PROGRAM TO COMPUTE RATIO ANALYSES OF BUSINESS
30 REM *********************************************************
40 PRINT
50 PRINT
60   A$="***********************************************"
70 PRINT "THE FOLLOWING RATIOS ARE AVAIABLE"
80 PRINT
90 PRINT "#          RATIO";TAB(35);"FORMULA"
100 PRINT
110 PRINT "1....CURRENT RATIO............";TAB(30);
120 PRINT "CURRENT ASSETS/CURRENT LIABILITIES"
130 PRINT
140 PRINT "2....ACID TEST...............";TAB(30);
150 PRINT "CASH+RECEIVABLES+OTHER LIQUID ASSETS"
160 PRINT TAB(35);"/CURRENT LIABILITIES"
170 PRINT
180 PRINT "3....NET PROFIT ON SALES......";TAB(30);"NET PROFIT/NET SALES"
190 PRINT
200 PRINT "4....INVESTMENT TURNOVER......";TAB(30);"NET SALES/TOTAL ASSETS"
210 PRINT
220 PRINT "5....RETURN ON INVESTMENT.....";TAB(30);"NET PROFIT/TOTAL ASSETS"
230 PRINT
240 PRINT "6....INVENTORY TURNOVER.......";TAB(30);
250 PRINT "COST OF GOODS SOLD/AVERAGE INVENTORY"
260 PRINT
270 PRINT
280 PRINT
290 PRINT "ENTER THE NUMBER OF THE RATIO TO BE COMPUTED";
300 O=0
310 INPUT O
320 PRINT
330 IF O=0 THEN 420
340 IF O=1 THEN GOSUB 510
350 IF O=2 THEN GOSUB 600
360 IF O=3 THEN GOSUB 730
370 IF O=4 THEN GOSUB 820
380 IF O=5 THEN GOSUB 910
390 IF O=6 THEN GOSUB 1000
```

```
400 PRINT
410 GOTO 290
420 REM *************PROGRAM TERMINATION POINT  ******************
430 PRINT
440 PRINT
450 PRINT "PROCESSING COMPLETE"
460 PRINT
470 STOP


480 REM ****************************************************************
490 REM                    SUBROUTINES FOLLOW
500 REM ****************************************************************
510 REM ******************COMPUTE CURRENT RATIO  ******************
520 PRINT "ENTER CURRENT ASSETS";
530 INPUT C
540 PRINT "ENTER CURRENT LIABILITIES";
550 INPUT L
560 R1=C/L
570 PRINT A$
580 PRINT "CURRENT RATIO =";R1
590 RETURN
600 REM ******************** COMPUTE ACID TEST RATIO  *************
610 PRINT "ENTER CASH AMOUNT";
620 INPUT C1
630 PRINT "ENTER RECEIVABLES";
640 INPUT R
650 PRINT "ENTER OTHER CURRENT ASSETS";
660 INPUT A1
670 PRINT "ENTER CURRENT LIABILITIES"
680 INPUT L
690 R2=(C1+R+A1)/L
700 PRINT A$
710 PRINT "ACID TEST RATIO =";R2
720 RETURN


730 REM ********************COMPUTE NET PROFIT ON SALES  ***********
740 PRINT "ENTER NET PROFIT";
750 INPUT P
760 PRINT"ENTER NET SALES";
770 INPUT S
780 R3=P/S
790 PRINT A$
800 PRINT "NET PROFIT ON SALES =";R3
810 RETURN


820 REM ******************** COMPUTE INVESTMENT TURNOVER  *********
830 PRINT "ENTER NET SALES";
840 INPUT S
850 PRINT "ENTER TOTAL ASSETS";
860 INPUT A
870 R4=S/A
880 PRINT A$
890 PRINT "INVESTMENT TURNOVER =";R4
900 RETURN


910 REM ***************** COMPUTE RETURN ON INVESTMENT   **********
920 PRINT "ENTER NET PROFIT";
930 INPUT P
940 PRINT "ENTER TOTAL ASSETS";
950 INPUT A
960 R5=P/A
970 PRINT A$
980 PRINT "RETURN ON INVESTMENT =";R5
990 RETURN
```

```
1000 REM ***************** COMPUTE INVENTORY TURNOVER ***********
1010 PRINT "ENTER COST OF GOODS SOLD";
1020 INPUT G
1030 PRINT "ENTER TOTAL ASSETS";
1040 INPUT A
1050 R6=G/A
1060 PRINT A$
1070 PRINT "INVENTORY TURNOVER =";R6
1080 RETURN


RUN "RATIO"


THE FOLLOWING RATIOS ARE AVAIABLE

*        RATIO                    FORMULA

1....CURRENT RATIO............CURRENT ASSETS/CURRENT LIABILITIES

2....ACID TEST...............CASH+RECEIVABLES+OTHER LIQUID ASSETS
                                  /CURRENT LIABILITIES

3....NET PROFIT ON SALES......NET PROFIT/NET SALES

4....INVESTMENT TURNOVER......NET SALES/TOTAL ASSETS

5....RETURN ON INVESTMENT.....NET PROFIT/TOTAL ASSETS

6....INVENTORY TURNOVER.......COST OF GOODS SOLD/AVERAGE INVENTORY


ENTER THE NUMBER OF THE RATIO TO BE COMPUTED? 1

ENTER CURRENT ASSETS? 1000
ENTER CURRENT LIABILITIES? 2000
***************************************************
CURRENT RATIO = .5

ENTER THE NUMBER OF THE RATIO TO BE COMPUTED? 6

ENTER COST OF GOODS SOLD? 500
ENTER TOTAL ASSETS? 1000
***************************************************
INVENTORY TURNOVER = .5

ENTER THE NUMBER OF THE RATIO TO BE COMPUTED? 5

ENTER NET PROFIT? 1000
ENTER TOTAL ASSETS? 20000
***************************************************
RETURN ON INVESTMENT = .05

ENTER THE NUMBER OF THE RATIO TO BE COMPUTED? 3

ENTER NET PROFIT? 1000
ENTER NET SALES? 10000
***************************************************
NET PROFIT ON SALES = .1

ENTER THE NUMBER OF THE RATIO TO BE COMPUTED?


PROCESSING COMPLETE

BREAK IN 470
OK
```

```
MAJOR SYMBOL TABLE - RATIO                              FUNCTIONS USED
I-------------------------------------------------I     I----------------I
I NAME    .. DESCRIPTION                          I     I  NAME          I
I-------------------------------------------------I     I----------------I
I   A     .. TOTAL ASSETS                         I     I TAB            I
I   A$    .. A LINE OF ASTERISKS                  I     I----------------I
I   A1    .. OTHER CURRENT ASSETS                 I
I   C     .. CURRENT ASSETS                       I
I   C1    .. CASH ON HAND                         I
I   G     .. COST OF GOODS SOLD                   I
I   L     .. CURRENT LIABILITIES                  I
I   O     .. RATIO NUMBER TO BE COMPUTED          I
I   P     .. NET PROFITS                          I
I   R     .. CURRENT RECEIVABLES                  I
I   R1    .. CURRENT RATIO                        I
I   R2    .. ACID TEST RATIO                      I
I   R3    .. NET PROFIT ON SALES                  I
I   R4    .. INVESTMENT TURNOVER                  I
I   R5    .. RETURN ON INVESTMENT                 I
I   R6    .. INVENTORY TURNOVER                   I
I   S     .. NET SALES                            I
I-------------------------------------------------I
```

Equipment Comparisons

Program Name: ECOMP

This program compares alternative equipment investments. Typical investments in capital equipment involve receipts and disbursements of funds over a wide span of time. To allow a common basis for their comparison, this program converts all fund receipts and payments into their present value (using the specified interest rate), thereby offering equality of the dollars at stake. Since the various items of many investments have unequal economic lives, the present values of the alternatives are then converted into an equivalent, uniform annual amount for direct comparison.

This program can also be used to compare BUY and LEASE alternatives whenever a lease can be considered an annual expense at the end of each year.

Files Affected: None

```
10 REM            SAVED AT ECOMP
20 REM   EQUIPMENT COST (PRESENT VALUE) PROGRAM
30 X$="*****************************************************"
40 REM ***********************************************************
50 REM               ENTER INITIALIZATION DATA
60 REM ***********************************************************
70 PRINT
```

```
80 PRINT "ENTER THE NUMBER OF ITEMS TO COMPARE";
90 INPUT N
100 DIM L(N)
110 PRINT "DO THEY HAVE DIFFERENT ECONOMIC LIVES (Y OR N)";
120 INPUT A$
130 IF A$="Y" THEN 200
140 PRINT "ENTER ECONOMIC LIFE OF THE EQUIPMENT";
150 INPUT L(1)
160 L0=L(1)
170 FOR J=2 TO N
180   L(J)=L(1)
190 NEXT J
200 PRINT "ENTER THE INTEREST RATE";
210 INPUT R
220 IF R>1 THEN R=R/100
230 PRINT
240 IF A$<>"Y" THEN 300
250 FOR J=1 TO N
260   PRINT "ENTER THE LIFE FOR ITEM #";J;
270   INPUT L(J)
280   IF L(J)>L0 THEN L0=L(J)
290 NEXT J
300 DIM P(L0,N),D(L0,N),I1(N),S(N),S1(N),T1(N),T(N),D$(N),T0(N),E(N)
310 FOR J=1 TO N
320   PRINT "ENTER THE DESCRIPTION FOR ITEM #";J
330   INPUT D$(J)
340 NEXT J
350 PRINT
360 REM *******************************************************************
370 REM                    ENTER COST DATA
380 REM *******************************************************************
390 FOR J=1 TO N
400   PRINT "ENTER FOR *****";D$(J);"*****"
410   PRINT
420   PRINT "ENTER INITIAL COSTS";
430   INPUT I1(J)
440   PRINT
450   PRINT "ENTER DISBURSEMENTS FOR EACH YEAR"
460   FOR I=1 TO L(J)
470     PRINT "YEAR";I;
480     INPUT D(I,J)
490   NEXT I
500   PRINT
510   PRINT "ENTER SALVAGE VALUE";
520   INPUT S(J)
530   PRINT
540 NEXT J
550 REM *******************************************************************
560 REM              COMPUTE PRESENT VALUES
570 REM *******************************************************************
580 FOR J=1 TO N
590   FOR I=1 TO L(J)
600     P(I,J)=D(I,J)*((1+R)^(-(I)))
610     T1(J)=T1(J)+P(I,J)
620   NEXT I
630   S1(J)=S(J)*((1+R)^(-(L(J))))
640   T(J)=I1(J)+T1(J)
650 NEXT J
660 REM *******************************************************************
670 REM              PRINT OF RESULTS
680 REM *******************************************************************
690 FOR J=1 TO N
700   PRINT
710   PRINT X$
720   PRINT
730   PRINT TAB(10);D$(J)
740   PRINT
750   PRINT "PRESENT VALUE OF EQUIPMENT COSTS"
```

```
760    PRINT
770    PRINT "ITEM";TAB(15);"COST";TAB(25);"PRESENT VALUE"
780    PRINT
790    PRINT "INITIAL";TAB(15);I1(J);TAB(27);I1(J)
800    PRINT "DISBURSEMENTS"
810    FOR I=1 TO L(J)
820      PRINT "YEAR";I;TAB(15);D(I,J);TAB(27);P(I,J)
830    NEXT I
840    PRINT "----------------------------------------------"
850    PRINT "PRESENT VALUE COSTS";TAB(27);T(J)
860    PRINT "LESS SALVAGE VALUE";TAB(15);S(J);TAB(27);S1(J)
870    PRINT "----------------------------------------------"
880    TO(J)=T(J)-S1(J)
890    PRINT "PRESENT VALUE NET COSTS";TAB(27);TO(J)
900    PRINT
910 NEXT J
920 PRINT X$
930 PRINT
940 REM ****************************************************************
950 REM                  PRINT EQUIVALENT ANNUAL AMOUNTS
960 REM ****************************************************************
970 PRINT "EQUIVALENT ANNUAL EXPENDITURES"
980 PRINT
990 PRINT TAB(10);"ITEM";TAB(25);"ANNUAL COST"
1000 FOR J=1 TO N
1010    F=(1+R)^L(J)
1020    A=(R*F)/(F-1)
1030    E(J)=TO(J)*A
1040    PRINT D$(J);TAB(27);E(J)
1050 NEXT J
1060 REM ****************************************************************
1070 REM                  PROGRAM TERMINATION POINT
1080 REM ****************************************************************
1090 PRINT
1100 PRINT
1110 PRINT "PROCESSING COMPLETE"
1120 PRINT
1130 STOP
```

```
RUN "ECOMP"

ENTER THE NUMBER OF ITEMS TO COMPARE? 2
DO THEY HAVE DIFFERENT ECONOMIC LIVES (Y OR N)? N
ENTER ECONOMIC LIFE OF THE EQUIPMENT? 2
ENTER THE INTEREST RATE? 14

ENTER THE DESCRIPTION FOR ITEM # 1
? MACHINE TYPE 1
ENTER THE DESCRIPTION FOR ITEM # 2
? MACHINE TYPE 2

ENTER FOR *****MACHINE TYPE 1*****

ENTER INITIAL COSTS? 1000

ENTER DISBURSEMENTS FOR EACH YEAR
YEAR 1 ? 100
YEAR 2 ? 200

ENTER SALVAGE VALUE? 250

ENTER FOR *****MACHINE TYPE 2*****

ENTER INITIAL COSTS? 2000
```

```
ENTER DISBURSEMENTS FOR EACH YEAR
YEAR 1 ? 50
YEAR 2 ? 50

ENTER SALVAGE VALUE? 1250


*********************************************************

            MACHINE TYPE 1

PRESENT VALUE OF EQUIPMENT COSTS

ITEM              COST        PRESENT VALUE

INITIAL           1000        1000
DISBURSEMENTS
YEAR 1            100         87.7193
YEAR 2            200         153.894
------------------------------------------------------
PRESENT VALUE COSTS           1241.61
LESS SALVAGE VALUE 250        192.367
------------------------------------------------------
PRESENT VALUE NET COSTS       1049.25


*********************************************************

            MACHINE TYPE 2

PRESENT VALUE OF EQUIPMENT COSTS

ITEM              COST        PRESENT VALUE

INITIAL           2000        2000
DISBURSEMENTS
YEAR 1            50          43.8597
YEAR 2            50          38.4734
------------------------------------------------------
PRESENT VALUE COSTS           2082.33
LESS SALVAGE VALUE 1250       961.835
------------------------------------------------------
PRESENT VALUE NET COSTS       1120.5


*********************************************************


EQUIVALENT ANNUAL EXPENDITURES

         ITEM              ANNUAL COST
MACHINE TYPE 1            637.197
MACHINE TYPE 2            680.468


PROCESSING COMPLETE

BREAK IN 1130
OK
```

```
                                                        FUNCTIONS USED
I-------------------------------------------------------I    I-----------------I
I NAME    .. DESCRIPTION                                I    I  NAME           I
I-------------------------------------------------------I    I-----------------I
I  A      .. ANNUAL INTEREST FACTOR                     I    I TAB             I
I  A$     .. INPUT ANSWER VARIABLE                      I    I DIM             I
I  D$()   .. DESCRIPTION OF ITEM                        I    I-----------------I
I  D()    .. DISBURSEMENT COST ARRAY                    I
I  E()    .. EQUIVALENT ANNUAL COSTS                    I
I  F      .. INTEREST FACTOR                            I
I  I      .. INDEX AND ARRAY POINTER                    I
I  I1()   .. INITIAL COST ARRAY                         I
I  J      .. INDEX AND ARRAY POINTER                    I
I  L()    .. ECONOMIC LIFE                              I
I  LO     .. MAXIMUM LIFE OF EQUIPMENT                  I
I  N      .. NUMBER OF ITEMS TO COMPARE                 I
I  P()    .. PRESENT VALUE OF DISBURSEMENTS             I
I  R      .. INTEREST RATE                              I
I  S()    .. SALVAGE VALUE                              I
I  S1()   .. PRESENT VALUE OF SALVAGE                   I
I  T()    .. TOTAL COSTS                                I
I  TO()   .. TOTAL PRESENT COST - SALVAGE              I
I  T1()   .. TOTAL PRESENT VALUE OF DISBURSEMENTS       I
I  X$     .. LINE OF ASTERISKS                          I
I-------------------------------------------------------I
```

Depreciation

Program Name: DEPREC

This program computes the depreciation of an asset by using any one (or all) of three methods. It also assesses the differences in the effect of these methods on taxes and profit figures and calculates the depreciation for year-end accounting. All data is entered in response to program messages through the keyboard.

Comment: The double-declining balance method is based on the straight-line rate. It is calculated by multiplying the straight-line depreciation rate for a given year by a given factor. Check current tax laws for the asset being depreciated, and enter the appropriate factor in response to the program's message.

Files Affected: None

```
10 REM            SAVED AT DEPREC
20 REM         DEPRECIATION COMPUTATION PROGRAM
30 REM **************** DATA INITIALIZATION ***********************
40 X$="***********************************************************"
50 PRINT "ENTER THE INITIAL COST OF THE ASSETS";
60 INPUT C
```

```
70 PRINT "ENTER THE LIFE OF THE ASSET (IN YEARS)";
80 INPUT L
90 DIM D(L),T$(3),D1(L+1)
100 T$(1)="STRAIGHT-LINE DEPRECIATION"
110 T$(2)="SUM-OF-THE-YEARS-DIGITS"
120 T$(3)="DOUBLE-DECLINING BALANCE"
130 PRINT "ENTER THE SALVAGE VALUE";
140 INPUT S
150 PRINT
160 PRINT "THE FOLLOWING ALTERNATIVE DEPRECIATION METHODS ARE AVAILABLE"
170 PRINT
180 PRINT "1...STRAIGHT-LINE"
190 PRINT "2...SUM-OF-THE-YEARS-DIGITS"
200 PRINT "3...DOUBLE-DECLINING BALANCE"
210 PRINT "4...ALL OF THE ABOVE"
220 PRINT
230 PRINT "ENTER THE NUMBER OF THE METHOD TO USE (4 FOR ALL)";
240 O=0
250 INPUT O
260 PRINT
270 IF O=0 THEN 360
280 IF O=1 THEN GOSUB 440               'STRAIGHT-LINE
290 IF O=2 THEN GOSUB 560               'SUM OF YEARS DIGITS
300 IF O=3 THEN GOSUB 720               'DOUBLE-DECLINING
310 IF O<4 THEN 350
320 GOSUB 440                    'STRAIGHT-LINE
330 GOSUB 560                    'SUM-OF-YEARS-DIGITS
340 GOSUB 720                    'DOUBLE-DECLINING
350 REM *****************************************************************
360 REM              PROGRAM TERMINATION POINT
370 REM *****************************************************************
380 PRINT
390 PRINT
400 PRINT "PROCESSING COMPLETE"
410 PRINT
420 STOP


430 REM *****************************************************************
440 REM              STRAIGHT-LINE DEPRECIATION
450 REM *****************************************************************
460 D0=C-S
470 D1(1)=C
480 FOR I=1 TO L
490   D(I)=D0/L
500   D1(I+1)=D1(I)-D(I)
510 NEXT I
520 K=1
530 GOSUB 850                       'PRINT RESULTS
540 RETURN


550 REM *****************************************************************
560 REM             SUM-OF-THE-YEARS-DIGITS
570 REM *****************************************************************
580 D1(1)=C
590 D0=C-S
600 FOR I=1 TO L
610   N=N+I
620 NEXT I
630 FOR I=1 TO L
640   F=(L+1-I)/N
650   D(I)=D0*F
660   D1(I+1)=D1(I)-D(I)
670 NEXT I
680 K=2
690 GOSUB 850                       'PRINT RESULTS
700 RETURN
```

```
710 REM **********************************************************
720 REM           DOUBLE-DECLINING BALANCE
730 REM **********************************************************
740 D1(1)=C
750 PRINT "ENTER THE FACTOR  TO BE APPLIED TO S-L RATE  I.E. 1.5";
760 INPUT F
770 FOR I=1 TO L
780    D(I)=(D1(I)/(L))*F
790    D1(I+1)=D1(I)-D(I)
800 NEXT I
810 K=3
820 GOSUB 850                    'PRINT RESULTS
830 RETURN


840 REM **********************************************************
850 REM                 PRINT OF RESULTS
860 REM **********************************************************
870 PRINT X$
880 PRINT
890 PRINT T$(K)
900 PRINT
910 PRINT "INITIAL VALUE ";C
920 PRINT
930 PRINT TAB(10);"DEPREC";TAB(20);"REM VALUE"
940 PRINT
950 FOR I=1 TO L
960 PRINT "YEAR";I;TAB(10);D(I);TAB(20);D1(I+1)
970 NEXT I
980 PRINT
990 PRINT "SALVAGE VALUE =";D1(I)
1000 PRINT X$
1010 PRINT
1020 RETURN




RUN "DEPREC"
ENTER THE INITIAL COST OF THE ASSETS? 10000
ENTER THE LIFE OF THE ASSET (IN YEARS)? 5
ENTER THE SALVAGE VALUE? 2500

THE FOLLOWING ALTERNATIVE DEPRECIATION METHODS ARE AVAILABLE

1...STRAIGHT-LINE
2...SUM-OF-THE-YEARS-DIGITS
3...DOUBLE-DECLINING BALANCE
4...ALL OF THE ABOVE

ENTER THE NUMBER OF THE METHOD TO USE (4 FOR ALL)? 4

**************************************************************

STRAIGHT-LINE DEPRECIATION

INITIAL VALUE  10000

          DEPREC     REM VALUE

YEAR 1    1500       8500
YEAR 2    1500       7000
YEAR 3    1500       5500
YEAR 4    1500       4000
YEAR 5    1500       2500

SALVAGE VALUE = 2500
**************************************************************
```

```
***************************************************************
SUM-OF-THE-YEARS-DIGITS

INITIAL VALUE   10000

            DEPREC    REM VALUE

YEAR 1      2500      7500
YEAR 2      2000      5500
YEAR 3      1500      4000
YEAR 4      1000      3000
YEAR 5      500       2500

SALVAGE VALUE = 2500
***************************************************************

ENTER THE FACTOR  TO BE APPLIED TO S-L RATE  I.E. 1.5? 1.5
***************************************************************

DOUBLE-DECLINING BALANCE

INITIAL VALUE   10000

            DEPREC    REM VALUE

YEAR 1      3000      7000
YEAR 2      2100      4900
YEAR 3      1470      3430
YEAR 4      1029      2401
YEAR 5      720.3     1680.7

SALVAGE VALUE = 1680.7
***************************************************************


PROCESSING COMPLETE

BREAK IN 420
OK
```

```
    MAJOR SYMBOL TABLE - DEPREC                              FUNCTIONS USED
I-----------------------------------------------I       I-----------------I
I NAME   .. DESCRIPTION                          I       I  NAME           I
I-----------------------------------------------I       I-----------------I
I  C     .. INITIAL COST OF ASSETS               I       I TAB             I
I  D()   .. DEPRECIATION ARRAY                   I       I GOSUB           I
I  D0    .. AMOUNT TO DEPRECIATE                 I       I RETURN          I
I  D1()  .. UNDEPRECIATED VALUE ARRAY            I       I DIM             I
I  F     .. DEPRECIATION FACTOR                  I       I-----------------I
I  I     .. INDEX AND ARRAY POINTER              I
I  K     .. INDEX POINTER TO METHOD USED         I
I  L     .. LIFE OF THE ASSET                    I
I  O     .. OPTION NUMBER                        I
I  S     .. SALVAGE VALUE                        I
I  T$()  .. DEPRECIATION METHOD NAME ARRAY       I
I  X$    .. LINE OF ASTERISKS                    I
I-----------------------------------------------I
```

Expected Value Computation

Program Name: EXPECT

This program analyzes business decisions by using the statistical technique of expected value. The possible outcomes of a decision are evaluated by multiplying their value, should they occur, by the probability of their occurring and comparing the results. To use this program, therefore, it is necessary to determine each of the possible outcomes and its value to the firm should it occur as well as the probability of its occurrence. Note that the sum of all probabilities must be 1 for the computation to yield accurate results.

Files Affected: None

```
10 REM           SAVED AT EXPECT
20 REM      EXPECTED VALUE COMPUTATION
30 REM ********************************************************
40 PRINT
50 PRINT
60 PRINT "ENTER THE NUMBER OF OUTCOMES THAT ARE POSSIBLE";
70 INPUT N
80 PRINT
90 DIM P(N),V(N),D$(N),E(N)
100 X$="********************************************************"
110 FOR I=1 TO N
120    PRINT "FOR OUTCOME";I;"ENTER:"
130    PRINT"DESCRIPTION OF OUTCOME";
140    INPUT D$(I)
150    PRINT "VALUE OF RESULT";
160    INPUT V(I)
170    PRINT "PROBABILITY OF IT HAPPENING";
180    INPUT P(I)
190    PRINT
200 NEXT I
210 REM ********************************************************
220 REM               COMPUTE RESULT
230 REM ********************************************************
240 PRINT
250 PRINT X$
260 PRINT
270 PRINT TAB(10);"EXPECTED VALUE COMPUTATION"
280 PRINT
290 PRINT "DESCRIPTION OF OUTCOME";TAB(40);"VALUE";TAB(50);"PROB";
300 PRINT TAB(58);"EX. VALUE"
310 PRINT
320 FOR I=1 TO N
330    E(I)=P(I)*V(I)
340    PRINT D$(I);TAB(40);V(I);TAB(50);P(I);TAB(58);E(I)
350    PO=PO+P(I)
360    T=T+E(I)
370 NEXT I
380 PRINT "---------------------------------------------------------------"
390 PRINT TAB(25);"EXPECTED VALUE";TAB(50);PO;TAB(58);T
400 PRINT X$
410 REM ********************************************************
420 REM            PROGRAM TERMINATION POINT
430 REM ********************************************************
440 PRINT
450 PRINT
460 PRINT "PROCESSING COMPLETE"
470 PRINT
480 STOP
```

```
RUN "EXPECT"


ENTER THE NUMBER OF OUTCOMES THAT ARE POSSIBLE? 3

FOR OUTCOME 1 ENTER:
DESCRIPTION OF OUTCOME? THE PRODUCT SELLS SUCCESSFULLY
VALUE OF RESULT? 1000
PROBABILITY OF IT HAPPENING? .50

FOR OUTCOME 2 ENTER:
DESCRIPTION OF OUTCOME? THE PRODUCT DOES NOT SELL TO SENIORS
VALUE OF RESULT? 100
PROBABILITY OF IT HAPPENING? .25

FOR OUTCOME 3 ENTER:
DESCRIPTION OF OUTCOME? THE PRODUCT DOES NOT SELL
VALUE OF RESULT? -2000
PROBABILITY OF IT HAPPENING? .25


*******************************************************************
             EXPECTED VALUE COMPUTATION

DESCRIPTION OF OUTCOME                  VALUE     PROB    EX. VALUE

THE PRODUCT SELLS SUCCESSFULLY          1000       .5       500
THE PRODUCT DOES NOT SELL TO SENIORS     100       .25       25
THE PRODUCT DOES NOT SELL               -2000      .25      -500
-----------------------------------------------------------------
                         EXPECTED VALUE              1        25
*******************************************************************


PROCESSING COMPLETE

BREAK IN 480
OK




    MAJOR SYMBOL TABLE - EXPECT                  FUNCTIONS USED
I------------------------------------------I    I----------------I
I NAME    .. DESCRIPTION                   I    I NAME           I
I------------------------------------------I    I----------------I
I  D$()   .. OUTCOME DESCRIPTION ARRAY     I    I TAB            I
I  E()    .. OUTCOME EXPECTED VALUE ARRAY  I    I DIM            I
I  I      .. INDEX AND ARRAY POINTER       I    I----------------I
I  N      .. NUMBER OF OUTCOMES            I
I  P()    .. PROBABILITY ARRAY             I
I  PO     .. TOTAL PROBABILITY             I
I  T      .. TOTAL EXPECTED VALUE          I
I  V()    .. OUTCOME VALUE ARRAY           I
I  X$     .. LINE OF ASTERISKS             I
I------------------------------------------I
```

Amortization

Program Name: AMORT

This program computes an amortization schedule for a debt, including repayment amounts and remaining balances for the life of the debt. All data is entered through the keyboard in response to program messages.

Files Affected: None

```
10 REM            SAVED AT AMORT
20 REM     AMORTIZATION PROGRAM
30 X$="*******************************************"
40 CO=.5
50 PRINT "ENTER INITIAL DEBT";
60 INPUT D
70 PRINT "ENTER INTEREST RATE";
80 INPUT R
90 IF R>1 THEN R=R/100
100 PRINT "ARE THE PAYMENTS MONTHLY (M), QUARTERLY (Q), OR ANNUALLY (A)"
110 PRINT "COMPOUNDING WILL FOR THE SAME PERIOD";
120 INPUT A$
130 IF A$="M" THEN C=12
140 IF A$="A" THEN C=1
150 IF A$="Q" THEN C=4
160 IF C=0 THEN 100
170 PRINT "NUMBER OF PAYMENTS TO BE MADE";
180 INPUT N
190 R1=R/C
200 PRINT
210 REM ********************************************
220 REM              PROCESSING AREA
230 REM ********************************************
240 PRINT X$
250 PRINT
260 PRINT TAB(10);"AMORTIZATION SCHEDULE"
270 PRINT
280 PRINT "PERIOD";TAB(10);"PAYMENT";TAB(20);"INTEREST";TAB(30);
290 PRINT "TO PRINC.";TAB(41);"BAL. AFTER"
300 PRINT TAB(40);D
310 P=INT(CO+D*(R1/(1-(1+R1)^(-N)))*100)/100
320 FOR I=1 TO N
330    I1=INT(CO+D*R1*100)/100
340    PRINT I;TAB(10);P;TAB(20);I1;TAB(30);P-I1;
350    D=INT(CO+(D-(P-I1))*100)/100
360    PRINT TAB(40);D
370 NEXT I
380 PRINT X$
390 REM ********************************************
400 REM             PROGRAM TERMINATION POINT
410 REM ********************************************
420 PRINT
430 PRINT
440 PRINT "PROCESSING COMPLETE"
450 PRINT
460 STOP
```

```
RUN "AMORT"
ENTER INITIAL DEBT? 5000
ENTER INTEREST RATE? 12
ARE THE PAYMENTS MONTHLY (M), QUARTERLY (Q), OR ANNUALLY (A)
COMPOUNDING WILL FOR THE SAME PERIOD? M
NUMBER OF PAYMENTS TO BE MADE? 24

***********************************************************

        AMORTIZATION SCHEDULE

PERIOD    PAYMENT    INTEREST    TO PRINC.    BAL. AFTER
                                             5000
  1       235.37     50          185.37       4814.63
  2       235.37     48.15       187.22       4627.41
  3       235.37     46.27       189.1        4438.31
  4       235.37     44.38       190.99       4247.32
  5       235.37     42.47       192.9        4054.42
  6       235.37     40.54       194.83       3859.59
  7       235.37     38.6        196.77       3662.82
  8       235.37     36.63       198.74       3464.08
  9       235.37     34.64       200.73       3263.35
 10       235.37     32.63       202.74       3060.61
 11       235.37     30.61       204.76       2855.85
 12       235.37     28.56       206.81       2649.04
 13       235.37     26.49       208.88       2440.16
 14       235.37     24.4        210.97       2229.19
 15       235.37     22.29       213.08       2016.11
 16       235.37     20.16       215.21       1800.9
 17       235.37     18.01       217.36       1583.54
 18       235.37     15.84       219.53       1364.01
 19       235.37     13.64       221.73       1142.28
 20       235.37     11.42       223.95       918.33
 21       235.37     9.18        226.19       692.14
 22       235.37     6.92        228.45       463.69
 23       235.37     4.64        230.73       232.96
 24       235.37     2.33        233.04       -.08
***********************************************************


PROCESSING COMPLETE

BREAK IN 460
OK
```

```
MAJOR SYMBOL TABLE - AMORT                                    FUNCTIONS USED
I---------------------------------------------------------I   I----------------I
I NAME   .. DESCRIPTION                                   I   I  NAME          I
I---------------------------------------------------------I   I----------------I
I A$     .. ANSWER VARIABLE                               I   I INT            I
I C      .. NUMBER OF COMPOUNDS PER YEAR                  I   I TAB            I
I CO     .. ROUNDING CONSTANT                             I   I----------------I
I D      .. AMOUNT OWED                                   I
I I1     .. INTEREST PAID                                 I
I P      .. PAYMENT                                       I
I R      .. INTEREST RATE                                 I
I R1     .. INTEREST RATE PER COMPOUNDING PERIOD          I
I X$     .. LINE OF ASTERISKS                             I
I---------------------------------------------------------I
```

Return on Investment

Program Name: RETURN

This program calculates the rate of return for a specified cost and income stream by means of a formula that examines the dollar flow and determines the interest rate necessary to equate income and expenses. This time-based interest rate can then be used to compare multiple investment alternatives. The section of the program beginning at statement 590 continues to home in on the interest rate until an acceptable level of accuracy is achieved.

Files Affected: None

```
10 REM            SAVED AT RETURN
20 REM      CALCULATES RATE OF RETURN FOR COST AND INCOME STREAM
30 X$="**********************************************"
40 PRINT "ENTER THE NUMBER OF YEARS FOR THE CASH FLOWS";
50 INPUT Y
60 Y=Y+1
70 DIM C(Y),I(Y),N(Y),P(Y)
80 R0=0
90 R=.32
100 R1=2.56
110 PRINT "ENTER THE INITIAL INVESTMENT";
120 INPUT C(1)
130 N(1)=-C(1)
140 FOR J=2 TO Y
150    PRINT
160    PRINT "ENTER FOR YEAR ";J-1
170    PRINT "DISBURSEMENTS";
180    INPUT C(J)
190    PRINT "INCOME";
200    INPUT I(J)
210    N(J)=I(J)-C(J)
220 NEXT J
230 PRINT
240 PRINT "ENTER FOR TERMINATION CHARGES OR SALVAGE VALUES"
250 PRINT "DISBURSEMENTS";
260 INPUT C9
270 PRINT "INCOME";
280 INPUT I9
290 I(Y)=I(Y)+I9
300 C(Y)=C(Y)+C9
310 N(Y)=N(Y)+I9+C9
320 REM ***********************************************************
330 REM               PRINT OF CASH FLOW TABLE
340 REM ***********************************************************
350 PRINT
360 PRINT X$
370 PRINT
380 PRINT   TAB(10);"CASH FLOW TABLE"
390 PRINT
400 PRINT "YEAR";TAB(10);"RECEIPTS";TAB(20);"DISBURSE";TAB(30);"NET FLOW"
410 PRINT
420 FOR J=1 TO Y
430    PRINT J-1;TAB(10);I(J);TAB(20);C(J);TAB(30);N(J)
440    I0=I0+I(J)
450    C0=C0+C(J)
460    N0=N0+N(J)
```

```
470 NEXT J
480 PRINT   TAB(10);"----------";TAB(20);"----------";TAB(30);"----------"
490 PRINT TAB(10);IO;TAB(20);CO;TAB(30);NO
500 PRINT
510 PRINT X$
520 IF NO>0 THEN 550
530 PRINT "CASH FLOW PROVIDES A NET LOSS"
540 GOTO 840
550 PRINT "IS THIS CORRECT - SHALL I CONTINUE (Y OR N)";
560 INPUT A$
570 IF A$="N" THEN 840
580 REM ****************************************************************
590 REM             CALCULATE PRESENT VALUE AT INTEREST R
600 REM ****************************************************************
610 FOR J=1 TO Y
620    P(J)=N(J)*(1+R)^(-J)
630    T=T+P(J)
640 NEXT J
650 IF T-T1 <.01 AND T-T1 >-.01 THEN 780
660 T1=I
670 IF T>0 THEN 730
680 REM *********** INTEREST RATE IS HIGH  ************
690 R1=R
700 R=(R+R0)/2
710 T=0
720 GOTO 610
730 REM *********** INTEREST RATE IS LOW  ************
740 R0=R
750 R=(R1+R)/2
760 T=0
770 GOTO 610
780 REM ************* INTEREST RATE IS CORRECT  **********
790 PRINT
800 R2=INT(R*1000+.5)/10
810 PRINT "THE CALCULATED RATE OF RETURN IS ";R2;"%"
820 PRINT
830 PRINT X$
840 REM ****************************************************************
850 REM                 PROGRAM TERMINATION POINT
860 REM ****************************************************************
870 PRINT
880 PRINT
890 PRINT "PROCESSING COMPLETE"
900 PRINT
910 STOP
```

```
RUN "RETURN"
ENTER THE NUMBER OF YEARS FOR THE CASH FLOWS? 2
ENTER THE INITIAL INVESTMENT? 10000

ENTER FOR YEAR  1
DISBURSEMENTS? 500
INCOME? 5000

ENTER FOR YEAR  2
DISBURSEMENTS? 500
INCOME? 7000

ENTER FOR TERMINATION CHARGES OR SALVAGE VALUES
DISBURSEMENTS? 100
INCOME? 2000
```

```
**************************************************
            CASH FLOW TABLE

YEAR        RECEIPTS  DISBURSE   NET FLOW

0           0         10000      -10000
1           5000      500        4500
2           9000      600        8600
            --------  --------   --------
            14000     11100      3100

**************************************************
IS THIS CORRECT - SHALL I CONTINUE (Y OR N)? Y

THE CALCULATED RATE OF RETURN IS   17.9 %

**************************************************

PROCESSING COMPLETE

BREAK IN 910
OK
```

```
  MAJOR SYMBOL TABLE - RETURN                              FUNCTIONS USED
I-------------------------------------------------I      I----------------I
I NAME    .. DESCRIPTION                          I      I  NAME          I
I-------------------------------------------------I      I----------------I
I  A$     .. ANSWER VARIABLE                      I      I DIM            I
I  C()    .. COST/DISBURSEMENT ARRAY              I      I INT            I
I  C0     .. TOTAL COSTS/DISBURSEMENTS            I      I TAB            I
I  C9     .. TERMINATION CHARGES                  I      I----------------I
I  I()    .. INCOME/SAVINGS ARRAY                 I
I  I0     .. TOTAL INCOME/SAVINGS                 I
I  I9     .. SALVAGE INCOME                       I
I  J      .. INDEX AND ARRAY POINTER              I
I  N()    .. NET EFFECT ARRAY                     I
I  N0     .. TOTAL NET EFFECT                     I
I  P()    .. PRESENT WORTH OF NET EFFECT AMOUNT   I
I  R      .. INTEREST RATE BEING USED             I
I  R0     .. LOWER INTEREST RATE BOUND            I
I  R1     .. UPPER INTEREST RATE BOUND            I
I  R2     .. CALCULATED RATE OF RETURN            I
I  T      .. TOTAL PRESENT WORTH OF ACTION        I
I  T1     .. TOTAL PRESENT WORTH OF PREVIOUS ITERATION  I
I  X$     .. LINE OF ASTERISKS                    I
I  Y      .. NUMBER OF YEARS TO BE CONSIDERED     I
I-------------------------------------------------I
```

Property Comparisons

Program Name: PROPERTY

This program compares the costs of property investment actions. The individual costs of the property are accepted from the terminal, computations are completed, and a table is produced that summarizes the monthly and annual costs of maintaining and operating the property. In addition, the costs of several properties can be processed to produce comparative information for investment decisions.

Files Affected: None

```
10 REM           SAVED AT PROPERTY
20 REM           PROPERTY COMPARISON PROGRAM
30 REM    ***************  DATA INITIALIZATION  ******************
40 PRINT "ENTER PROPERTY NAME ( JUST PRESS RETURN WHEN DONE )"
50 RO= .005
60 N$=" "
70 INPUT N$
80 IF N$=" " THEN 840
90 PRINT "ENTER THE MORTGAGE AMOUNT"
100 P=0
110 INPUT P
120 PRINT "ENTER THE INTEREST RATE"
130 INPUT I1
140 IF I1>=1 THEN 160
150 I1=I1*100
160 I=(I1/100)/12
170 PRINT "ENTER THE YEARS OF THE MORTGAGE"
180 INPUT Y
190 PRINT "ENTER THE ANNUAL TAXES ON THE PROPERTY"
200 T=0
210 INPUT T
220 T=T/12
230 T=INT((T+RO)*100)
240 T=T/100
250 PRINT "ENTER THE ANNUAL INSURANCE COSTS FOR THE PROPERTY"
260 F=0
270 INPUT F
280 F=F/12
290 F=INT((F+RO)*100)
300 F=F/100
310 PRINT "ENTER THE ANNUAL MAINTENANCE AND REPAIR COSTS"
320 R=0
330 INPUT R
340 R=R/12
350 R=INT((R+RO)*100)
360 R=R/100
370 PRINT "ENTER AVERAGE *** MONTHLY *** UTILITY COSTS"
380 U=0
390 INPUT U
400 PRINT "ENTER ANY OTHER *** MONTHLY *** COSTS THAT APPLY"
410 S=0
420 INPUT S
430 PRINT "ENTER ANY OTHER  *** ANNUAL *** COSTS THAT APPLY"
440 A=0
450 INPUT A
460 PRINT
470 PRINT
480 PRINT
```

```
490 REM ***********************************************************
500 REM                       COMPUTATIONS
510 REM ***********************************************************
520 M=I/((1+I)^(Y*12)-1)+I
530 M1=M*P
540 M1=INT((M1+RO)*100)
550 M1=M1/100
560 O=U+S+R
570 T1=M1+T+F
580 T2=(T1+R+S+U)*12+A
590 REM ***********************************************************
600 REM                       PRINT RESULTS
610 REM ***********************************************************
620 PRINT "***********************************************************"
630 PRINT
640 PRINT N$,"INTEREST RATE";I1;"% - MORTGAGE YEARS";Y
650 PRINT
660 PRINT "MORTGAGE";TAB(10);" P I";TAB(20);"TAXES";TAB(30);"INS";
670 PRINT TAB(40);" PITI"
680 PRINT "--------";TAB(10);"------";TAB(20);"--------";TAB(30);
690 PRINT "-------";TAB(40);"--------"
700 PRINT P;TAB(10);M1;TAB(20);T;TAB(30);F;TAB(40);T1
710 PRINT
720 PRINT "UTILITIES";TAB(15);"  MAINT";TAB(25);" OTHER";TAB(38);
730 PRINT "OPERATING COSTS"
740 PRINT "-----------";TAB(15);"--------";TAB(25);"--------";
750 PRINT TAB(40);"-----------"
760 PRINT U;TAB(15);R;TAB(25);S;TAB(40);O
770 PRINT
780 PRINT "TOTAL MONTHLY COSTS: $";O+T1;"  ANNUAL COSTS: $";T2
790 PRINT
800 PRINT "***********************************************************"
810 PRINT
820 GOTO 40
830 REM ***********************************************************
840 REM                 PROGRAM TERMINATION POINT
850 REM ***********************************************************
860 PRINT
870 PRINT
880 STOP
```

```
RUN "PROPERTY"
ENTER PROPERTY NAME ( JUST PRESS RETURN WHEN DONE )
? 234 HARRISON STREET
ENTER THE MORTGAGE AMOUNT
? 10000
ENTER THE INTEREST RATE
? 10
ENTER THE YEARS OF THE MORTGAGE
? 10
ENTER THE ANNUAL TAXES ON THE PROPERTY
? 190
ENTER THE ANNUAL INSURANCE COSTS FOR THE PROPERTY
? 100
ENTER THE ANNUAL MAINTENANCE AND REPAIR COSTS
? 190
ENTER AVERAGE *** MONTHLY *** UTILITY COSTS
? 10
ENTER ANY OTHER *** MONTHLY *** COSTS THAT APPLY
? 10
ENTER ANY OTHER  *** ANNUAL *** COSTS THAT APPLY
? 100
```

```
**************************************************************

234 HARRISON STREET            INTEREST RATE 10 % - MORTGAGE YEARS 10

MORTGAGE    P I      TAXES      INS      PITI
--------    -----    -----      ---      ----
 10000     132.15    15.83      8.33    156.31

UTILITIES         MAINT     OTHER       OPERATING COSTS
---------         -----     -----       ---------------
 10               15.83      10              35.83

TOTAL MONTHLY COSTS: $ 192.14    ANNUAL COSTS: $ 2405.68

**************************************************************

ENTER PROPERTY NAME ( JUST PRESS RETURN WHEN DONE )
?


BREAK IN 880
OK
```

```
MAJOR SYMBOL TABLE - PROPERTY                                  FUNCTIONS USED
I-------------------------------------------------------I      I----------------I
I NAME   .. DESCRIPTION                                 I      I  NAME          I
I-------------------------------------------------------I      I----------------I
I  A     .. OTHER ANNUAL COSTS                          I      I TAB            I
I  F     .. ANNUAL INSURANCE                            I      I INT            I
I  I1    .. INTEREST RATE                               I      I----------------I
I  M1    .. PRINCIPAL AND INTEREST                      I
I  N$    .. NAME OF PROPERTY                            I
I  O     .. TOTAL UTILITIES/MAINT/OTHER                 I
I  P     .. MORTGAGE AMOUNT                             I
I  R     .. ANNUAL MAINT/REPAIR COSTS                   I
I  R0    .. ROUNDING CONSTANT                           I
I  S     .. OTHER MONTHLY COSTS                         I
I  T     .. ANNUAL TAXES                                I
I  T1    .. PRINCIPAL/INTEREST/TAXES/INSURANCE          I
I  T2    .. TOTAL ANNUAL COSTS                          I
I  U     .. UTILITY COSTS PER MONTH                     I
I  Y     .. YEARS OF THE MORTGAGE                       I
I-------------------------------------------------------I
```

Job Pricing/Bidding

Program Name: BIDDING

This program accepts overhead and fixed and variable cost information about a product or job to compute the price or bid it warrants in accordance with a specified markup percentage (or range of percentages). The program also provides a summary of costs for manual review and computation.

Files Affected: None

```
10 REM            SAVED AT BIDDING
20 REM COMPUTES BIDS BASED UPON FIXED AND VARIABLE COSTS
30 REM ****************************************************************
40 M=25
50 I=1
60 J=1
70 DIM F(M),F$(M),V(M),V$(M)
80 X$="****************************************************************"
90 REM                  ENTER INITIALIZING INFORMATION
100 REM ****************************************************************
110 PRINT "ENTER THE AMOUNT OF OVERHEAD DOLLARS TO APPLY";
120 INPUT O
130 PRINT "ENTER FIXED COSTS THAT APPLY AND THE TYPE OF COST"
140 PRINT "EXAMPLE  1000,SET UP CHARGES"
150 INPUT F(I),F$(I)
160 IF F(I)=0 THEN 190
170 I=I+1
180 GOTO 150
190 PRINT "ENTER VARIABLE COSTS THAT APPLY AND THE TYPE OF COST"
200 PRINT "EXAMPLE 10,MATERIALS"
210 INPUT V(J),V$(J)
220 IF V(J)=0 THEN 250
230 J=J+1
240 GOTO 210
250 PRINT "SHALL I PRINT BIDS FOR A RANGE OF MARK-UPS (Y OR N)";
260 INPUT A$
270 IF A$="Y" THEN 330
280 PRINT "ENTER MARK-UP";
290 INPUT P1
300 P2=P1
310 S=1
320 GOTO 390
330 PRINT "ENTER BEGINNING MARK-UP";
340 INPUT P1
350 PRINT "ENTER ENDING MARK-UP";
360 INPUT P2
370 PRINT "ENTER INTERVAL BETWEEN PRINTS";
380 INPUT S
390 PRINT "ENTER THE QUANTITY TO BE BID";
400 INPUT Q1
410 REM ****************************************************************
420 REM                    DISPLAY RESULTS
430 REM ****************************************************************
440 PRINT
450 J1=J-1
460 I1=I-1
470 PRINT X$
480 PRINT
490 PRINT TAB(15);"JOB COST"
```

```
500 PRINT
510 PRINT "OVERHEAD";TAB(30);O
520 PRINT
530 PRINT "FIXED COSTS"
540 FOR I=1 TO I1
550    PRINT " ";F$(I);TAB(30);F(I)
560    F9=F9+F(I)
570 NEXT I
580 PRINT TAB(30);"------------"
590 PRINT "TOTAL FIXED COSTS";TAB(30);F9
600 PRINT
610 PRINT "VARIABLE COSTS"
620 FOR J=1 TO J1
630    PRINT " ";V$(J);TAB(30);V(J)
640    V9=V9+V(J)
650 NEXT J
660 PRINT TAB(30);"------------"
670 PRINT "VARIABLE COSTS PER UNIT";TAB(30);V9
680 PRINT
690 PRINT X$
700 PRINT
710 REM **************** PRINT COST STRUCTURE  ******************
720 PRINT TAB(15);"SUMMARY OF COSTS"
730 PRINT
740 PRINT "QUANTITY";TAB(10);"OVERHEAD";TAB(20);"FIXED";
750 PRINT TAB(30);"VARIABLE";TAB(40);"TOT COSTS";TAB(50);"COST/UNIT"
760 T1=Q1*V9
770 T=O+F9+T1
780 PRINT
790 PRINT Q1;TAB(10);O;TAB(20);F9;TAB(30);T1;TAB(40);T;TAB(50);T/Q1
800 PRINT X$
810 PRINT
820 REM **************** PRINT RANGE OF BIDS  *****************
830 PRINT TAB(15);"COST/PROFITS/BIDS"
840 PRINT
850 PRINT "PERCENT";TAB(10);" COSTS";TAB(20);"PROFIT";TAB(30);"  BID"
860 PRINT
870 FOR K=P1 TO P2 STEP S
880    PO=(K/100*T)
890    B=PO+T
900    PRINT  TAB(2);K;TAB(10);T;TAB(20);PO;TAB(30);B
910 NEXT K
920 PRINT X$
930 REM ************************************************************
940 REM            PROGRAM TERMINATION POINT
950 REM ************************************************************
960 PRINT
970 PRINT
980 PRINT "PROCESSING COMPLETE"
990 PRINT
1000 STOP
```

```
RUN "BIDDING"
ENTER THE AMOUNT OF OVERHEAD DOLLARS TO APPLY? 1000
ENTER FIXED COSTS THAT APPLY AND THE TYPE OF COST
EXAMPLE  1000,SET UP CHARGES
? 1000,SET UP CHARGES
? 500,TRANSPORTATION
?
ENTER VARIABLE COSTS THAT APPLY AND THE TYPE OF COST
EXAMPLE 10,MATERIALS
? 10,MATERIALS
? 1,VARIABLE SHIPPING
?
SHALL I PRINT BIDS FOR A RANGE OF MARK-UPS (Y OR N)? Y
ENTER BEGINNING MARK-UP? 10
ENTER ENDING MARK-UP? 15
ENTER INTERVAL BETWEEN PRINTS? 1
ENTER THE QUANTITY TO BE BID? 100


***************************************************************

                   JOB COST

OVERHEAD                        1000

FIXED COSTS
  SET UP CHARGES                1000
  TRANSPORTATION                500
                              ------------
TOTAL FIXED COSTS               1500

VARIABLE COSTS
  MATERIALS                     10
  VARIABLE SHIPPING             1
                              ------------
VARIABLE COSTS PER UNIT         11

***************************************************************

                  SUMMARY OF COSTS

QUANTITY  OVERHEAD  FIXED    VARIABLE  TOT COSTS COST/UNIT

 100       1000      1500      1100      3600       36
***************************************************************

                 COST/PROFITS/BIDS

PERCENT    COSTS    PROFIT     BID

  10       3600      360      3960
  11       3600      396      3996
  12       3600      432      4032
  13       3600      468      4068
  14       3600      504      4104
  15       3600      540      4140
***************************************************************


PROCESSING COMPLETE

BREAK IN 1000
OK
```

```
MAJOR SYMBOL TABLE - BIDDING                            FUNCTIONS USED
I-----------------------------------------------------I  I------------------I
I NAME    .. DESCRIPTION                              I  I  NAME           I
I-----------------------------------------------------I  I------------------I
I  A$     .. OPTION-ANSWER VARIABLE                   I  I  TAB            I
I  F$()   .. FIXED COST NAME ARRAY                    I  I  DIM            I
I  F()    .. FIXED COST ARAY                          I  I------------------I
I  F9     .. TOTAL FIXED COSTS                        I
I  I      .. INDEX TO FIXED COSTS                     I
I  I1     .. NUMBER OF FIXED COSTS ENTERED            I
I  J      .. INDEX TO VARIABLE COSTS                  I
I  J1     .. NUMBER OF VARIABLE COSTS ENTERED         I
I  M      .. MAXIMUM ARRAY SIZE                       I
I  O      .. OVERHEAD  COSTS                          I
I  Q1     .. QUANTITY                                 I
I  P1     .. BEGINNING MARKUP TO PRINT                I
I  P2     .. ENDING MARKUP TO PRINT                   I
I  B      .. BID                                      I
I  PO     .. PROFIT                                   I
I  S      .. PRINT INTERVAL                           I
I  T      .. TOTAL COSTS                              I
I  T1     .. TOTAL VARIABLE COSTS                     I
I  V$()   .. VARIABLE COST NAME ARRAY                 I
I  V()    .. VARIABLE COST ARRAY                      I
I  V9     .. TOTAL VARIABLE COSTS PER UNIT            I
I  X$     .. LINE OF ASTERISKS                        I
I-----------------------------------------------------I
```

Mortgage Computation

Program Name: MCOMP1

This program computes monthly payments for mortgages, given the interest rate, the term of the mortgage, and the amount borrowed.

Files Affected: None

```
10 REM            SAVED AT MCOMP1
20 REM   MORTGAGE COMPUTATION PROGRAM -BASIC
30 REM ***********************************************************
40 REM            DATA INITIALIZATION
50 REM ***********************************************************
60 PRINT "ENTER THE MORTGAGE AMOUNT"
70 INPUT P
80 PRINT "ENTER THE INTEREST RATE"
90 INPUT I1
100 IF I1>1 THEN 120
110 I1=I1*100
120 I=(I1/100)/12
130 PRINT "ENTER THE YEARS OF THE MORTGAGE"
140 INPUT Y
150 PRINT
160 PRINT
170 PRINT
180 REM ***********************************************************
190 REM            COMPUTATION AND PRINT
200 REM ***********************************************************
```

```
210 M=I/((1+I)^(Y*12)-1)+I
220 M1=M*P
230 PRINT "****************************"
240 PRINT "MORTGAGE AMOUNT $";P
250 PRINT "INTEREST RATE ";I1;"%"
260 PRINT "MONTHLY PAYMENT $";M1
270 PRINT "****************************"
280 REM *********************** PROGRAM TERMINATION  **********
290 PRINT
300 PRINT
310 STOP


RUN "MCOMP1"
ENTER THE MORTGAGE AMOUNT
? 10000
ENTER THE INTEREST RATE
? 12
ENTER THE YEARS OF THE MORTGAGE
? 10


****************************
MORTGAGE AMOUNT $ 10000
INTEREST RATE  12 %
MONTHLY PAYMENT $ 143.472
****************************


BREAK IN 310
OK
```

```
   MAJOR SYMBOL TABLE - MCOMP1                         FUNCTIONS USED
I------------------------------------------------I    I----------------I
I NAME    .. DESCRIPTION                         I    I  NAME          I
I------------------------------------------------I    I----------------I
I  I      .. MONTHLY INTEREST RATE               I    I  NONE          I
I  I1     .. INTEREST RATE                       I    I----------------I
I  M      .. MORTGAGE MULTIPLICATION FACTOR      I
I  M1     .. MONTHLY PAYMENT                     I
I  P      .. MORTGAGE AMOUNT                     I
I  Y      .. NUMBER OF YEARS FOR THE MORTGAGE    I
I------------------------------------------------I
```

Mortgage Comparison Program

Program Name: MORTCOMP

This program produces a series of outputs that are useful for comparing mortgage alternatives in terms of the effects of amount, interest rate, or mortgage year changes on the monthly principal and interest payment and also on the total interest paid over the term of the mortgage. All data is entered in response to program prompting.

Files Affected: None

```
10 REM           SAVED AT MORTCOMP
20 REM MORTGAGE COMPARISON PROGRAM
30 REM    NOTE ROUNDING ERRORS MAY OCCUR IN COMPUTED NUMBERS
40 REM ************************************************************
50 REM           DATA INITIALIZATION
60 REM ************************************************************
70 PRINT "ENTER THE ITEM TO VARY-AMOUNT(A), INT RATE(I), OR YEARS(Y)"
80 S1=1
90 S2=1
100 S3=1
110 INPUT A$
120 REM ************************************************************
130 REM           ENTER VARIABLE ITEMS
140 REM ************************************************************
150 IF A$<>"A" THEN 210
160  PRINT "ENTER THE BEGINNING AMOUNT, ENDING AMOUNT TO CONSIDER"
170 INPUT A0,A1
180 PRINT "ENTER THE INTERVAL BETWEEN PRINTS I.E. 1000"
190 INPUT S1
200 GOTO 390
210 IF A$<>"I" THEN 270
220 PRINT "ENTER THE LOWEST,HIGHEST INTEREST RATE TO CONSIDER"
230 INPUT R0,R1
240 PRINT "ENTER THE INTERVAL BETWEEN PRINTS I.E., .25 FOR 1/4"
250 INPUT S2
260 GOTO 350
270 IF A$<>"Y" THEN 330
280 PRINT "ENTER THE LOWEST,HIGHEST NUMBER OF YEARS TO CONSIDER"
290 INPUT Y0,Y1
300 PRINT "ENTER THE INTERVAL BETWEEN PRINTS I.E., 5"
310 INPUT S3
320 REM ************************************************************
330 REM           ENTER CONSTANT ITEMS
340 REM ************************************************************
350 PRINT "ENTER THE MORTGAGE AMOUNT"
360 INPUT P
370 A0=P
380 IF A$="I" THEN 450
390 PRINT "ENTER THE INTEREST RATE"
400 INPUT I1
410 IF I1>=1 THEN 430
420 I1=I1*100
430 R0=I1
440 IF A$="Y" THEN 480
450 PRINT "ENTER THE YEARS OF THE MORTGAGE"
460 INPUT Y
470 Y0=Y
480 PRINT
490 PRINT
500 PRINT
510 REM ************************************************************
520 REM           PROCESSING LOOP
530 REM ************************************************************
540 FOR Y=Y0 TO Y1 STEP S3
550    PRINT"FOR A MORTGAGE OF";Y;"YEARS"
560    PRINT
570    FOR I1=R0 TO TO R1 STEP S2
580      PRINT"USING THE INTEREST RATE";I1;"%"
590      PRINT
600      PRINT "MORTGAGE";TAB(15);"MONTHLY PI";TAB(30);" TOTAL"
610      PRINT " AMOUNT";TAB(15);" PAYMENT";TAB(30);"INTEREST"
620      PRINT "--------";TAB(15);"----------";TAB(30);"----------"
630      FOR P=A0 TO A1 STEP S1
640        REM ****** COMPUTATION AND PRINT    *************
650        I=(I1/100)/12
660        M=I/((1+I)^(Y*12)-1)+I
670        M1=M*P
680        I3=M1*Y*12-P
```

120   BASIC Computer Programs for Business

```
690        PRINT P;TAB(15);M1;TAB(30);I3
700     NEXT P
710     PRINT "****************************************"
720      PRINT
730   NEXT I1
740 NEXT Y
750 REM **************************************************************
760 REM              PROGRAM TERMINATION POINT
770 REM **************************************************************
780 PRINT
790 PRINT
800 STOP
```

```
RUN "MORTCOMP"
ENTER THE ITEM TO VARY-AMOUNT(A), INT RATE(I), OR YEARS(Y)
? I
ENTER THE LOWEST,HIGHEST INTEREST RATE TO CONSIDER
? 10,12
ENTER THE INTERVAL BETWEEN PRINTS I.E., .25 FOR 1/4
? .5
ENTER THE MORTGAGE AMOUNT
? 10000
ENTER THE YEARS OF THE MORTGAGE
? 10


FOR A MORTGAGE OF 10 YEARS

USING THE INTEREST RATE 10 %

MORTGAGE         MONTHLY PI       TOTAL
 AMOUNT           PAYMENT         INTEREST
--------         ----------       --------
 10000            132.153          5858.35
****************************************

USING THE INTEREST RATE 10.5 %

MORTGAGE         MONTHLY PI       TOTAL
 AMOUNT           PAYMENT         INTEREST
--------         ----------       --------
 10000            134.935          6192.26
****************************************

USING THE INTEREST RATE 11 %

MORTGAGE         MONTHLY PI       TOTAL
 AMOUNT           PAYMENT         INTEREST
--------         ----------       --------
 10000            137.75           6529.96
****************************************

USING THE INTEREST RATE 11.5 %

MORTGAGE         MONTHLY PI       TOTAL
 AMOUNT           PAYMENT         INTEREST
--------         ----------       --------
 10000            140.597          6871.67
```

```
********************************************

USING THE INTEREST RATE 12 %

MORTGAGE          MONTHLY PI        TOTAL
 AMOUNT            PAYMENT        INTEREST
----------        ----------     ----------
  10000           143.472         7216.62
********************************************


BREAK IN 800
OK




RUN "MORTCOMP"
ENTER THE ITEM TO VARY-AMOUNT(A), INT RATE(I), OR YEARS(Y)
? A
ENTER THE BEGINNING AMOUNT, ENDING AMOUNT TO CONSIDER
? 10000,30000
ENTER THE INTERVAL BETWEEN PRINTS I.E. 1000
? 5000
ENTER THE INTEREST RATE
? 12
ENTER THE YEARS OF THE MORTGAGE
? 10


FOR A MORTGAGE OF 10 YEARS

USING THE INTEREST RATE 12 %

MORTGAGE          MONTHLY PI        TOTAL
 AMOUNT            PAYMENT        INTEREST
----------        ----------     ----------
  10000           143.472         7216.62
  15000           215.208         10824.9
  20000           286.944         14433.2
  25000           358.68          18041.5
  30000           430.415         21649.9
********************************************


BREAK IN 800
OK
```

```
  MAJOR SYMBOL TABLE - MORTCOMP                              FUNCTIONS USED
I-------------------------------------------------------I   I---------------I
I NAME   .. DESCRIPTION                                 I   I  NAME         I
I-------------------------------------------------------I   I---------------I
I  A0    .. FIRST AMOUNT CONSIDERED                     I   I TAB           I
I  A1    .. LAST AMOUNT CONSIDERED                      I   I---------------I
I  I1    .. SINGLE INTEREST RATE                        I
I  I3    .. TOTAL INTEREST PAID                         I
I  M1    .. COMPUTED MONTHLY PAYEMNT                    I
I  P     .. SINGLE  MORTGAGE AMOUNT                     I
I  R0    .. LOWEST RATE CONSIDERED                      I
I  R1    .. HIGHEST RATE CONSIDERED                     I
I  S1    .. INTERVAL BETWEEN MORTAGE AMOUNTS            I
I  S2    .. INTERVAL BETWEEN INTEREST RATES             I
I  S3    .. INTERVAL BETWEEN MORTGAGE YEARS             I
I  Y     .. SINGLE NUMBER OF YEARS TO CONSIDER          I
I  Y0    .. LOWEST NUMBER OF YEARS CONSIDERED           I
I  Y1    .. HIGHEST NUMBER OF YEARS CONSIDERED          I
I-------------------------------------------------------I
```

II
Inventory Control and Analysis

5 Perpetual Inventory System

The two programs in this chapter perform all functions necessary for the processing of a perpetual inventory system, including querying the file to determine the availability of specific inventory items in response to customer requests.

The programs have been designed to accept and display information throughout the month and to update the files as each transaction is entered. At the end of each inventory period (usually monthly), the inventory transactions are summarized and monthly status reports are produced. Reports in the format of these monthly reports can be produced at any time, but the account close-out option may be run only at the end of the inventory period.

Since the security of inventory information may be critical to the effective operation of a business, care must be taken to insure the recovery of the information in cases of system (or file) failures. It is recommended that the file be copied after any significant activity and that a record of transactions be maintained for audit trail and recovery purposes.

Operation of the System

The following two programs have been provided for your use:

1. Inventory processing (INVPROC)—This program permits adding new inventory items, correcting existing items, and listing all current items in the file; it also provides a query/update capability.
2. Inventory reporting (INVPRNT)—This program produces month-end reports, closes the files at the end of the period, and allows the inventory files to be copied for recovery purposes.

Initialization of the files occurs as a normal part of the system's operation (whenever a new file name is entered); it does not require a specific initialization procedure.

Normal operation of the system throughout the month involves the execution of INVPROC to add new items and to query and update the current file. At the end of each month (or inventory period), INVPRNT must be executed to produce statements and then close the inventory records prior to the entry of the next period's transactions. Note that the monthly statements must be prepared before the item records are closed. The close option summarizes the transactions but does not allow the detail necessary to produce normal monthly reports. At a minimum, the recovery (file copy) option should be executed just before the files for each period are closed. These "copies" can then be maintained to provide a snapshot of the system's status at the end of each period. Furthermore, they act as the basis for system recovery and can be used later for inventory analysis purposes.

The flowcharts in Figs. 5-1 and 5-2 illustrate the processing of the perpetual inventory system.

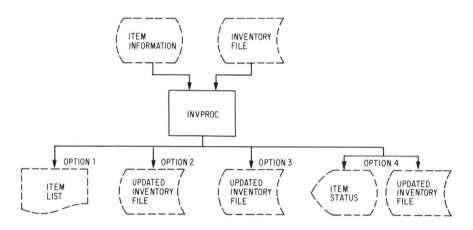

Fig. 5-1 Operation of the inventory processing program

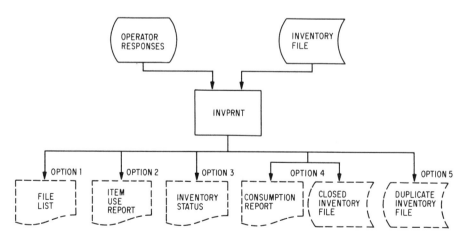

Fig. 5-2 Operation of the inventory reporting program

Files Used by the Perpetual Inventory System

The perpetual inventory system requires only one file for its operation, a random access file that contains a record for each inventory item. The format of the record is shown in Fig. 5-3.

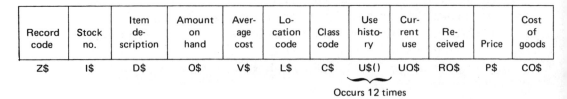

Record code	Stock no.	Item de-scription	Amount on hand	Aver-age cost	Lo-cation code	Class code	Use histo-ry	Cur-rent use	Re-ceived	Price	Cost of goods
Z$	I$	D$	O$	V$	L$	C$	U$( )	UO$	RO$	P$	CO$

Occurs 12 times

Fig. 5-3 Record format

```
        MAJOR SYMBOL TABLE - PERPETUAL INVENTORY            FUNCTIONS USED
I-----------------------------------------------------I    I-----------------I
I NAME     .. DESCRIPTION                             I    I    NAME         I
I-----------------------------------------------------I    I-----------------I
I   A1$    .. TEMP ANSWER VARIABLE                    I    I TAB             I
I   C$     .. INV CLASS CODE - IN FILE                I    I GOSUB           I
I   C0     .. NUMERIC C0$                             I    I RETURN          I
I   C1     .. TOTAL COST OF GOODS SOLD                I    I OPEN            I
I   C0$    .. COST OF GOODS - IN FILE                 I    I FIELD           I
I   C9$    .. INPUT CLASS CODE                        I    I CLOSE           I
I   D$     .. DESCRIPTION - IN FILE                   I    I GET             I
I   D1$    .. PROCESSING DATE                         I    I PUT             I
I   D9$    .. INPUT DESCRIPTION                       I    I LEN             I
I   F$     .. INPUT FILE NAME                         I    I LOF(1)          I
I   F1$    .. OUTPUT COPY FILE NAME                   I    I CVI             I
I   I      .. INDEX AND ARRAY POINTER                 I    I CVS             I
I   I$     .. ITEM NUMBER -IN FILE                    I    I MKI$            I
I   I1$()  .. ITEM NUMBER ARRAY                       I    I MKS$            I
I   I9$    .. ITEM NUMBER IN                          I    I LSET            I
I   J      .. INDEX AND ARRAY POINTER                 I    I DIM             I
I   K      .. RECORD # TO READ/WRITE                  I    I SPACE$          I
I   K1     .. RECORD NUMBER TO ADD                    I    I-----------------I
I   L$     .. LOCATION CODE - IN FILE                 I
I   L1     .. LAST RECORD NUMBER USED                 I
I   L9     .. LENGTH OF VARIABLE                      I
I   L9$    .. INPUT LOCATION                          I
I   M1     .. MAX NUMBER OF ITEMS                     I
I   M3     .. NUMBER OF INVENTORY ITEMS               I
I   0      .. NUMERIC O$                              I
I   O$     .. ON-HAND - IN FILE                       I
I   01     .. OPTION NUMBER                           I
I   P      .. NUMERIC P$                              I
I   P$     .. SELLING PRICE - IN FILE                 I
I   P9     .. PRICE PAID PER UNIT                     I
I   Q      .. QUANTITY OF TRANSACTION                 I
I   R      .. NUMERIC R$                              I
I   R$     .. REORDER POINT - IN FILE                 I
I   R0     .. NUMERIC R0$                             I
I   R0$    .. RCVD CURRENT PERIOD - IN FILE           I
I   R1$()  .. RECORD POINTER ARRAY                    I
I   T8$    .. ACTION CODE                             I
I   T9$    .. ACTION CODE                             I
```

```
I   U$()    .. USE ARRAY - IN FILE          I
I   U()     .. NUMERIC USE ARRAY            I
I   U0      .. NUMERIC U0$                  I
I   U0$     .. USE CURRENT PERIOD - IN FILE I
I   V       .. NUMERIC V$                   I
I   V$      .. UNIT AVG COST - IN FILE      I
I   V9      .. NEW AVERAGE COST PER UNIT    I
I   X$      .. LINE OF ASTERISKS            I
I   X1$     .. DUMMY VARIABLE               I
I   X2$     .. LINE OF HYPHENS              I
I   Z$      .. RECORD CODE - IN FILE        I
I   Z0$     .. 0 CONSTANT IN CHARACTER FORM I
I   Z1$     .. INPUT COPY RECORD            I
I   Z2$     .. OUTPUT COPY RECORD           I
I-------------------------------------------I
```

Inventory Processing

Program Name: INVPROC

This program performs the day-to-day processing functions of the perpetual inventory system. Four options are available to the operator through keyboard responses to program messages:

Option 1 lists all current records with their associated record numbers (in the file).

Option 2 adds new inventory items to the file. The program requests all necessary information from the operator.

Option 3 corrects information in the inventory record.

Option 4 allows the operator to query the status of an inventory item or update the inventory record to indicate the usage or receipt of additional supplies.

```
10 REM            SAVED AT INVPROC
20 REM            PERPETUAL INVENTORY SYSTEM
30 REM ***************************************************************
40 X$="***************************************************************"
50 X2$="-------------------------------------------------------------"
60 Z0$=MKI$(0)
70 M3=50
80 M1=200
90 DIM I1$(M1),R1(M1),U$(12)
100 PRINT "ENTER INVENTORY FILE NAME";
110 INPUT F$
120 GOSUB 430                    'FILE OPEN AND DEFINE
130 GOSUB 560                    'BUILD ITEM TABLE
140 PRINT
150 PRINT X$
160 PRINT
```

```
170 PRINT "THE FOLLOWING OPTIONS ARE AVAILABLE:"
180 PRINT
190 PRINT TAB(5);"1..ITEM LIST (WITH RECORD NUMBERS)"
200 PRINT TAB(5);"2..ADDING NEW ITEMS"
210 PRINT TAB(5);"3..CORRECTING ITEM INFORMATION"
220 PRINT TAB(5);"4..QUERY AND UPDATE PROCESS"
230 PRINT
240 PRINT "ENTER OPTION DESIRED";
250 INPUT O1
260 IF O1=1 THEN GOSUB 2200          'ITEM LIST
270 IF O1=2 THEN GOSUB 1040          'ADD NEW ITEMS
280 IF O1=3 THEN GOSUB 2340          'CORRECT ITEM INFO
290 IF O1=4 THEN GOSUB 1630          'ADD TRANSACTIONS
300 PRINT
310 PRINT "DO YOU WISH TO CONTINUE (Y OR N)";
320 INPUT A1$
330 IF A1$="Y" THEN 240
340 REM *****************************************************************
350 REM              PROGRAM TERMINATION POINT
360 REM *****************************************************************
370 PRINT
380 PRINT
390 PRINT "PROCESSING COMPLETE"
400 PRINT
410 STOP


420 REM *****************************************************************
430 REM              OPEN AND DEFINE FILES
440 REM *****************************************************************
450 OPEN "R",1,F$,0
460 FIELD#1,2 AS Z$,8 AS I$,30 AS D$,2 AS O$,4 AS V$,4 AS L$,4 AS C$
470 FOR I=1 TO 12
480   FIELD#1,(I-1)*2+54 AS X1$,2 AS U$(I)
490 NEXT I
500 FIELD#1,78 AS X1$,2 AS UO$,2 AS RO$,4 AS P$,4 AS CO$,2 AS R$
510 GET#1,1
520 L1=CVI(Z$)
530 IF L1<1 THEN L1=1
540 RETURN


550 REM *****************************************************************
560 REM              TABLE BUILD
570 REM *****************************************************************
580 I=1
590 FOR K=2 TO LOF(1)
600   GOSUB 800              'FILE READ
610   IF Z$<>"**" THEN 650
620   I1$(I)=I$
630   R1(I)=K
640   I=I+1
650 NEXT K
660 M3=I-1
670 RETURN


680 REM *****************************************************************
690 REM              FIND ITEM
700 REM *****************************************************************
710 K=0
720 FOR I=1 TO M3
730   IF I9$=I1$(I) THEN 770
740 NEXT I
750 PRINT "ITEM NOT FOUND"
760 GOTO 780
770 K=R1(I)
780 RETURN
```

```
790 REM ***************************************************************
800 REM               FILE READ
810 REM ***************************************************************
820 GET#1,K
830 O=CVI(O$)
840 V=CVS(V$)
850 UO=CVI(UO$)
860 P=CVS(P$)
870 CO=CVS(CO$)
880 RO=CVI(RO$)
890 R=CVI(R$)
900 RETURN

910 REM ***************************************************************
920 REM               FILE WRITE
930 REM ***************************************************************
940 LSET O$=MKI$(O)
950 LSET V$=MKS$(V)
960 LSET UO$=MKI$(UO)
970 LSET P$=MKS$(P)
980 LSET CO$=MKS$(CO)
990 LSET RO$=MKI$(RO)
1000 LSET R$=MKI$(R)
1010 PUT#1,K
1020 RETURN

1030 REM ***************************************************************
1040 REM          ADD NEW INVENTORY ITEMS
1050 REM ***************************************************************
1060 PRINT "***** ADD NEW INVENTORY ITEMS *****"
1070 PRINT
1080 PRINT "ENTER THE ITEM STOCK NUMBER";
1090 I9$=""
1100 INPUT I9$
1110 IF I9$="" THEN 1460
1120 M3=M3+1
1130 IF LEN(I9$)<8 THEN I9$=I9$+SPACE$(8-LEN(I9$))
1140 I1$(M3)=I9$
1150 PRINT "ENTER THE ITEM DESCRIPTION";
1160 INPUT D9$
1170 GOSUB 1480             'FIND RECORD #
1180 PRINT "ENTER THE AMOUNT ON HAND";
1190 INPUT O
1200 PRINT "ENTER  UNIT COST";
1210 INPUT V
1220 PRINT "ENTER LOCATION CODE";
1230 INPUT L9$
1240 PRINT "ENTER INVENTORY CLASS CODE";
1250 INPUT C9$
1260 PRINT "ENTER SELLING PRICE";
1270 INPUT P
1280 PRINT "ENTER REORDER POINT";
1290 INPUT R
1300 FOR I=1 TO 12
1310   LSET U$(I)=Z0$
1320 NEXT I
1330 LSET D$=D9$
1340 LSET I$=I9$
1350 LSET Z$="**"
1360 LSET L$=L9$
1370 LSET C$=C9$
1380 CO=0
1390 R1(M3)=K1
1400 K=K1
1410 GOSUB 920              'FILE WRITE
1420 K=1
1430 LSET Z$=MKI$(L1)
1440 GOSUB 920              'FILE WRITE
```

```
1450 GOTO 1080
1460 RETURN

1470 REM ***********************************************************
1480 REM                    FIND RECORD NUMBERS
1490 REM ***********************************************************
1500 I=2
1510 J=1
1520 IF I<=L1 THEN 1560
1530 L1=L1+1
1540 I=L1+1
1550 GOTO 1600
1560 K=I
1570 GOSUB 800              'FILE READ
1580 I=I+1
1590 IF Z$="**" THEN 1520
1600 K1=I-1
1610 RETURN

1620 REM ***********************************************************
1630 REM                    QUERY AND UPDATE
1640 REM ***********************************************************
1650 PRINT "***** QUERY AND UPDATE *****"
1660 PRINT
1670 K=0
1680 PRINT "ITEM NUMBER";
1690 I9$=" "
1700 INPUT I9$
1710 IF I9$="STOP" THEN 2180
1720 L9=LEN(I9$)
1730 IF L9<8 THEN I9$=I9$+SPACE$(8-L9)
1740 GOSUB 690              'FIND ITEM
1750 IF K=0 THEN 1670
1760 PRINT "ENTER QUERY(Q), UPDATE(U), OR QUERY/UPDATE (QU)";
1770 INPUT T9$
1780 IF T9$="Q" OR T9$="U" OR T9$="QU" THEN 1810
1790 PRINT "ERRONEOUS CODE - TRY AGAIN"
1800 GOTO 1760
1810 GOSUB 800              'FILE READ
1820 PRINT
1830 IF T9$="U" THEN 1890
1840 REM ******************* QUERY RECORD   ********************
1850 PRINT "STK #";TAB(10);"DESCRIPTION";TAB(41);"ON-HAND";
1860 PRINT TAB(50);"PRICE";TAB(60);"LOCATION"
1870 PRINT I$;TAB(10);D$;TAB(41);O;TAB(50);P;TAB(60);L$
1880 PRINT
1890 IF T9$="Q" THEN 2170
1900 REM ******************* UPDATE RECORD   ********************
1910 PRINT "ITEM RECEIVED (R), OR SOLD (S)";
1920 T8$=""
1930 INPUT T8$
1940 IF T8$="R" OR T8$="S" THEN 1970
1950 PRINT "ERRONEOUS CODE - TRY AGAIN"
1960 GOTO 1910
1970 PRINT "ENTER QUANTITY";
1980 Q=0
1990 INPUT Q
2000 IF T8$="R" THEN 2080
2010 U0=U0+Q
2020 C0=C0+Q*V
2030 LSET C0$=MKS$(C0)
2040 O=O-Q
2050 PRINT "PRICE IS:";Q*P
2060 PRINT
2070 GOTO 2160
2080 R0=R0+Q
2090 PRINT "ENTER UNIT PRICE";
2100 INPUT P9
```

```
2110 V9=(Q*P9+O*V)/(O+Q)
2120 PRINT "INVENTORY VALUE OLD-";V;" NEW-";V9
2130 PRINT
2140 V=V9
2150 O=O+Q
2160 GOSUB 920                    'FILE REWRITE
2170 GOTO 1670
2180 RETURN

2190 REM ***********************************************************
2200 REM                 PRINT ACCOUNT NUMBERS
2210 REM ***********************************************************
2220 PRINT "***** INVENTORY ITEM LIST *****"
2230 PRINT
2240 PRINT
2250 PRINT X$
2260 PRINT
2270 PRINT "NBR";TAB(10);"ITEM";TAB(20);"REC #"
2280 PRINT
2290 FOR I=1 TO M3
2300   PRINT I;TAB(10);I1$(I);TAB(20);R1(I)
2310 NEXT I
2320 RETURN

2330 REM ***********************************************************
2340 REM               CORRECT ACCOUNT INFORMATION
2350 REM ***********************************************************
2360 PRINT "***** CORRECTIONS *****"
2370 PRINT
2380 I9$=""
2390 PRINT "ENTER ITEM NUMBER";
2400 INPUT I9$
2410 IF I9$="" THEN 2990
2420 L9=LEN(I9$)
2430 IF L9<8 THEN I9$=I9$+SPACE$(8-L9)
2440 GOSUB 690                    'FIND ITEM
2450 IF K=0 THEN 2380
2460 PRINT "DELETE THE ITEM(Y OR N)";
2470 A1$=""
2480 INPUT A1$
2490 IF A1$<>"Y" THEN 2530
2500 LSET Z$="   "
2510 I1$(I)="********"
2520 GOTO 2970
2530 PRINT "ENTER THE INFORMATION TO BE CHANGED"
2540 PRINT "ITEM(I), DESC(D), LOC(L), CLASS(C), ";
2550 PRINT "PRICE(P), REORDER(R)"
2560 A1$=""
2570 INPUT A1$
2580 IF A1$="" THEN 2390
2590 GOSUB 800                    'FILE READ
2600 IF A1$<>"L" THEN 2660
2610 REM ***************** CHANGE LOCATION *********************
2620 PRINT "ENTER NEW LOCATION CODE";
2630 INPUT L9$
2640 LSET L$=L9$
2650 GOTO 2970
2660 IF A1$<>"D" THEN 2720
2670 REM ***************** CHANGE DESCRIPTION *******************
2680 PRINT "ENTER NEW PRODUCT DESCRIPTION";
2690 INPUT D9$
2700 LSET D$=D9$
2710 GOTO 2970
2720 IF A1$<>"C" THEN 2780
2730 REM ******************* CHANGE CLASS *********************
2740 PRINT "ENTER NEW CLASS CODE";
2750 INPUT C9$
2760 LSET C$=C9$
```

```
2770 GOTO 2970
2780 IF A1$<>"P" THEN 2840
2790 REM ******************** CHANGE PRICE ************************
2800 PRINT "ENTER NEW PRICE";
2810 INPUT P
2820 LSET P$=MKS$(P)
2830 GOTO 2970
2840 IF A1$<>"R" THEN 2900
2850 REM ******************** CHANGE REORDER POINT ***************
2860 PRINT "ENTER NEW REORDER POINT";
2870 INPUT R
2880 LSET R$=MKI$(R)
2890 GOTO 2970
2900 IF A1$<>"I" THEN 2990
2910 REM ***************** CHANGE ITEM NUMBER   ******************
2920 PRINT "ENTER NEW ITEM NUMBER";
2930 INPUT I9$
2940 IF LEN(I9$)<8 THEN I9$=I9$+SPACE$(8-LEN(I9$))
2950 I1$(I)=I9$
2960 LSET I$=I9$
2970 GOSUB 920                          'REWRITE FILE
2980 GOTO 2370
2990 RETURN
```

```
RUN "INVPROC"
ENTER INVENTORY FILE NAME? INVFILE

**************************************************************

THE FOLLOWING OPTIONS ARE AVAILABLE:

        1..ITEM LIST (WITH RECORD NUMBERS)
        2..ADDING NEW ITEMS
        3..CORRECTING ITEM INFORMATION
        4..QUERY AND UPDATE PROCESS

ENTER OPTION DESIRED? 2
***** ADD NEW INVENTORY ITEMS *****

ENTER THE ITEM STOCK NUMBER? 11111
ENTER THE ITEM DESCRIPTION? SUPER WIDGET
ENTER THE AMOUNT ON HAND? 10
ENTER   UNIT COST? 9.95
ENTER LOCATION CODE? B515
ENTER INVENTORY CLASS CODE? A
ENTER SELLING PRICE? 29.99
ENTER REORDER POINT? 5
ENTER THE ITEM STOCK NUMBER? 22222
ENTER THE ITEM DESCRIPTION? MIDDLE CLASS WIDGET
ENTER THE AMOUNT ON HAND? 20
ENTER   UNIT COST? 6.51
ENTER LOCATION CODE? B514
ENTER INVENTORY CLASS CODE? B
ENTER SELLING PRICE? 19.95
ENTER REORDER POINT? 10
ENTER THE ITEM STOCK NUMBER? 33333
ENTER THE ITEM DESCRIPTION? BUDGET WIDGET
ENTER THE AMOUNT ON HAND? 50
ENTER   UNIT COST? 1.98
ENTER LOCATION CODE? B513
ENTER INVENTORY CLASS CODE? C
ENTER SELLING PRICE? 4.98
ENTER REORDER POINT? 60
ENTER THE ITEM STOCK NUMBER?
```

```
DO YOU WISH TO CONTINUE (Y OR N)? Y
ENTER OPTION DESIRED? 1
***** INVENTORY ITEM LIST *****


*****************************************************************

NBR       ITEM       REC #

1         11111       2
2         22222       3
3         33333       4

DO YOU WISH TO CONTINUE (Y OR N)? N


PROCESSING COMPLETE

BREAK IN 410
OK




RUN "INVPROC"
ENTER INVENTORY FILE NAME? INVFILE

*****************************************************************

THE FOLLOWING OPTIONS ARE AVAILABLE:

     1..ITEM LIST (WITH RECORD NUMBERS)
     2..ADDING NEW ITEMS
     3..CORRECTING ITEM INFORMATION
     4..QUERY AND UPDATE PROCESS

ENTER OPTION DESIRED? 3
***** CORRECTIONS *****

ENTER ITEM NUMBER? 11111
DELETE THE ITEM(Y OR N)? N
ENTER THE INFORMATION TO BE CHANGED
ITEM(I), DESC(D), LOC(L), CLASS(C), PRICE(P), REORDER(R)
? L
ENTER NEW LOCATION CODE? B500

ENTER ITEM NUMBER?

DO YOU WISH TO CONTINUE (Y OR N)? Y
ENTER OPTION DESIRED? 4
***** QUERY AND UPDATE *****

ITEM NUMBER? 11111
ENTER QUERY(Q), UPDATE(U), OR QUERY/UPDATE (QU)? Q

STK #     DESCRIPTION                    ON-HAND  PRICE      LOCATION
11111     SUPER WIDGET                      10    29.99      B500

ITEM NUMBER? 11111
ENTER QUERY(Q), UPDATE(U), OR QUERY/UPDATE (QU)? QU

STK #     DESCRIPTION                    ON-HAND  PRICE      LOCATION
11111     SUPER WIDGET                      10    29.99      B500

ITEM RECEIVED (R), OR SOLD (S)? S
ENTER QUANTITY? 1
PRICE IS: 29.99
```

Perpetual Inventory System   133

```
ITEM NUMBER? 11111
ENTER QUERY(Q), UPDATE(U), OR QUERY/UPDATE (QU)? Q

STK #      DESCRIPTION                      ON-HAND   PRICE      LOCATION
11111      SUPER WIDGET                        9        29.99     B500

ITEM NUMBER? 11111
ENTER QUERY(Q), UPDATE(U), OR QUERY/UPDATE (QU)? U

ITEM RECEIVED (R), OR SOLD (S)? R
ENTER QUANTITY? 5
ENTER UNIT PRICE? 11.45
INVENTORY VALUE OLD- 9.95  NEW- 10.4857

ITEM NUMBER?
ITEM NOT FOUND
ITEM NUMBER? STOP

DO YOU WISH TO CONTINUE (Y OR N)? N

PROCESSING COMPLETE

BREAK IN 410
OK
```

Inventory Reporting

Program Name: INVPRNT

This program performs end-of-month (end-of-inventory-period) processing. It produces inventory reports and permits the inventory file to be copied for recovery purposes. Five options are available to the operator through keyboard responses to program messages:

Option 1 lists the current contents of the inventory file.

Option 2 prints an Inventory Use Report for the current period and also provides prior usage information.

Option 3 prepares a report portraying the status of all inventory items as of the date the report is run.

Option 4 closes the inventory records for the current period. Current period usage is given a history status, and the current period fields are set to zero. In addition, the option produces a summary report detailing the usage and cost of each item sold during this period. Once the option has been executed, the Inventory Use Report loses much of its value.

Option 5 allows the operator to create a duplicate of the inventory file. At a minimum, this option should be executed monthly, just prior to closing the accounts.

```
10 REM              SAVED AT INVPRNT
20 REM          PERPETUAL INVENTORY SYSTEM -- REPORTS PROGRAM
30 REM ***********************************************************
40 X$="*********************************************************************"
50 X2$="--------------------------------------------------------------------- "
60 Z0$=MKI$(0)
70 M3=50
80 M1=200
90 DIM I1$(M1),R1(M1),U$(12),U(12)
100 PRINT "ENTER INVENTORY FILE NAME";
110 INPUT F$
120 PRINT "ENTER TODAY'S DATE";
130 INPUT D1$
140 GOSUB 470                    'FILE OPEN AND DEFINE
150 GOSUB 600                    'BUILD ITEM TABLE
160 PRINT
170 PRINT X$
180 PRINT
190 PRINT "THE FOLLOWING OPTIONS ARE AVAILABLE:"
200 PRINT
210 PRINT TAB(5);"1..FILE LIST"
220 PRINT TAB(5);"2..USE REPORT"
230 PRINT TAB(5);"3..INVENTORY STATUS REPORT"
240 PRINT TAB(5);"4..CLOSE ACCOUNTS (END OF MONTH)"
250 PRINT TAB(5);"5..COPY INVENTORY FILE"
260 PRINT
270 PRINT "ENTER OPTION DESIRED";
280 INPUT O1
290 IF O1=1 THEN GOSUB 1100          'FILE PRINT
300 IF O1=2 THEN GOSUB 1430          'PRINT USE INFO
310 IF O1=3 THEN GOSUB 1710          'STATUS REPORT
320 IF O1=4 THEN GOSUB 1920          'CLOSE ACCOUNTS
330 IF O1=5 THEN GOSUB 2270          'COPY FILE
340 PRINT
350 PRINT "DO YOU WISH TO CONTINUE (Y OR N)";
360 INPUT A1$
370 IF A1$="Y" THEN 270
380 REM ***********************************************************
390 REM              PROGRAM TERMINATION POINT
400 REM ***********************************************************
410 PRINT
420 PRINT
430 PRINT "PROCESSING COMPLETE"
440 PRINT
450 STOP


460 REM ***********************************************************
470 REM            OPEN AND DEFINE FILES
480 REM ***********************************************************
490 OPEN "R",1,F$,0
500 FIELD#1,2 AS Z$,8 AS I$,30 AS D$,2 AS O$,4 AS V$,4 AS L$,4 AS C$
510 FOR I=1 TO 12
520    FIELD#1,(I-1)*2+54 AS X1$,2 AS U$(I)
530 NEXT I
540 FIELD#1,78 AS X1$,2 AS U0$,2 AS R0$,4 AS P$,4 AS C0$,2 AS R$
550 GET#1,1
560 L1=CVI(Z$)
570 IF L1<1 THEN L1=1
580 RETURN


590 REM ***********************************************************
600 REM                  TABLE BUILD
610 REM ***********************************************************
620 I=1
630 FOR K=2 TO LOF(1)
640    GOSUB 840              'FILE READ
650    IF Z$<>"**" THEN 690
```

```
660    I1$(I)=I$
670    R1(I)=K
680    I=I+1
690 NEXT K
700 M3=I-1
710 RETURN

720 REM *******************************************************
730 REM                  FIND ITEM
740 REM *******************************************************
750 K=0
760 FOR I=1 TO M3
770    IF I9$=I1$(I) THEN 810
780 NEXT I
790 PRINT "ITEM NOT FOUND
800 GOTO 820
810 K=R1(I)
820 RETURN

830 REM *******************************************************
840 REM                 FILE READ
850 REM *******************************************************
860 GET#1,K
870 O=CVI(O$)
880 V=CVS(V$)
890 UO=CVI(UO$)
900 P=CVS(P$)
910 CO=CVS(CO$)
920 RO=CVI(RO$)
930 R=CVI(R$)
940 FOR J=1 TO 12
950    U(J)=CVI(U$(J))
960 NEXT J
970 RETURN

980 REM *******************************************************
990 REM                 FILE WRITE
1000 REM *******************************************************
1010 FOR J=1 TO 12
1020    LSET U$(J)=MKI$(U(J))
1030 NEXT J
1040 LSET UO$=MKI$(O)
1050 LSET CO$=MKS$(O)
1060 LSET RO$=MKI$(O)
1070 PUT#1,K
1080 RETURN

1090 REM *******************************************************
1100 REM                  FILE PRINT
1110 REM *******************************************************
1120 PRINT "POSITION PAPER NOW";
1130 INPUT A1$
1140 PRINT
1150 PRINT X$
1160 PRINT
1170 PRINT TAB(15);"FILE CONTENTS - ";F$;"    AS OF:";D1$
1180 PRINT
1190 PRINT X2$
1200 PRINT "ITEM";TAB(10);"DESCRIPTION";TAB(41);"ON-HAND";TAB(50);"ITEM COST";
1210 PRINT TAB(60);"LOC";TAB(65);"CLASS"
1220 PRINT X2$
1230 PRINT "    USE FOR PREVIOUS PERIODS - EARLIEST FIRST"
1240 PRINT X2$
1250 PRINT "CUR USE";TAB(10);"RCVD";TAB(20);"PRICE";TAB(30);"COST-GOODS";
1260 PRINT TAB(42);"REORDER AT"
1270 PRINT X2$
1280 FOR I=1 TO M3
1290    K=R1(I)
```

```
1300    GOSUB 840                    'READ FILE
1310    PRINT I$;TAB(10);D$;TAB(41);O;TAB(50);V;TAB(60);L$;TAB(65);C$
1320    FOR J=1 TO 12
1330       PRINT TAB((J-1)*6+1);U(J);
1340    NEXT J
1350    PRINT
1360    PRINT UO;TAB(10);RO;TAB(20);P;TAB(32);CO;TAB(44);R
1370    PRINT X2$
1380 NEXT I
1390 PRINT
1400 PRINT X$
1410 RETURN


1420 REM ****************************************************************
1430 REM               USE REPORT
1440 REM ****************************************************************
1450 PRINT "POSITION PAPER NOW";
1460 INPUT A1$
1470 PRINT
1480 PRINT X$
1490 PRINT
1500 PRINT TAB(25);"INVENTORY USE REPORT    AS OF:";D1$
1510 PRINT
1520 PRINT X2$
1530 PRINT "ITEM";TAB(10);"CUR USE ";TAB(20);"COST-GOODS";TAB(31);"ON-HAND";
1540 PRINT TAB(42);"REORDER AT"
1550 PRINT "   USE FOR PREVIOUS PERIODS -  EARLIEST FIRST"
1560 PRINT X2$
1570 FOR I=1 TO M3
1580    K=R1(I)
1590    GOSUB 840                    'READ FILE
1600    PRINT I$;TAB(12);UO;TAB(24);CO;TAB(34);O;TAB(44);R
1610    FOR J=1 TO 12
1620       PRINT TAB((J-1)*6+1);U(J);
1630    NEXT J
1640    PRINT
1650    PRINT X2$
1660 NEXT I
1670 PRINT
1680 PRINT X$
1690 RETURN


1700 REM ****************************************************************
1710 REM               STATUS REPORT
1720 REM ****************************************************************
1730 PRINT "POSITION PAPER NOW";
1740 INPUT A1$
1750 PRINT
1760 PRINT X$
1770 PRINT
1780 PRINT TAB(15);"INVENTORY STATUS REPORT  AS OF:";D1$
1790 PRINT
1800 PRINT "ITEM";TAB(10);"DESCRIPTION";TAB(42);"ON-HAND";TAB(50);
1810 PRINT "AVG COST";TAB(60);"REORDER AT"
1820 PRINT X2$
1830 FOR I=1 TO M3
1840    K=R1(I)
1850    GOSUB 840                    'READ FILE
1860    PRINT I$;TAB(10);D$;TAB(44);O;TAB(50);V;TAB(63);R
1870 NEXT I
1880 PRINT
1890 PRINT X$
1900 RETURN


1910 REM ****************************************************************
1920 REM               CLOSE OUT INVENTORY MONTHLY
1930 REM ****************************************************************
1940 PRINT "ARE YOU CERTAIN THAT YOU WANT TO CLOSE ACCOUNTS (Y OR N)";
```

```
1950 A1$=""
1960 INPUT A1$
1970 IF A1$<>"Y" THEN 2460
1980 PRINT
1990 PRINT "***** CLOSING INVENTORY ACCOUNTS FOR PERIOD *****"
2000 PRINT
2010 PRINT X$
2020 PRINT
2030 PRINT "INVENTORY CONSUMPTION   AS OF:";D1$
2040 PRINT TAB(5);"(AT CLOSING)"
2050 PRINT
2060 PRINT "ITEM";TAB(10);"USE";TAB(20);"COST OF GOODS"
2070 PRINT
2080 FOR I=1 TO M3
2090   K=R1(I)
2100   GOSUB 840                  'READ FILE
2110   FOR J=1 TO 11
2120     U(J)=U(J+1)
2130   NEXT J
2140   U(12)=U0
2150   GOSUB 990                  'FILE WRITE
2160   PRINT I$;TAB(10);U(12);TAB(20);C0
2170   C1=C1+C0
2180 NEXT I
2190 PRINT
2200 PRINT X2$
2210 PRINT "TOT COST OF GOODS";TAB(20);C1
2220 PRINT
2230 PRINT X$
2240 PRINT
2250 RETURN

2260 REM *************************************************************
2270 REM                 FILE COPY ROUTINE
2280 REM *************************************************************
2290 CLOSE 1
2300 PRINT "ENTER FILE TO BE COPIED TO";
2310 INPUT F1$
2320 OPEN"R",1,F$,0
2330 OPEN"R",2,F1$,0
2340 FIELD#1,128 AS Z1$
2350 FIELD#2,128 AS Z2$
2360 FOR K=1 TO LOF(1)
2370   GET#1,K
2380   LSET Z2$=Z1$
2390   PUT#2,K
2400 NEXT K
2410 PRINT
2420 PRINT "FILE COPY COMPLETE"
2430 CLOSE 1,2
2440 GOSUB 470                  'REOPEN FILE
2450 PRINT
2460 RETURN
```

```
RUN "INVPRNT"
ENTER INVENTORY FILE NAME? INVFILE
ENTER TODAY'S DATE? 02/28/81

******************************************************************************

THE FOLLOWING OPTIONS ARE AVAILABLE:

        1..FILE LIST
        2..USE REPORT
        3..INVENTORY STATUS REPORT
        4..CLOSE ACCOUNTS (END OF MONTH)
        5..COPY INVENTORY FILE

ENTER OPTION DESIRED? 1
POSITION PAPER NOW?

******************************************************************************

                FILE CONTENTS - INVFILE    AS OF:02/28/81

-------------------------------------------------------------------------------
ITEM       DESCRIPTION                        ON-HAND  ITEM COST LOC  CLASS
-------------------------------------------------------------------------------
    USE FOR PREVIOUS PERIODS - EARLIEST FIRST
-------------------------------------------------------------------------------
CUR USE   RCVD       PRICE     COST-GOODS  REORDER AT
-------------------------------------------------------------------------------
11111      SUPER WIDGET                        14       10.4857  B500 A
   0      0     0      0      0      0      0      0      0      0     0
   1      5       29.99        9.95          5
-------------------------------------------------------------------------------
22222      MIDDLE CLASS WIDGET                 20        6.51    B514 B
   0      0     0      0      0      0      0      0      0      0     0
   0      0       19.95        0            10
-------------------------------------------------------------------------------
33333      BUDGET WIDGET                       50        1.98    B513 C
   0      0     0      0      0      0      0      0      0      0     0
   0      0        4.98        0            60
-------------------------------------------------------------------------------

******************************************************************************

DO YOU WISH TO CONTINUE (Y OR N)? Y
ENTER OPTION DESIRED? 2
POSITION PAPER NOW?

******************************************************************************

                 INVENTORY USE REPORT    AS OF:02/28/81

-------------------------------------------------------------------------------
ITEM      CUR USE   COST-GOODS ON-HAND   REORDER AT
    USE FOR PREVIOUS PERIODS -  EARLIEST FIRST
-------------------------------------------------------------------------------
11111       1           9.95      14        5
   0      0     0      0      0      0      0      0      0      0     0
-------------------------------------------------------------------------------
22222       0           0         20       10
   0      0     0      0      0      0      0      0      0      0     0
-------------------------------------------------------------------------------
33333       0           0         50       60
   0      0     0      0      0      0      0      0      0      0     0
-------------------------------------------------------------------------------
```

Perpetual Inventory System   139

```
****************************************************************

DO YOU WISH TO CONTINUE (Y OR N)? Y
ENTER OPTION DESIRED? 3
POSITION PAPER NOW?

****************************************************************

              INVENTORY STATUS REPORT   AS OF:02/28/81

  ITEM      DESCRIPTION                ON-HAND AVG COST  REORDER AT
  ------    ----------------------     ------- --------  ----------
  11111     SUPER WIDGET                  14   10.4857       5
  22222     MIDDLE CLASS WIDGET           20    6.51         10
  33333     BUDGET WIDGET                 50    1.98         60

****************************************************************

DO YOU WISH TO CONTINUE (Y OR N)? Y
ENTER OPTION DESIRED? 4
ARE YOU CERTAIN THAT YOU WANT TO CLOSE ACCOUNTS (Y OR N)? Y

***** CLOSING INVENTORY ACCOUNTS FOR PERIOD *****

****************************************************************

INVENTORY CONSUMPTION   AS OF:02/28/81
       (AT CLOSING)

  ITEM      USE      COST OF GOODS

  11111      1        9.95
  22222      0        0
  33333      0        0

  --------------------------------------------------------------
  TOT COST OF GOODS    9.95

****************************************************************


DO YOU WISH TO CONTINUE (Y OR N)? Y
ENTER OPTION DESIRED? 5
ENTER FILE TO BE COPIED TO? INV-SAVE



FILE COPY COMPLETE

DO YOU WISH TO CONTINUE (Y OR N)? N

PROCESSING COMPLETE

BREAK IN 450
OK
```

6 Periodic Inventory System

This series of programs is designed to provide the processing required to monitor and control an inventory in an environment that lends itself to a weekly, monthly, or other periodic update. Records of incoming stock accumulated during the period are processed in one batch at the end of the period along with inventory-on-hand information. At the end of each period, a physical inventory is taken of all stock items (using the recording log provided by program ILOG), and the current inventory (on-hand) amounts are entered in the files (using program IDATA). After these transactions have been entered, program IREPORT updates the inventory files and prints an inventory report for the period. Subsequently, any or all of the optional reporting programs may be executed.

A procedure to help you protect your inventory files is provided. File problems can often be eliminated by using program ISTATUS, but to assure full file protection and recovery, the critical master files should be copied after all major updates.

Inventory valuation and computations for the cost of goods sold are based on the FIFO (First In, First Out) method, a method that can be changed by modifying the section of program IREPORT beginning at statement 1320.

Projected-usage computations are based on a weighted-average method. The usage for each period is weighted by multiplying it by a factor that gives the most weight to the most recent periods. For example, the sample outputs record usage information for twelve previous months ($M1 = 12$). The weighted-averaging method causes the most recent month to be multiplied by 12, the month before that by 11, the one before that by 10, and so forth, until the earliest month is multiplied by 1. This method can be modified by changing lines 320–380 of program ICOMP.

All programs given here assign fixed values to a number of variables. You may wish to change these values to suit your processing needs. The variables involved and the values presently assigned are as follows:

141

1. Variable M0 controls the number of master files to be maintained for recovery purposes. For the programs given, its value is 2.
2. Variable M1 controls the number of previous periods for which data is to be stored. For the programs given, its value is 12.
3. Variable M2 controls the number of inventory values to be recorded. For the programs given, its value is 8. (The master file contains several records listing inventory values for each item so that both FIFO and LIFO valuation methods may be accommodated.)
4. The index file is named "MINDEX." This name can be changed by modifying the value of variable F$.

Operation of the System

Initialization of inventory files

The following programs provide for the initialization of the system and for the entry of initial-inventory master-file items. This step must be completed before the other inventory programs can be run. You will need to gather your inventory records in advance and assign an inventory code to each. These codes, which have a maximum length of eight characters, are the primary means of record identification within the computer. Since the inventory items must be entered in alphabetic order (based on this code), it would be wise to set up the code so that various types of inventory items are grouped logically.

Two other four-letter codes can be used to separate items in the inventory by type and location. These codes are meant solely for use in the reports. Unlike the codes for the inventory master file, they are not used by the computer and consequently can be eliminated from the files and programs, if desired.

As illustrated in the flowchart of Fig. 6-1, the programs INITIAL, ITRANS, and IUPDTE perform the initialization processes that create the file structures and enter the original inventory items in the inventory master file.

As-Required Processing

These programs allow for the maintenance of the inventory master file and for recovery capability in case of file problems.

Programs ITRANS and IUPDTE are used to add, delete, and replace items in the inventory master file [see Fig. 6-2(a)]. They are the same programs that were used during the initial file-building process.

Program ISTATUS verifies the status of the index and the master files, allowing the operator to step back to a previous version of the inventory master file in case of difficulties [see Fig. 6-2(b)]. The

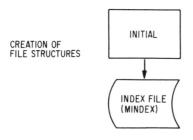

CREATION OF
FILE STRUCTURES

ENTERING ITEMS TO
THE MASTER FILE

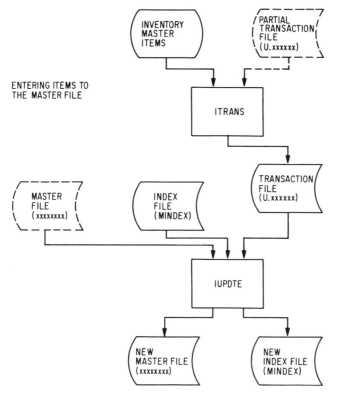

Fig. 6-1 Initialization of inventory files

amount of protection offered by this program is determined by the number of files you choose to maintain (variable M0).

End-of-Period Processing

These programs allow the physical inventory amounts to be entered at the end of each period and the quantities and costs of items received to be entered during the period. After the data is entered, the files are updated and the inventory report produced.

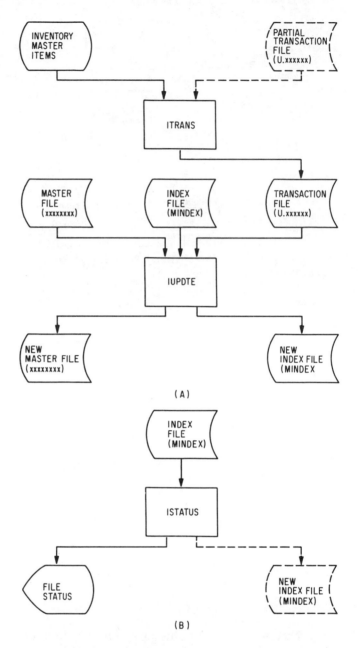

Fig. 6-2 As-required processing: (a) adding to, deleting from, and correcting the master file; and (b) verifying file status and recovering

Program IDATA records the end-of-period inventory amounts in a transaction file for later update.

Program IREPORT processes the transactions and produces the inventory report for the period.

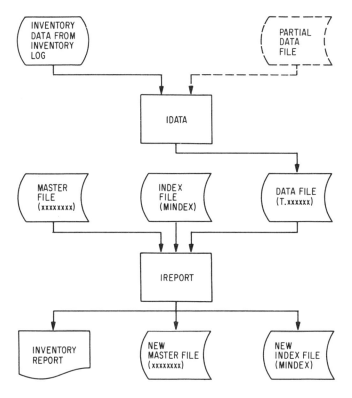

Fig. 6-3 End-of-period processing

To perform these processes (see Fig. 6-3), it is first necessary to take a physical inventory at the end of each period and to prepare a log indicating the quantity of each item on hand and the quantity received from suppliers during the period.

Printing Reports

A basic inventory report is produced during end-of-period processing, but other reports for specific purposes may also be desired. Several report-producing programs are thus provided for your use, as shown in Fig. 6-4. All these programs are optional, although ILOG, which helps record the end-of-period quantities on hand, is strongly recommended. Since this log is in item-code order, it also facilitates the entry of inventory data.

Program ILIST produces a formatted list of the contents of the master inventory file for validation and review.

Program ICOMP provides a skeletal aid for computer-assisted analyses of inventory trouble spots. In its present form, it produces useful statistics and projections.

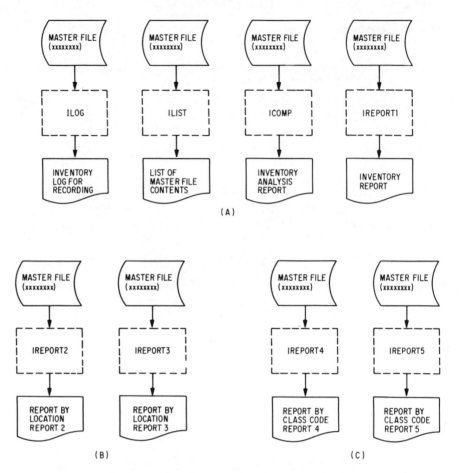

(A)

(B)   (C)

Fig. 6-4 Printing reports: (a) miscellaneous reports,
(b) reports by location, and (c) reports by class code

Programs IREPORT1 through IREPORT5 produce reports of various formats, most of which are ordered by class or location codes.

Files Used by the Periodic Inventory System

Four basic files are used by these inventory programs, each of which is described below.

Index file

The name of this file is determined by the value assigned to variable F$; in these examples, it is MINDEX. Only one copy of this file is provided by the system. Its function is to maintain a record of the various copies of the inventory master files, their creation dates, and the version to be used for the next update/processing cycle. It consists of multiple occurrences of a file name and file creation date. The first occurrence is considered to be the latest, and the last occurrence is considered to be the earliest. The number of file names included in the index file is determined by the value of variable M0. Occasionally, the file will contain the name of a transaction file that is being used for updating the inventory master file. If a transaction file name is present, it will be the last entry in the file, and the name will begin with a "T." or a "U.".

Inventory master file

The name of this file is determined by the value entered during the execution of the initialization program. The number of versions of the file is determined by the value of variable M0. The actual file name is determined by adding a version number (for example, 1) to the end of the file name entered. In the case of the examples provided, the file name MASTER was modified to be MASTER 1 and MASTER 2 to accommodate the two versions of the file.

The master file contains one record for each inventory item. Its sequence is based on an alphabetic ordering by item code. All records are identical in format (but not in length), except for the first. The first record contains the creation date of the file. All other records are of the form shown in Fig. 6-5.

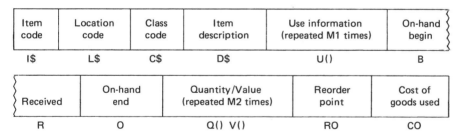

Item code	Location code	Class code	Item description	Use information (repeated M1 times)	On-hand begin
I$	L$	C$	D$	U()	B

Received	On-hand end	Quantity/Value (repeated M2 times)	Reorder point	Cost of goods used
R	O	Q() V()	RO	CO

Fig. 6-5 Record format

Transaction files

Both the transaction file for updating (correcting) the inventory master file and the transaction file for entering inventory data share the same characteristics. They are temporary files that are not accessible after they have been processed. They are also sequential files that contain essentially mirror images of the transactions entered at the terminal. Their formats vary according to the transaction entered. Their names are determined by appending a special character just before the first of the six characters of the master file name to denote the file type (a "T." or a "U."). Therefore, when the master file name is MASTER, the transaction file for updating the master file is U.MASTER, and the file that contains the period's data for processing is T.MASTER. All programs for the periodic inventory system are listed in Fig. 6-6, along with their functions. The symbol and function tables are consolidated for the entire group. Symbol usage is consistent throughout.

Program Name	Function	Remarks
INITIAL	Initializes files	Program list in section introduction
IDATA	Records inventory transactions	
IREPORT	Processes periodic inventory	IDATA must be run first
ISTATUS	Prints file status and swaps files for recovery	
ILIST	Prints contents of master file	
ITRANS	Enters update corrections for master file	IUPDTE processes transactions
ILOG	Produces list to record transactions	In order by item code
ICOMP	Inventory analysis program	Optional
IREPORT1	Prints inventory report	Optional
IREPORT2	Prints report by location code	Optional
IREPORT3	Prints report by location code	Optional
IREPORT4	Prints report by class code	Optional
IREPORT5	Prints report by class code	Optional
IUPDTE	Corrects master file	Requires ITRANS first

FIG. 6-6 Programs for the periodic inventory system

```
MAJOR SYMBOL TABLE - INVENTORY                                    FUNCTIONS USED
I-------------------------------------------------------I        I-----------------I
I NAME     .. DESCRIPTION                                I        I NAME            I
I-------------------------------------------------------I        I-----------------I
I  A0      .. AVERAGE USE                                I        I CLOSE           I
I  A       .. TEMP ANSWER VARIABLE                       I        I DIM             I
I  A9      .. TEMP VARIABLE                              I        I EOF()           I
I  A$      .. TEMP ANSWER VARIABLE                       I        I GOSUB           I
I  A1$     .. TEMP ANSWER VARIABLE                       I        I INPUT#          I
I  A2$     .. TEMP ANSWER VARIABLE                       I        I INT             I
I  B       .. ON HAND BEGINNING - MASTER FILE            I        I KILL            I
I  B9      .. ON HAND BEGINNING - TRANS FILE             I        I LEFT$           I
I  C0      .. COST OF GOODS SOLD                         I        I LEN             I
I  C0$()   .. CLASS CODE ARRAY                           I        I LINEINPUT       I
I  C9      .. COUNTER                                    I        I NAME            I
I  C9$     .. CLASS CODE - TRANS FILE                    I        I OPEN            I
I  C$      .. CLASS CODE - MASTER FILE                   I        I PRINT#          I
I  D$      .. DESCRIPTION - MASTER FILE                  I        I RETURN          I
I  D0$     .. TEMP DATE VARIABLE                         I        I TAB             I
I  D1$()   .. MASTER FILE - DATES                        I        I SPACE$          I
I  D8$     .. DESCRIPTION - TRANS FILE                   I        I STRING$         I
I  D9$     .. CURRENT DATE                               I        I                 I
I  E       .. ERROR CODE                                 I        I-----------------I
I  F$      .. INDEX FILE NAME                            I
I  F0$     .. TEMP FILE NAME                             I
I  F1$     .. MASTER FILE FILENAMES                      I
I  I$      .. ITEM CODE - MASTER FILE                    I
I  I8$     .. INPUT ITEM CODE                            I
I  I9$     .. ITEM CODE - TRANS FILE                     I
I  L0      .. COUNTER                                    I
I  L$      .. LOCATION CODE - MASTER FILE                I
I  L0$()   .. LOCATION CODE ARRAY                        I
I  L9$     .. LOCATION CODE - TRANS FILE                 I
I  M0      .. NUMBER OF MASTER FILES                     I
I  M1      .. NUMBER OF PERIODS RECORDED                 I
I  M2      .. NUMBER OF INVENTORY VALUES RECORDED        I
I  M3      .. MAXIMUM NUMBER OF CLASSES/LOCATIONS        I
I  M0$     .. MONTH NAME                                 I
I  O       .. ON HAND END - MASTER FILE                  I
I  O9      .. ON HAND END - TRANS FILE                   I
I  P       .. NUMBER OF PERIODS TO RECORD                I
I  P9      .. PROJECTED USE                              I
I  Q()     .. QUANTITY PURCHASED - MASTER FILE           I
I  Q9()    .. QTY PURCHASED - TRANS FILE                 I
I  R       .. RECEIVED DURING PERIOD - MASTER FILE       I
I  R0      .. REORDER POINT                              I
I  R9      .. RECEIVED DURING PERIOD - TRANS FILE        I
I  S7      .. EOF INDICATOR                              I
I  S8      .. EOF INDICATOR                              I
I  T()     .. TOTAL DOLLAR ARRAY                         I
I  T0      .. TOTAL DOLLARS                              I
I  T0$     .. OLD TRANS FILE NAME                        I
I  T1      .. LENGTH OF FILE NAME                        I
I  T1$     .. TRANS FILE NAME                            I
I  T2$     .. TEMP FILE NAME                             I
I  T9$     .. TRANSACTION TYPE CODE                      I
I  U()     .. USE STATISTICS - MASTER FILE               I
I  U0      .. USE DURING CURRENT PERIOD                  I
I  U9()    .. USE STATISTICS - MASTER FILE               I
I  V()     .. UNITS VALUE -MASTER FILE                   I
I  V0      .. VALUE OF GOODS                             I
I  V9      .. TRANSACTION VALUE                          I
I  V9()    .. VALUES - TRANS FILE                        I
I  X       .. TEMP VARIABLE                              I
I  X$      .. TEMP VARIABLE                              I
I-------------------------------------------------------I
```

Initialization of Inventory Files

Program Name: INITIAL

This program initializes files for use by the periodic inventory system and contains an unused capability to create other files as well. In its present form, it produces master and index files using the file names provided by the operator at the time of initialization. Multiple copies of the master file are created for use during recovery processing. The number of master files for recovery cycling is specified by the value of variable M0.

Files Affected: Index file (created)

Inventory master files (created)

```
10 REM            SAVED AT INITIAL
20 REM ***********************************************************
30 REM                   INITIALIZE
40 REM ***********************************************************
50 M0=2
60 M=3
70 DIM F$(M)
80 DIM D7$(M)
90 D7$(1)="INVENTORY"
100 D7$(2)="UNUSED"
110 D7$(3)="UNUSED"
120 F$(1)="MINDEX"
130 F$(2)="OINDEX"
140 F$(3)="SINDEX"
150 DIM F1$(M0),D1$(M0)
160 REM ***********************************************************
170 REM            PROCESSING AREA
180 REM ***********************************************************
190 PRINT
200 PRINT
210 PRINT "WE CAN INITIALIZE THE FOLLOWING TYPES OF FILES"
220 PRINT
230 FOR I= 1 TO M
240    PRINT TAB(10);I;D7$(I)
250 NEXT I
260 PRINT
270 PRINT "ENTER THE CODE NUMBER OF THE FILE TO BE INITIALIZED ";
280 INPUT T
290 IF T > M THEN 210
300 IF T = 0 THEN 640
310 PRINT
320 PRINT
330 PRINT "YOU ARE INITIALIZING ";D7$(T);" MASTER FILES"
340 PRINT
350 PRINT "THE NAME OF THE ID FILE WILL BE ....... ";F$(T)
360 PRINT "ENTER THE NAME TO BE USED FOR THE MASTER FILE";
370 INPUT F0$
380 PRINT "ENTER TODAY'S DATE MM/DD/YY";
390 INPUT D1$(1)
400 FOR I=1 TO M0
410    F1$(I)=F0$+STR$(I)
420 NEXT I
430 PRINT
440 PRINT "I AM PREPARED TO CREATE THE FOLLOWING FILES:"
```

```
450 PRINT TAB(5);"INDEX FILE..................";F$(T)
460 PRINT TAB(5);D7$(T);" FILES (";MO;")..";
470 FOR I= 1 TO MO
480    PRINT "...";F1$(I);" ";
490 NEXT I
500 PRINT
510 PRINT
520 PRINT "SHALL I CREATE THEM (Y OR N)?";
530 INPUT A$
540 PRINT
550 IF A$="N" THEN 640
560 GOSUB 680                     'FILE OPEN
570 GOSUB 740                     'FILE WRITE
580 REM ***********************************************************
590 REM                  PROGRAM TERMINATES
600 REM ***********************************************************
610 GOSUB 800                     'FILE CLOSE
620 PRINT "FILE CREATION COMPLETE"
630 PRINT
640 STOP



650 REM ***********************************************************
660 REM               FILE HANDLING PROCEDURES
670 REM ***********************************************************
680 REM************** FILE OPENS   ***************************
690 OPEN "O",MO+1,F$(T)
700 FOR I= 1 TO MO
710    OPEN "O",I,F1$(I)
720 NEXT I
730 RETURN


740 REM *****************  FILE WRITE   ***********************
750 PRINT#MO+1,F1$(1);",";D1$(1);",";F1$(2);",";D1$(2)
760 FOR I = 1 TO MO
770    PRINT#I,0;0;0;0;0
780 NEXT I
790 RETURN


800 REM ***************   FILE CLOSES   ***********************
810 FOR I= 1 TO MO+1
820    CLOSE I
830 NEXT I
840 RETURN





RUN "INITIAL"

WE CAN INITIALIZE THE FOLLOWING TYPES OF FILES

          1 INVENTORY
          2 UNUSED
          3 UNUSED

ENTER THE CODE NUMBER OF THE FILE TO BE INITIALIZED ? 1

YOU ARE INITIALIZING INVENTORY MASTER FILES
```

```
THE NAME OF THE ID FILE WILL BE ....... MINDEX
ENTER THE NAME TO BE USED FOR THE MASTER FILE? MASTER
ENTER TODAY'S DATE MM/DD/YY? 11/30/80

I AM PREPARED TO CREATE THE FOLLOWING FILES:
        INDEX FILE.................MINDEX
        INVENTORY FILES ( 2 ).....MASTER 1 ...MASTER 2

SHALL I CREATE THEM (Y OR N)?? Y

FILE CREATION COMPLETE

BREAK IN 640
OK
```

File Status and Recovery

Program Name: ISTATUS

This program prints the status of files, including the creation dates, as recorded in the index file and also prints the first record of the master file itself. The latest file information is printed first. A file recovery routine exists as an option. If you choose to execute it, the index file must be changed to indicate that the latest file is invalid and the next newest file is the correct one. Future processing against this file will then occur automatically. Note, however, that further processing may be required to insure the currency of the file.

Files Affected: Index file (recovery option only)

```
10 REM            SAVED AT ISTATUS
20 REM ***********************************************************
30 REM                  INITIALIZATION
40 REM ***********************************************************
50 M0=2
60 M1=12
70 M2=8
80 DIM U(M1),Q(M2),V(M2),F1$(M0),D1$(M0)
90 F$="MINDEX"
100 REM ***********************************************************
110 REM                 PROCESSING AREA
120 REM ***********************************************************
130 PRINT
140 PRINT
150 PRINT "              INVENTORY FILE STATUS PROGRAM"
160 PRINT
170 REM                 ACCESS FILES
180 OPEN "I",1,F$
190 PRINT "THE FOLLOWING FILES ARE AVAILABLE"
200 PRINT
210 PRINT TAB(10);"FILE NAME";TAB(25);"CREATION DATE";TAB(45);"CREATION DATE"
220 PRINT TAB(25);"(FROM INDEX)";TAB(45);"(FROM FILE)"
230 PRINT TAB(10);"---------";TAB(25);"--------------";TAB(45);"-------------"
240 PRINT "*LATEST*";
250 FOR I=1 TO M0
```

```
260    INPUT#1,F1$(I),D1$(I)
270    OPEN"I",2,F1$(I)
280    INPUT#2,DO$
290    CLOSE 2
300    IF I=MO THEN PRINT "*OLDEST*";
310    PRINT TAB(10);F1$(I);TAB(25);D1$(I);TAB(45);DO$
320 NEXT I
330 IF NOT EOF(1) THEN INPUT#1,T1$
340 PRINT
350 PRINT "DO YOU WISH TO ENTER THE RECOVERY ROUTINE (Y OR N)"
360 INPUT A$
370 IF A$<>"Y" THEN 550
380 A$="N"
390 PRINT
400 PRINT "DO YOU WISH TO DISCARD THE LATEST FILE (Y OR N)";
410 INPUT A$
420 IF A$<>"Y" THEN 550
430 A$="N"
440 PRINT "ARE YOU ABSOLUTELY POSITIVE";
450 INPUT A$
460 IF A$<>"Y" THEN 550
470 PRINT
480 CLOSE 1
490 OPEN "O",1,F$
500 PRINT "THE LATEST FILE ";F1$(1);" IS BEING DISCARDED"
510 FOR I= 2 TO MO
520    PRINT#1,F1$(I);",";D1$(I);",";
530 NEXT I
540 PRINT#1,F1$(1);",BAD FILE,";T1$
550 PRINT
560 REM ***********************************************************
570 REM                    TERMINATION POINT
580 REM ***********************************************************
590 PRINT
600 PRINT
610 CLOSE
620 IF A$="Y" THEN PRINT "RECOVERY COMPLETE"
630 STOP
OK
```

RUN "ISTATUS"

```
              INVENTORY FILE STATUS PROGRAM

THE FOLLOWING FILES ARE AVAILABLE

              FILE NAME      CREATION DATE      CREATION DATE
                             (FROM INDEX)       (FROM FILE)
              ---------      -------------      -------------
*LATEST*  MASTER 1     11/30/80           0  0  0  0  0
*OLDEST*  MASTER 2                        0  0  0  0  0

DO YOU WISH TO ENTER THE RECOVERY ROUTINE (Y OR N)
? Y

DO YOU WISH TO DISCARD THE LATEST FILE (Y OR N)? Y
ARE YOU ABSOLUTELY POSITIVE? Y

THE LATEST FILE MASTER 1 IS BEING DISCARDED

RECOVERY COMPLETE
BREAK IN 630
OK
```

```
RUN "ISTATUS"
```

                    INVENTORY FILE STATUS PROGRAM

THE FOLLOWING FILES ARE AVAILABLE

                 FILE NAME   CREATION DATE   CREATION DATE
                                (FROM INDEX)   (FROM FILE)
                 ---------   ----------------   ---------------
LATEST MASTER 2   0 0 0 0 0
OLDEST MASTER 1   BAD FILE   0 0 0 0 0

DO YOU WISH TO ENTER THE RECOVERY ROUTINE (Y OR N)
? N

BREAK IN 630
OK

Updating Transactions for Master File

Program Name: ITRANS

This program enters initial records in the inventory master file and corrects the contents of that file later on. It accepts records that are written to an update transaction file for later processing by program IUPDTE. It allows the entry of transaction types that add, delete, or replace records in the master file. These types are entered by keying in the item code first and then an "A," "D," or "R" to indicate the specific type. Add and replace transactions will then prompt the operator to enter the remaining information in the inventory master records. This program will combine the transactions from several runs into one file for updating, but the transactions must be entered by item code in the same alphabetic sequence as that of the master file.

Files Affected: Update transaction file (created)

```
10 REM           SAVED AT ITRANS
20 REM *************************************************************
30 REM           INITIALIZATION
40 REM *************************************************************
50 M0=2
60 M1=12
70 M2=8
80 DIM U(M1),Q(M2),V(M2),F1$(M0),D1$(M0)
90 F$="MINDEX"
100 REM *************************************************************
110 REM                     PROCESSING AREA
120 REM *************************************************************
```

```
130 PRINT "HAVE UPDATES ALREADY BEEN PARTIALLY ENTERED (Y OR N)";
140 INPUT A$
150 GOSUB 710                      'ACCESS FILES
160 IF A$="N" THEN 180
170 GOSUB 940                      'FIND PLACE IN FILES
180 PRINT "ENTER";TAB(10);"ITEM CODE:";
190 I9$=I$
200 I8$=""
210 INPUT I8$
220 IF I8$="" THEN 600
230 IF I8$="STOP" THEN 630
240 I$=I8$+SPACE$(8-LEN(I8$))
250 IF I$>I9$ THEN 280
260 PRINT"ITEM OUT OF SEQUENCE - NOT PROCESSED"
270 GOTO 180
280 PRINT "ADD (A), DELETE (D), OR REPLACE (R)";
290 INPUT T9$
300 IF T9$<>"D" THEN 330
310 GOSUB 1040                     'FILE WRITE
320 GOTO 180
330 PRINT TAB(10);"LOCATION CODE:";
340 INPUT L$
350 PRINT TAB(10);"CLASS:";
360 INPUT C$
370 PRINT TAB(10);"DESCRIPTION:";
380 INPUT D$
390 PRINT TAB(10);"WILL YOU ENTER USE INFORMATION (Y OR N)";
400 INPUT A$
410 IF A$<>"Y" THEN 480
420 PRINT "HOW MANY PERIODS OF USE SHALL I RECORD";
430 INPUT P
440 PRINT "ENTER LATEST PERIOD FIRST"
450 FOR I=1 TO P
460   INPUT U(I)
470 NEXT I
480 PRINT TAB(10);"ON HAND:";
490 INPUT O
500 Q(1)=O
510 PRINT TAB(10);"UNIT COST:";
520 INPUT V(1)
530 PRINT TAB(10);"REORDER POINT";
540 INPUT RO
550 PRINT "*************************"
560 PRINT
570 GOSUB 1040                     'FILE WRITE
580 GOTO 180
590 REM ****************************************************************
600 REM              TERMINATION POINT
610 REM ****************************************************************
620 GOSUB 850                      'REWRITE INDEX
630 PRINT
640 PRINT
650 PRINT "PROGRAM TERMINATING"
660 PRINT
670 STOP


680 REM ****************************************************************
690 REM              FILE HANDLING PROCEDURES
700 REM ****************************************************************
710 REM              ACCESS FILES
720 OPEN "I",1,F$
730 FOR I= 1 TO MO
740   INPUT#1,F1$(I),D1$(I)
750 NEXT I
760 T1=LEN(F1$(1))
770 IF T1>6 THEN T1=6
780 TO$="0."+LEFT$(F1$(1),T1)
```

```
790 T1$="U."+LEFT$(F1$(1),T1)
800 IF A$<>"Y" THEN 830
810 NAME T1$ AS T0$
820 OPEN "I",4,T0$
830 OPEN "O",3,T1$
840 RETURN


850 REM *********** REWRITE INDEX ******************************
860 CLOSE 1
870 OPEN "O",1,F$
880 FOR I= 1 TO M0
890   PRINT#1,F1$(I);",";D1$(I);",";
900 NEXT I
910 PRINT#1,T1$
920 CLOSE 1,2,3
930 RETURN


940 REM *********** FIND PLACE IN FILES **************************
950 IF EOF(4) THEN 1000
960 INPUT#4,T9$,I$
970 LINEINPUT#4,X$
980 PRINT#3,T9$;",";I$;",";X$
990 GOTO 950
1000 PRINT "LAST RECORD WAS ";T9$;" ";I$
1010 CLOSE 4
1020 KILL T0$
1030 RETURN


1040 REM ******************** FILE WRITE *********************
1050 PRINT#3,T9$;",";I$;",";L$;",";C$;",";D$;",";
1060 FOR I=1 TO M1
1070   PRINT#3,U(I);
1080   U(I)=0
1090 NEXT I
1100 PRINT#3,B;R;O;
1110 FOR I = 1 TO M2
1120   PRINT#3,Q(I);V(I);
1130 NEXT I
1140 PRINT#3,R0,C0
1150 RETURN
```

```
RUN "ITRANS"
HAVE UPDATES ALREADY BEEN PARTIALLY ENTERED (Y OR N)? N
ENTER     ITEM CODE:? 11111
ADD (A), DELETE (D), OR REPLACE (R)? A
          LOCATION CODE:? 1234
          CLASS:? ABCD
          DESCRIPTION:? SUPER DELUXE WIDGET
          WILL YOU ENTER USE INFORMATION (Y OR N)? Y
HOW MANY PERIODS OF USE SHALL I RECORD? 12
ENTER LATEST PERIOD FIRST
? 78
? 65
? 74
? 85
? 47
? 67
```

```
? 58
? 59
? 61
? 52
? 80
? 45
            ON HAND:? 100
            UNIT COST:? 12.15
            REORDER POINT? 90
*************************

ENTER    ITEM CODE:? 22222
ADD (A), DELETE (D), OR REPLACE (R)? A
            LOCATION CODE:? 1233
            CLASS:? ABCD
            DESCRIPTION:? MIDDLE CLASS WIDGET
            WILL YOU ENTER USE INFORMATION (Y OR N)? N
            ON HAND:? 50
            UNIT COST:? 56.67
            REORDER POINT? 52
*************************

ENTER    ITEM CODE:? 33333
ADD (A), DELETE (D), OR REPLACE (R)? A
            LOCATION CODE:? 1234
            CLASS:? ABXX
            DESCRIPTION:? GOLD-PLATED WIDGET
            WILL YOU ENTER USE INFORMATION (Y OR N)? N
            ON HAND:? 50
            UNIT COST:? 88.43
            REORDER POINT? 10
*************************

ENTER    ITEM CODE:?


PROGRAM TERMINATING

BREAK IN 670
OK
```

Updating of Master File

Program Name: IUPDTE

This program accepts transactions previously entered in an update transaction file by program ITRANS and performs the necessary addition, deletion, and replacement of records in the inventory master file. At the completion of this processing, the index file is updated to reflect the name and date of the most recent (updated) version of the inventory master file.

Files Affected: Inventory master file
Index file

```
10 REM                    SAVED AT IUPDTE
20 REM ****************************************************************
30 REM              INITIALIZATION
40 REM ****************************************************************
50 M0=2
60 M1=12
70 M2=8
80 DIM U(M1),Q(M2),V(M2),U9(M1),Q9(M2),V9(M2),F1$(M0),D1$(M0)
90 F$="MINDEX"
100 REM ****************************************************************
110 REM                    PROCESSING AREA
120 REM ****************************************************************
130 PRINT
140 PRINT "       INVENTORY UPDATE PROCESSING"
150 PRINT
160 PRINT "HAVE ALL UPDATE TRANSACTIONS BEEN ENTERED (Y OR N)";
170 INPUT A$
180 PRINT "ENTER TODAY'S DATE MM/DD/YY"
190 INPUT D0$
200 IF A$="Y" THEN 250
210 PRINT "THE INVENTORY FILE CAN ONLY BE UPDATED FROM TRANSACTIONS IN"
220 PRINT "THE UPDATE FILE.  SHALL I GO AHEAD AND PROCESS THESE (Y OR N)";
230 INPUT A$
240 IF A$="N" THEN 390
250 GOSUB 430                     'ACCESS FILES
260 GOSUB 1220                    'READ MASTER FILE
270 GOSUB 970                     'READ TRANSACTION FILE
280 IF I$<I9$ THEN GOSUB 1120     'WRITE FROM MASTER
290 IF I$>I9$ THEN  GOSUB 830     'WRITE FROM TRANSACTION
300 IF S8=1 AND S7=1 THEN 340
310 IF I$=I9$ THEN GOSUB 1370     'EQUAL COMPARE
320 GOTO 280
330 REM ****************************************************************
340 REM              TERMINATION POINT
350 REM ****************************************************************
360 GOSUB 570                     'REWRITE INDEX
370 PRINT "INVENTORY UPDATE COMPLETE"
380 PRINT
390 STOP


400 REM ****************************************************************
410 REM              FILE HANDLING PROCEDURES
420 REM ****************************************************************
430 REM              ACCESS FILES
```

```
440 OPEN "I",1,F$
450 FOR I= 1 TO MO
460    INPUT#1,F1$(I),D1$(I)
470 NEXT I
480 OPEN "I",2,F1$(1)
490 LINEINPUT#2,X$
500 OPEN "O",4,F1$(2)
510 PRINT#4,DO$
520 T1=LEN(F1$(1))
530 IF T1>6 THEN T1=6
540 T1$="U."+LEFT$(F1$(1),T1)
550 OPEN "I",3,T1$
560 RETURN


570 REM ************ REWRITE INDEX    *****************************
580 CLOSE 1
590 OPEN "O",1,F$
600 D1$(2)=DO$
610 PRINT#1,F1$(MO);",";D1$(MO);",",";
620 IF MO=2 THEN 660
630 FOR I=2 TO MO-1
640    PRINT#1,F1$(I);",";D1$(I);",";
650 NEXT I
660 PRINT #1,F1$(1);",";D1$(1);",",";
670 PRINT#1,T1$
680 CLOSE 1,2,3,4
690 RETURN


700 REM ****************** ERROR ROUTINE    ********************
710 IF E <>1 THEN GOTO 770
720 PRINT "**** ERROR CODE 1 - ADD ERROR *****"
730 PRINT "ITEM CODE ";I9$;" ALREADY EXISTED IN THE FILE"
740 PRINT "PROCESSING IGNORED."
750 PRINT
760 GOTO 820
770 IF E<>2 THEN 820
780 PRINT "**** ERROR CODE 2 - REPLACE/DELETE ERROR ****"
790 PRINT "ITEM CODE ";I9$;" DID NOT EXIST IN THE MASTER FILE"
800 PRINT "PROCESSING IGNORED"
810 PRINT
820 RETURN


830 REM  **************** WRITE FROM TRANS FILE   ******************
840 IF T9$="A" THEN 880
850 E=2
860 GOSUB 700                        'ERROR ROUTINE
870 GOTO 970
880 PRINT#4,I9$;",";L9$;",";C9$;",";D8$;",";
890 FOR I=1 TO M1
900    PRINT#4,U9(I);
910 NEXT I
920 PRINT#4,B9;R9;O9;
930 FOR I=1 TO M2
940    PRINT#4,Q9(I);V9(I);
950 NEXT I
960 PRINT#4,RO,CO
970 REM  **************** TRANSACTION READ ROUTINE   *************
980 IF NOT EOF(3) THEN 1020
990 S8=1
1000 I9$=STRING$(8,128)
1010 GOTO 1110
1020 INPUT #3,T9$,I9$,L9$,C9$,D8$
1030 FOR I=1 TO M1
1040    INPUT#3,U9(I)
1050 NEXT I
```

```
1060 INPUT#3,B9,R9,O9
1070 FOR I = 1 TO M2
1080    INPUT#3,Q9(I),V9(I)
1090 NEXT I
1100 INPUT#3,RO,CO
1110 RETURN


1120 REM ************** WRITE FROM MASTER FILE   *****************
1130 PRINT#4,I$;",";L$;",";C$;",";D$;",";
1140 FOR I=1 TO M1
1150    PRINT#4,U(I);
1160 NEXT I
1170 PRINT#4,B;R;O;
1180 FOR I = 1 TO M2
1190    PRINT#4,Q(I);V(I);
1200 NEXT I
1210 PRINT#4,RO,CO
1220 REM ************** MASTER FILE READ ROUTINE   **************
1230 IF NOT EOF(2) THEN 1270
1240 S7=1
1250 I$=STRING$(8,128)
1260 GOTO 1360
1270 INPUT#2,I$,L$,C$,D$
1280 FOR I = 1 TO M1
1290    INPUT#2,U(I)
1300 NEXT I
1310 INPUT#2,B,R,O
1320 FOR I = 1 TO M2
1330    INPUT#2,Q(I),V(I)
1340 NEXT I
1350 INPUT#2,RO,CO
1360 RETURN


1370 REM  ************* EQUAL COMPARE OF ITEM CODES   ************
1380 IF T9$<>"A" THEN 1430
1390 E=1
1400 GOSUB 700                    'ERROR ROUTINE
1410 GOSUB 970                    'READ NEXT TRANS
1420 GOTO 1500
1430 IF T9$<>"D" THEN 1470
1440 GOSUB 970                    'READ NEXT TRANSACTION
1450 GOSUB 1220                   'READ NEXT MASTER
1460 GOTO 1500
1470 IF T9$<>"R" THEN 1500
1480 GOSUB 880                    'WRITE FROM TRANSACTION
1490 GOSUB 1220                   'READ NEXT MASTER
1500 RETURN




RUN "IUPDTE"

        INVENTORY UPDATE PROCESSING

HAVE ALL UPDATE TRANSACTIONS BEEN ENTERED (Y OR N)? Y
ENTER TODAY'S DATE MM/DD/YY
? 11/30/80
INVENTORY UPDATE COMPLETE

BREAK IN 390
OK
```

Inventory Log

Program Name: ILOG

This program produces a log for use in recording the receipt of inventory items and the quantities on hand during the end-of-period inventory. Since the log is ordered by item number, it provides an ideal data-entry document for entering the inventory data for the period.

Files Affected: None

```
10 REM                    SAVED AT ILOG
20 REM ***************************************************************
30 REM                    INITIALIZATION
40 REM ***************************************************************
50 M0=2
60 M1=12
70 M2=8
80 DIM U(M1),Q(M2),V(M2),F1$(M0),D1$(M0)
90 F$="MINDEX"
100 REM ***************************************************************
110 REM                   PROCESSING AREA
120 REM ***************************************************************
130 PRINT
140 PRINT
150 PRINT "             INVENTORY LOG PROGRAM"
160 PRINT "ENTER THE MONTH FOR THE INVENTORY LOG";
170 INPUT M0$
180 PRINT "ALIGN TO TOP-OF-PAGE AND PRESS THE RETURN"
190 INPUT A$
200 PRINT
210 GOSUB 420                    'ACCESS FILES
220 GOSUB  620                   'PRINT HEADINGS
230 GOSUB 500                    'READ FILE
240 PRINT
250 PRINT I$;TAB(10);L$;TAB(18);D$;TAB(47);"--------- ---------   ------- "
260 L0=L0+1
270 GOTO 230
280 REM ***************************************************************
290 REM                    TERMINATION POINT
300 REM ***************************************************************
310 PRINT
320 PRINT
330 PRINT
340 PRINT "INVENTORY LOG IS COMPLETE"
350 PRINT "           ";L0;"RECORDS PRINTED"
360 PRINT
370 CLOSE 1,2
380 STOP

390 REM ***************************************************************
400 REM                    SUBROUTINES FOLLOW
410 REM ***************************************************************
420 REM                    ACCESS FILES
430 OPEN "I",1,F$
440 FOR I=1 TO MO
450    INPUT#1,F1$(I),D1$(I)
460 NEXT I
470 OPEN "I",2,F1$(1)
480 INPUT #2,D0$
490 RETURN
```

```
500 REM ******************** READ FILE  **************************
510 IF EOF(2) THEN 290
520 INPUT#2,I$,L$,C$,D$
530 FOR I=1 TO M1
540    INPUT#2,U(I)
550 NEXT I
560 INPUT#2,B,R,O
570 FOR I=1 TO M2
580    INPUT#2,Q(I),V(I)
590 NEXT I
600 INPUT#2,RO,CO
610 RETURN


620 REM ******************** PRINT HEADING *********************
630 PRINT
640 PRINT
650 PRINT "        INVENTORY LOG  -  MONTH OF: ";MO$
660 PRINT
670 PRINT
680 PRINT STRING$(72,42)
690 PRINT "ITEM";TAB(10);"LOC";TAB(25);"DESCRIPTION";
700 PRINT TAB(47);"RCVD/UNIT COST";TAB(65);"ON-HAND"
710 PRINT STRING$(72,42)
720 PRINT
730 RETURN




RUN "ILOG"


                    INVENTORY LOG PROGRAM
ENTER THE MONTH FOR THE INVENTORY LOG? DECEMBER
ALIGN TO TOP-OF-PAGE AND PRESS THE RETURN
?




          INVENTORY LOG  -  MONTH OF: DECEMBER

*********************************************************************
ITEM      LOC          DESCRIPTION       RCVD/UNIT COST     ON-HAND
*********************************************************************

11111     1234     SUPER DELUXE WIDGET      -------- --------   --------

22222     1233     MIDDLE CLASS WIDGET      -------- --------   --------

33333     1234     GOLD-PLATED WIDGET       -------- --------   --------


INVENTORY LOG IS COMPLETE
          3 RECORDS PRINTED

BREAK IN 380
OK
```

Inventory Transaction Recording

Program Name: IDATA

This program accepts data that reflects the amount of inventory on hand at the end of a period and the quantities received from suppliers during the period. The information is written from the terminal to a data transaction file for later use by program IREPORT in updating the inventory and producing inventory reports for the period. It allows multiple runs of the program to combine several batches of data in one file; all entries must be in item-code order.

Files Affected: Data transaction file

```
10 REM           SAVED AT IDATA
20 REM ***************************************************************
30 REM        INITIALIZATION
40 REM ***************************************************************
50 M0=2
60 M1=12
70 M2=8
80 DIM U(M1),Q(M2),V(M2),F1$(M0),D1$(M0)
90 F$="MINDEX"
100 REM ***************************************************************
110 REM                    PROCESSING AREA
120 REM ***************************************************************
130 PRINT "HAVE TRANSACTION ALREADY BEEN PARTIALLY ENTERED (Y OR N)";
140 INPUT A$
150 PRINT
160 GOSUB 570                    'ACCESS FILES
170 IF A$="N" THEN 300
180 PRINT "SHALL I PRINT THE PREVIOUS ENTRIES (Y OR N)";
190 INPUT A2$
200 PRINT "DO YOU WISH TO CORRECT PREVIOUS ENTRIES (Y OR N)"
210 INPUT A1$
220 IF A1$<> "Y" THEN 260
230 PRINT "ENTER ITEM NUMBER TO CORRECT"
240 INPUT I8$
250 I8$=I8$+SPACE$(8-LEN(I8$))
260 GOSUB 820                    'FIND PLACE IN FILES
270 IF A1$="Y" THEN 200
280 CLOSE 4
290 KILL TO$
300 PRINT "ENTER QUANTITY RECEIVED, UNIT PRICE, ENDING INVENTORY"
310 PRINT "*****  0,0,0 TO STOP  *****"
320 GOSUB 970                    'READ FILE
330 PRINT I$;
340 INPUT R,V9,O
350 IF R<>0 THEN 430
360 IF V9<>0 THEN 430
370 IF O<>0 THEN 430
380 PRINT "DO YOU WISH TO STOP NOW (Y OR N)"
390 INPUT A$
400 IF A$<>"Y" THEN 430
410 PRINT "PROGRAM TERMINATING "
420 GOTO 530
430 PRINT#3,I$;",";R;V9;O
440 GOTO 320
450 REM ***************************************************************
460 REM            TERMINATION POINT
470 REM ***************************************************************
```

```
480 GOSUB 730                      'REWRITE INDEX
490 PRINT
500 PRINT
510 PRINT "TRANSACTION ENTRY IS COMPLETE"
520 PRINT
530 STOP


540 REM ****************************************************************
550 REM                 FILE HANDLING PROCEDURES
560 REM ****************************************************************
570 REM                 ACCESS FILES
580 OPEN "I",1,F$
590 FOR I= 1 TO MO
600    INPUT#1,F1$(I),D1$(I)
610 NEXT I
620 OPEN "I",2,F1$(1)
630 LINEINPUT#2,X$
640 T1=LEN(F1$(1))
650 IF T1>6 THEN T1=6
660 TO$="X."+LEFT$(F1$(1),T1)
670 T1$="T."+LEFT$(F1$(1),T1)
680 IF A$<>"Y" THEN 710
690 NAME T1$ AS TO$
700 OPEN "I",4,TO$
710 OPEN "O",3,T1$
720 RETURN


730 REM ************ REWRITE INDEX   *****************************
740 CLOSE 1
750 OPEN "O",1,F$
760 FOR I= 1 TO MO
770    PRINT#1,F1$(I);",";D1$(I);",";
780 NEXT I
790 PRINT#1,T1$
800 CLOSE 1,2,3
810 RETURN


820 REM *********** FIND PLACE IN FILES ************************
830 IF EOF(4) THEN 950
840 LINEINPUT#2,X$
850 INPUT#4,I9$
860 LINEINPUT#4,X$
870 IF A2$="Y" THEN PRINT I9$,X$
880 IF A1$<>"Y" OR I9$<>I8$ THEN 930
890 PRINT "ENTER CORRECT RECEIPTS,UNIT COST,ON HAND"
900 INPUT R,V9,O
910 PRINT#3,I9$;",";R;V9;O
920 GOTO 960
930 PRINT#3,I9$;",";X$
940 GOTO 830
950 PRINT "LAST RECORD WAS ";I$,I9$
960 RETURN


970 REM ********************** READ MASTER FILE  *****************
980 IF EOF(2) THEN 460
990 INPUT#2,I$,L$,C$,D$
1000 FOR  I=1 TO M1
1010    INPUT#2,U(I)
1020 NEXT I
1030 INPUT#2,B,R,O
1040 FOR I=1 TO M2
1050    INPUT#2,Q(I),V(I)
1060 NEXT I
1070 INPUT#2,RO,CO
1080 RETURN
```

```
RUN "IDATA"
HAVE TRANSACTION ALREADY BEEN PARTIALLY ENTERED (Y OR N)? N

ENTER QUANTITY RECEIVED, UNIT PRICE, ENDING INVENTORY
*****  0,0,0 TO STOP  *****
11111    ? 15,67.50,45
22222    ? 0,0,0
DO YOU WISH TO STOP NOW (Y OR N)
? Y
PROGRAM TERMINATING
BREAK IN 530
OK




RUN "IDATA"
HAVE TRANSACTION ALREADY BEEN PARTIALLY ENTERED (Y OR N)? Y

SHALL I PRINT THE PREVIOUS ENTRIES (Y OR N)? Y
DO YOU WISH TO CORRECT PREVIOUS ENTRIES (Y OR N)
? N
11111           15   67.5   45
LAST RECORD WAS             11111
ENTER QUANTITY RECEIVED, UNIT PRICE, ENDING INVENTORY
*****  0,0,0 TO STOP  *****
22222    ? 50,55.66,40
33333    ? 10,15.11,90


TRANSACTION ENTRY IS COMPLETE

BREAK IN 530
OK
```

Updating of Inventory Master File

Program Name: IREPORT

This program accepts the end-of-period inventory data from the data transaction file and makes the computations necessary for the update of the inventory master file to reflect usage for the period. It produces an inventory report of this usage.

Files Affected: Inventory master file
Index file

```
10 REM                    SAVED AT IREPORT
20 REM ******************************************************************
30 REM                   INITIALIZATION
40 REM ******************************************************************
50 MO=2
60 M1=12
70 M2=8
80 DIM U(M1),Q(M2),V(M2),F1$(MO),D1$(MO)
90 F$="MINDEX"
100 REM ******************************************************************
110 REM                   PROCESSING AREA
120 REM ******************************************************************
130 PRINT
140 PRINT
150 PRINT "              INVENTORY REPORT PROGRAM"
160 PRINT
170 PRINT "ENTER THE MONTH FOR THE REPORT ";
180 INPUT MO$
190 PRINT "ENTER TODAY'S DATE";
200 INPUT D9$
210 PRINT "ALIGN TO TOP-OF-PAGE AND PRESS THE RETURN"
220 INPUT A$
230 PRINT
240 GOSUB 600                    'ACCESS FILES
250 GOSUB  950                   'PRINT HEADINGS
260 GOSUB 810                    'READ FILE
270 U0=B+R-O
280 GOSUB 1100                   'UPDATE FILE
290 TO=TO+CO
300 PRINT I$;TAB(10);D$;TAB(37);B;TAB(45);R;TAB(52);O;TAB(59);UO;TAB(62);
310 PRINT CO
320 LO=LO+1
330 GOTO 260
340 REM ******************************************************************
350 REM                   TERMINATION POINT
360 REM ******************************************************************
370 PRINT
380 PRINT STRING$(72,45)
390 PRINT TAB(38);"TOTAL COSTS OF GOODS SOLD ";TAB(62);TO
400 PRINT
410 PRINT
420 CLOSE 1
430 OPEN "O",1,F$
440 D1$(MO)=D9$
450 PRINT#1,F1$(MO);",";D1$(MO);",";
460 IF MO=2 THEN 500
470 FOR I=2 TO MO-1
480 PRINT#1,F1$(I);",";D1$(I);",";
```

166   BASIC Computer Programs for Business

```
490 NEXT I
500 PRINT#1,F1$(1);",";D1$(1);",";
510 PRINT#1,T1$
520 PRINT "INVENTORY REPORT IS COMPLETE"
530 PRINT "              ";L0;"RECORDS PRINTED"
540 PRINT
550 CLOSE 1,2,3,4
560 STOP


570 REM ******************************************************************
580 REM                    SUBROUTINES FOLLOW
590 REM ******************************************************************
600 REM                    ACCESS FILES
610 OPEN "I",1,F$
620 FOR I=1 TO MO
630    INPUT#1,F1$(I),D1$(I)
640 NEXT I
650 INPUT#1,T1$
660 OPEN "I",2,F1$(1)
670 T1=LEN(F1$(1))
680 IF T1>6 THEN T1=6
690 T2$="T."+LEFT$(F1$(1),T1)
700 IF T1$=T2$ THEN 750
710 PRINT "TRANSACTION FILE NOT COMPLETE.  ALL TRANSACTIONS"
720 PRINT "MUST BE ENTERED BEFORE PROCEEDING."
730 PRINT
740 GOTO 540
750 OPEN "I",3,T1$
760 T1$="********"
770 INPUT #2,D0$
780 OPEN "O",4,F1$(MO)
790 PRINT#4,D9$
800 RETURN


810 REM ******************** READ FILE   ***************************
820 IF EOF(2) THEN 350
830 INPUT#2,I$,L$,C$,D$
840 FOR I=1 TO M1
850    INPUT#2,U(I)
860 NEXT I
870 INPUT#2,B,R,0
880 B=0
890 FOR I=1 TO M2
900    INPUT#2,Q(I),V(I)
910 NEXT I
920 INPUT#2,R0,C0
930 INPUT#3,I9$,R,V9,0
940 RETURN


950 REM ******************** PRINT HEADING ********************
960 PRINT
970 PRINT
980 PRINT "      INVENTORY REPORT  -  MONTH OF: ";MO$
990 PRINT "                PREPARED: ";D9$
1000 PRINT
1010 PRINT
1020 PRINT STRING$(72,42)
1030 PRINT "ITEM";;TAB(10);"DESCRIPTION";
1040 PRINT TAB(36);"BEGIN";TAB(45);"RCVD";TAB(53);"END";TAB(59);"USED";
1050 PRINT TAB(65);"COST OF"
1060 PRINT TAB(36);" INV";TAB(53);"INV";TAB(66);"GOODS"
1070 PRINT STRING$(72,42)
1080 PRINT
1090 RETURN
```

```
1100 REM ***************** UPDATE FILE   *************************
1110 REM                 UPDATE USE DATA
1120 FOR I=2 TO M1
1130   U(I-1)=U(I)
1140 NEXT I
1150 U(M1)=U0

1160 REM ***************** UPDATE RECEIPTS ***********************
1170 FOR I=M2 TO 1 STEP -1
1180   IF Q(I)<>0 THEN 1200
1190 NEXT I
1200 IF V9<>V(I) THEN 1220
1210 Q(I)=Q(I)+R
1220 IF I+1<>6 THEN 1300
1230 X=(Q(1)*V(1)+Q(2)*V(2))/(V(1)+V(2))
1240 Q(1)=Q(1)+Q(2)
1250 V(1)=X
1260 FOR I=2 TO 5
1270   Q(I)=Q(I+1)
1280   V(I)=V(I+1)
1290 NEXT I
1300 Q(I+1)=R
1310 V(I+1)=V9

1320 REM ***************** UPDATE COSTS/VALUES *******************
1330 C0=0
1340 IF U0=0 THEN 1500
1350 I=1
1360 IF Q(I)<>0 THEN 1390
1370 PRINT "***ERROR*** COST DATA NOT COMPLETE FOR ";I$
1380 GOTO 1500
1390 IF Q(I)<=U0 THEN 1430
1400 Q(I)=Q(I)-U0
1410 C0=C0+U0*V(I)
1420 GOTO 1500
1430 C0=C0+Q(I)*V(I)
1440 U0=U0-Q(I)
1450 FOR I=2 TO M2
1460   Q(I-1)=Q(I)
1470   V(I-1)=V(I)
1480 NEXT I
1490 IF U0<>0 THEN 1350
1500 U0=U(M1)

1510 REM*********************** FILE WRITE  *****************
1520 PRINT#4,I$;",";L$;",";C$;",";D$;",";
1530 FOR I=1 TO M1
1540   PRINT#4,U(I);",";
1550 NEXT I
1560 PRINT#4,B;",";R;",";O;",";
1570 FOR I=1 TO M2
1580   PRINT#4,Q(I);",";V(I);",";
1590 NEXT I
1600 PRINT#4,R0,C0
1610 RETURN




RUN "IREPORT"



        INVENTORY REPORT PROGRAM

ENTER THE MONTH FOR THE REPORT ? NOVEMBER
ENTER TODAY'S DATE? 12/06/80
ALIGN TO TOP-OF-PAGE AND PRESS THE RETURN
?
```

168   BASIC Computer Programs for Business

```
INVENTORY REPORT  -  MONTH OF: NOVEMBER
        PREPARED: 12/06/80


*************************************************************************
ITEM        DESCRIPTION                  BEGIN    RCVD    END    USED    COST OF
                                          INV             INV             GOODS
*************************************************************************

11111       SUPER DELUXE WIDGET          100      15      45      70     850.5
22222       MIDDLE CLASS WIDGET           50      50      40      60    3390.1
33333       GOLD-PLATED WIDGET            50      10      90     -30   -2652.9

----------------------------------------------------------------------------
                                TOTAL COSTS OF GOODS SOLD    1587.7


INVENTORY REPORT IS COMPLETE
        3 RECORDS PRINTED

BREAK IN 560
OK
```

Printing of Master File

Program Name: ILIST

This program produces a formatted list of the index file and inventory master file, with headings for ease of use. The list can be used for historical purposes or for review and validation.

Files Affected: None

```
10 REM                 SAVED AT ILIST
20 REM *****************************************************************
30 REM                 INITIALIZATION
40 REM *****************************************************************
50 M0=2
60 M1=12
70 M2=8
80 DIM U(M1),Q(M2),V(M2),F1$(M0),D1$(M0)
90 F$="MINDEX"
100 REM ****************************************************************
110 REM                 PROCESSING AREA
120 REM ****************************************************************
130 PRINT
140 PRINT
150 PRINT "          INVENTORY FILE LIST PROGRAM"
160 PRINT
170 GOSUB 360              'ACCESS FILES
180 GOSUB  830             'PRINT HEADINGS
190 GOSUB 520              'READ FILE
200 GOSUB 640              'PRINT ROUTINE
210 GOTO 190
```

```
220 REM ***************************************************************
230 REM                     TERMINATION POINT
240 REM ***************************************************************
250 PRINT
260 PRINT
270 PRINT
280 PRINT "INVENTORY MASTER LIST COMPLETE"
290 PRINT "              ";LO;"RECORDS PRINTED"
300 PRINT
310 CLOSE 1,2
320 STOP


330 REM ***************************************************************
340 REM                     SUBROUTINES FOLLOW
350 REM ***************************************************************
360 REM                     ACCESS FILES
370 OPEN "I",1,F$
380 PRINT "THE FOLLOWING FILES ARE AVAILABLE"
390 PRINT
400 PRINTTAB(10);"FILE NAME";TAB(25);"CREATION DATE"
410 PRINT TAB(10);"----------";TAB(25);"-------------"
420 FOR I=1 TO MO
430   INPUT#1,F1$(I),D1$(I)
440 PRINT TAB(10);F1$(I);TAB(25);D1$(I)
450 NEXT I
460 PRINT
470 PRINT "ENTER THE FILE NAME TO BE LISTED;
480 INPUT FO$
490 OPEN "I",2,FO$
500 INPUT #2,DO$
510 RETURN


520 REM ********************** READ FILE   **************************
530 IF EOF(2) THEN 230
540 INPUT#2,I$,L$,C$,D$
550 FOR I=1 TO M1
560   INPUT#2,U(I)
570 NEXT I
580 INPUT#2,B,R,O
590 FOR I=1 TO M2
600   INPUT#2,Q(I),V(I)
610 NEXT I
620 INPUT#2,RO,CO
630 RETURN


640 REM ********************** PRINT ROUTINE   *******************
650 LO=LO+1
660 PRINT I$;TAB(10);L$;TAB(15);C$;TAB(20);D$;TAB(45);B;TAB(52);R;TAB(60);O
670 PRINT STRING$(72,45)
680 FOR I=1 TO M1
690   PRINT U(I);TAB(I*5);
700 NEXT I
710 PRINT
720 PRINT STRING$(72,45)
730 FOR I=1 TO 4
740   PRINT Q(I);"/";V(I);TAB(I*15);
750 NEXT I
760 PRINT
770 FOR I= 5 TO M2
780   PRINT Q(I);"/";V(I);TAB((I-4)*15);
790 NEXT I
800 PRINT TAB(62);RO
810 PRINT STRING$(72,42)
820 RETURN
```

```
830 REM ******************** HEADING ROUTINE  *********************
840 PRINT
850 PRINT
860 PRINT "      INVENTORY FILE LIST-";FO$;"          DATE OF FILE-";DO$
870 PRINT
880 PRINT
890 PRINT STRING$(72,42)
900 PRINT "ITEM";TAB(10);"LOC";TAB(15);"CLASS";TAB(25);"DESCRIPTION";
910 PRINT TAB(45);"BEGIN";
920 PRINT TAB(52);"RCVD";TAB(60);"ON-HAND"
930 PRINT STRING$(72,45)
940 PRINT "QUANTITIES USED FOR";M1;"PERIODS  - OLDEST FIRST"
950 PRINT STRING$(72,45)
960 PRINT "INVENTORY VALUE - OLDEST FIRST  QUANTITY/UNIT COST";
970 PRINT TAB(60);"REORDER AT"
980 PRINT STRING$(72,42)
990 PRINT
1000 RETURN
```

RUN "ILIST"

                    INVENTORY FILE LIST PROGRAM

THE FOLLOWING FILES ARE AVAILABLE

            FILE NAME   CREATION DATE
            ----------   -------------
            MASTER 2   12/06/80
            MASTER 1   11/30/80

ENTER THE FILE NAME TO BE LISTED;
? MASTER 2

            INVENTORY FILE LIST-MASTER 2   DATE OF FILE-12/06/80

****
ITEM   LOC CLASS   DESCRIPTION   BEGIN RCVD   ON-HAND

QUANTITIES USED FOR 12 PERIODS - OLDEST FIRST

INVENTORY VALUE - OLDEST FIRST QUANTITY/UNIT COST   REORDER AT
****

11111   1234 ABCD SUPER DELUXE WIDGET   100   15   45
----
 65   74   85   47   67   58   59   61   52   80   45   70
----
 30 / 12.15   15 / 67.5   0 / 0   0 / 0
 0 / 0   0 / 0   0 / 0   0 / 0   90
****
22222   1233 ABCD MIDDLE CLASS WIDGET   50   50   40
----
 0   0   0   0   0   0   0   0   0   0   0   60
----
 40 / 55.66   0 / 0   0 / 0   0 / 0
 0 / 0   0 / 0   0 / 0   0 / 0   52
****

                    Periodic Inventory System   171

```
33333     1234 ABXX GOLD-PLATED WIDGET          50      10        90
------------------------------------------------------------------------
0     0     0     0     0     0     0     0     0     0     0   -30
------------------------------------------------------------------------
80 / 88.43       10 / 15.11       0 / 0          0 / 0
0 / 0            0 / 0            0 / 0          0 / 0            10
************************************************************************


INVENTORY MASTER LIST COMPLETE
        3 RECORDS PRINTED

BREAK IN 320
OK
```

Inventory Reports

Program Name: IREPORT1, IREPORT2, IREPORT3, IREPORT4, IREPORT5

These programs produce a series of optional reports that provide various formats and organizations for the inventory master file data. Report examples can be reviewed to determine the applicability of particular formats to your inventory situation. Note that several reports provide breakdowns and subtotals by location or product class codes should you decide to use them.

Files Affected: None

```
10 REM           SAVED AT IREPORT1
20 REM ****************************************************************
30 REM                  INITIALIZATION
40 REM ****************************************************************
50 MO=2
60 M1=12
70 M2=8
80 DIM U(M1),Q(M2),V(M2),F1$(MO),D1$(MO)
90 F$="MINDEX"
100 REM ***************************************************************
110 REM                 PROCESSING AREA
120 REM ***************************************************************
130 PRINT
140 PRINT
150 PRINT "              INVENTORY REPORT PROGRAM"
160 PRINT
170 PRINT "ENTER THE MONTH FOR THE REPORT ";
180 INPUT MO$
190 PRINT "ENTER TODAY'S DATE";
200 INPUT D9$
210 PRINT "ALIGN TO TOP-OF-PAGE AND PRESS THE RETURN"
220 INPUT A$
```

```
230 PRINT
240 GOSUB 490                    'ACCESS FILES
250 GOSUB  690                   'PRINT HEADINGS
260 GOSUB 570                    'READ FILE
270 UO=B+R-O
280 TO=TO+CO
290 PRINT I$;;TAB(10);D$;TAB(37);B;TAB(45);R;TAB(52);O;TAB(59);UO;TAB(65);
300 PRINT CO
310 LO=LO+1
320 GOTO 260
330 REM ********************************************************************
340 REM                    TERMINATION POINT
350 REM ********************************************************************
360 PRINT
370 PRINT STRING$(72,45)
380 PRINT TAB(38);"TOTAL COSTS OF GOODS SOLD ";TAB(62);TO
390 PRINT
400 PRINT
410 PRINT "INVENTORY REPORT IS COMPLETE"
420 PRINT "           ";LO;"RECORDS PRINTED"
430 PRINT
440 CLOSE 1,2
450 STOP


460 REM ********************************************************************
470 REM                    SUBROUTINES FOLLOW
480 REM ********************************************************************
490 REM                    ACCESS FILES
500 OPEN "I",1,F$
510 FOR I=1 TO MO
520    INPUT#1,F1$(I),D1$(I)
530 NEXT I
540 OPEN "I",2,F1$(1)
550 INPUT #2,DO$
560 RETURN


570 REM ******************** READ FILE   *************************
580 IF EOF(2) THEN 340
590 INPUT#2,I$,L$,C$,D$
600 FOR I=1 TO M1
610    INPUT#2,U(I)
620 NEXT I
630 INPUT#2,B,R,O
640 FOR I=1 TO M2
650    INPUT#2,Q(I),V(I)
660 NEXT I
670 INPUT#2,RO,CO
680 RETURN


690 REM ******************** PRINT HEADING *********************
700 PRINT
710 PRINT
720 PRINT "                    REPORT 1"
730 PRINT "      INVENTORY REPORT   -   MONTH OF: ";MO$
740 PRINT "                PREPARED: ";D9$
750 PRINT
760 PRINT
770 PRINT STRING$(72,42)
780 PRINT "ITEM";;TAB(10);"DESCRIPTION";
790 PRINT TAB(36);"BEGIN";TAB(45);"RCVD";TAB(53);"END";TAB(59);"USED";
800 PRINT TAB(65);"COST OF"
810 PRINT TAB(36);" INV";TAB(53);"INV";TAB(66);"GOODS"
820 PRINT STRING$(72,42)
830 PRINT
840 RETURN
```

```
RUN "IREPORT1"


                     INVENTORY REPORT PROGRAM

ENTER THE MONTH FOR THE REPORT ? NOVEMBER
ENTER TODAY'S DATE? 12/06/80
ALIGN TO TOP-OF-PAGE AND PRESS THE RETURN
?





                        REPORT 1
           INVENTORY REPORT   -   MONTH OF: NOVEMBER
                 PREPARED: 12/06/80


***********************************************************************
ITEM      DESCRIPTION               BEGIN   RCVD    END    USED   COST OF
                                    INV            INV           GOODS
***********************************************************************

11111     SUPER DELUXE WIDGET        100     15     45     70     850.5
22222     MIDDLE CLASS WIDGET         50     50     40     60    3390.1
33333     GOLD-PLATED WIDGET          50     10     90    -30   -2652.9

----------------------------------------------------------------------
                              TOTAL COSTS OF GOODS SOLD   1587.7


INVENTORY REPORT IS COMPLETE
        3 RECORDS PRINTED

BREAK IN 450
OK
```

```
10 REM                    SAVED AT IREPORT2
20 REM *****************************************************************
30 REM                    INITIALIZATION
40 REM *****************************************************************
50 MO=2
60 M1=12
70 M2=8
80 M3=100
90 DIM U(M1),Q(M2),V(M2),LO$(M3),T(M3),F1$(MO),D1$(MO)
100 FOR I=1 TO M3
110    LO$(I)="*"
120 NEXT I
130 F$="MINDEX"
140 REM *****************************************************************
150 REM                    PROCESSING AREA
160 REM *****************************************************************
170 PRINT
180 PRINT
190 PRINT "             INVENTORY REPORT PROGRAM - BY LOCATION"
200 PRINT
210 PRINT "ENTER THE MONTH FOR THE REPORT ";
220 INPUT MO$
230 PRINT "ENTER TODAY'S DATE";
240 INPUT D9$
250 PRINT "ALIGN TO TOP-OF-PAGE AND PRESS THE RETURN"
260 INPUT A$
270 PRINT
280 GOSUB 690                  'ACCESS FILES
290 GOSUB 1040                 'INITIALIZE ARRAYS
300 FOR K=1 TO M3
310    IF LO$(K)="*" THEN 520
320    GOSUB  880              'PRINT HEADINGS
330    IF EOF(2) THEN 420
340    GOSUB 770               'READ FILE
350    IF LO$(K)<>L$ THEN 330
360    UO=B+R-O
370    T(K)=T(K)+CO
380    PRINT I$;;TAB(10);D$;TAB(37);B;TAB(45);R;TAB(52);O;TAB(59);UO;TAB(65);
390    PRINT CO
400    LO=LO+1
410    GOTO 330
420    CLOSE 2
430    GOSUB 740               'REOPEN FILE
440    PRINT STRING$(72,45)
450    PRINT TAB(30);"LOCATION ";LO$(K);" COST OF GOODS SOLD ";TAB(62);T(K)
460    TO=TO+T(K)
470    PRINT
480    PRINT
490    PRINT
500 NEXT K
510 REM *****************************************************************
520 REM                    TERMINATION POINT
530 REM *****************************************************************
540 PRINT
550 PRINT
560 PRINT
570 PRINT
580 PRINT STRING$(72,42)
590 PRINT TAB(38);"TOTAL COSTS OF GOODS SOLD ";TAB(62);TO
600 PRINT
610 PRINT "INVENTORY REPORT IS COMPLETE"
620 PRINT "          ";LO;"RECORDS PRINTED"
630 PRINT
640 CLOSE 1,2
650 STOP
660 REM *****************************************************************
670 REM                    SUBROUTINES FOLLOW
680 REM *****************************************************************
```

```
690 REM                    ACCESS FILES
700 OPEN "I",1,F$
710 FOR I=1 TO MO
720    INPUT#1,F1$(I),D1$(I)
730 NEXT I
740 OPEN "I",2,F1$(1)
750 INPUT #2,DO$
760 RETURN


770 REM ******************** READ FILE   *****************************
780 INPUT#2,I$,L$,C$,D$
790 FOR I=1 TO M1
800    INPUT#2,U(I)
810 NEXT I
820 INPUT#2,B,R,O
830 FOR I=1 TO M2
840    INPUT#2,Q(I),V(I)
850 NEXT I
860 INPUT#2,RO,CO
870 RETURN


880 REM ********************* PRINT HEADING ***********************
890 PRINT
900 PRINT
910 PRINT "                    REPORT 2"
920 PRINT "     INVENTORY REPORT  -  MONTH OF: ";MO$;TAB(60);"LOC: ";LO$(K)
930 PRINT "               PREPARED: ";D9$
940 PRINT
950 PRINT
960 PRINT STRING$(72,42)
970 PRINT "ITEM";TAB(10);"DESCRIPTION";
980 PRINT TAB(36);"BEGIN";TAB(45);"RCVD";TAB(53);"END";TAB(59);"USED";
990 PRINT TAB(65);"COST OF"
1000 PRINT TAB(36);" INV";TAB(53);"INV";TAB(66);"GOODS"
1010 PRINT STRING$(72,42)
1020 PRINT
1030 RETURN


1040 REM ************* INITIALIZE LOCATION ARRAYS ***************
1050 IF EOF(2) THEN 1130
1060 GOSUB 770                 'READ FILE
1070 FOR I = 1 TO M3
1080    IF L$ = LO$(I) THEN 1050
1090    IF LO$(I) <>"*" THEN 1120
1100    LO$(I)=L$
1110    GOTO 1050
1120 NEXT I
1130 CLOSE 2
1140 OPEN "I",2,F1$(1)
1150 INPUT#2,DO$
1160 RETURN




RUN "IREPORT2"


               INVENTORY REPORT PROGRAM - BY LOCATION

ENTER THE MONTH FOR THE REPORT ? NOVEMBER
ENTER TODAY'S DATE? 12/06/80
ALIGN TO TOP-OF-PAGE AND PRESS THE RETURN
?
```

```
                        REPORT 2
          INVENTORY REPORT  -  MONTH OF: NOVEMBER              LOC: 1234
                  PREPARED: 12/06/80


****************************************************************************
ITEM      DESCRIPTION              BEGIN    RCVD     END     USED   COST OF
                                   INV               INV            GOODS
****************************************************************************

11111     SUPER DELUXE WIDGET       100      15      45       70    850.5
33333     GOLD-PLATED WIDGET         50      10      90      -30   -2652.9
------------------------------------------------------------------------------
                           LOCATION 1234 COST OF GOODS SOLD -1802.4




                        REPORT 2
          INVENTORY REPORT  -  MONTH OF: NOVEMBER              LOC: 1233
                  PREPARED: 12/06/80


****************************************************************************
ITEM      DESCRIPTION              BEGIN    RCVD     END     USED   COST OF
                                   INV               INV            GOODS
****************************************************************************

22222     MIDDLE CLASS WIDGET        50      50      40       60   3390.1
------------------------------------------------------------------------------
                           LOCATION 1233 COST OF GOODS SOLD  3390.1





****************************************************************************
                           TOTAL COSTS OF GOODS SOLD  1587.7

INVENTORY REPORT IS COMPLETE
        3 RECORDS PRINTED

BREAK IN 650
OK
```

```
10 REM                     SAVED AT IREPORT3
20 REM ***********************************************************
30 REM                   INITIALIZATION
40 REM ***********************************************************
50 M0=2
60 M1=12
70 M2=8
80 M3=100
90 DIM U(M1),Q(M2),V(M2),LO$(M3),T(M3),F1$(M0),D1$(M0)
100 FOR I=1 TO M3
110    LO$(I)="*"
120 NEXT I
130 F$="MINDEX"
140 REM ***********************************************************
150 REM                   PROCESSING AREA
160 REM ***********************************************************
170 PRINT
180 PRINT
190 PRINT "              INVENTORY REPORT PROGRAM - BY LOCATION"
200 PRINT
210 PRINT "ENTER THE MONTH FOR THE REPORT ";
220 INPUT MO$
230 PRINT "ENTER TODAY'S DATE";
240 INPUT D9$
250 PRINT "ALIGN TO TOP-OF-PAGE AND PRESS THE RETURN"
260 INPUT A$
270 PRINT
280 GOSUB 810                     'ACCESS FILES
290 GOSUB 1160                    'INITIALIZE ARRAYS
300 FOR K=1 TO M3
310    IF LO$(K)="*" THEN 640
320    GOSUB  1000                'PRINT HEADINGS
330    IF EOF(2) THEN 540
340    GOSUB 890                  'READ FILE
350    IF LO$(K)<>L$ THEN 330
360    U0=B+R-0
370    FOR I=1 TO M1
380       IF U(I)<>0 AND X=0 THEN X=M1-I+1
390       IF X>0 THEN A0=A0+U(I)
400    NEXT I
410    IF X>0 THEN A0=INT(A0/X)
420    IF X=0 THEN A0=0
430    FOR I=1 TO M2
440       V0=V0+Q(I)*V(I)
450    NEXT I
460    T(K)=T(K)+V0
470    PRINT I$;;TAB(10);D$;TAB(37);U0;TAB(45);A0;TAB(51);R0;TAB(59);0;TAB(65);
480    PRINT V0
490    A0=0
500    V0=0
510    X=0
520    L0=L0+1
530    GOTO 330
540    CLOSE 2
550    GOSUB 860                  'REOPEN FILE
560    PRINT STRING$(72,45)
570    PRINT TAB(30);"LOCATION ";LO$(K);" VALUE OF GOODS ";TAB(62);T(K)
580    T0=T0+T(K)
590    PRINT
600    PRINT
610    PRINT
620 NEXT K
630 REM ***********************************************************
640 REM                   TERMINATION POINT
650 REM ***********************************************************
660 PRINT
670 PRINT
680 PRINT
```

```
690 PRINT
700 PRINT STRING$(72,42)
710 PRINT TAB(38);"TOTAL VALUE OF INVENTORY ";TAB(62);TO
720 PRINT
730 PRINT "INVENTORY REPORT IS COMPLETE"
740 PRINT "           ";LO;"RECORDS PRINTED"
750 PRINT
760 CLOSE 1,2
770 STOP


780 REM ******************************************************************
790 REM                  SUBROUTINES FOLLOW
800 REM ******************************************************************
810 REM                  ACCESS FILES
820 OPEN "I",1,F$
830 FOR I=1 TO MO
840    INPUT#1,F1$(I),D1$(I)
850 NEXT I
860 OPEN "I",2,F1$(1)
870 INPUT #2,DO$
880 RETURN


890 REM ******************** READ FILE   *************************
900 INPUT#2,I$,L$,C$,D$
910 FOR I=1 TO M1
920    INPUT#2,U(I)
930 NEXT I
940 INPUT#2,B,R,O
950 FOR I=1 TO M2
960    INPUT#2,Q(I),V(I)
970 NEXT I
980 INPUT#2,RO,CO
990 RETURN


1000 REM ********************** PRINT HEADING **********************
1010 PRINT
1020 PRINT
1030 PRINT "                         REPORT 3"
1040 PRINT "    INVENTORY REPORT   -   MONTH OF: ";MO$;TAB(60);"LOC: ";LO$(K)
1050 PRINT "               PREPARED: ";D9$
1060 PRINT
1070 PRINT
1080 PRINT STRING$(72,42)
1090 PRINT "ITEM";;TAB(10);"DESCRIPTION";
1100 PRINT TAB(36);"USED";TAB(45);"AVG";TAB(51);"ORDER";TAB(59);"END";
1110 PRINT TAB(64);"VALUE OF"
1120 PRINT TAB(45);"USE";TAB(51);"POINT";TAB(59);"INV";TAB(66);"GOODS"
1130 PRINT STRING$(72,42)
1140 PRINT
1150 RETURN


1160 REM ************* INITIALIZE LOCATION ARRAYS  *************
1170 IF EOF(2) THEN 1250
1180 GOSUB 890                'READ FILE
1190 FOR I = 1 TO M3
1200    IF L$ = LO$(I) THEN 1170
1210    IF LO$(I) <>"*" THEN 1240
1220    LO$(I)=L$
1230    GOTO 1170
1240 NEXT I
1250 CLOSE 2
1260 OPEN "I",2,F1$(1)
1270 INPUT#2,DO$
1280 RETURN
```

```
RUN "IREPORT3"

                    INVENTORY REPORT PROGRAM - BY LOCATION

ENTER THE MONTH FOR THE REPORT ? NOVEMBER
ENTER TODAY'S DATE? 12/06/80
ALIGN TO TOP-OF-PAGE AND PRESS THE RETURN
?




                              REPORT 3
               INVENTORY REPORT   -  MONTH OF: NOVEMBER            LOC: 1234
                      PREPARED: 12/06/80


**********************************************************************
ITEM        DESCRIPTION                   USED    AVG    ORDER   END   VALUE OF
                                                  USE    POINT   INV   GOODS
**********************************************************************

11111     SUPER DELUXE WIDGET             70      63     90      45    1377
33333     GOLD-PLATED WIDGET             -30     -30     10      90    7225.5
-----------------------------------------------------------------
                              LOCATION 1234 VALUE OF GOODS     8602.5




                              REPORT 3
               INVENTORY REPORT   -  MONTH OF: NOVEMBER            LOC: 1233
                      PREPARED: 12/06/80


**********************************************************************
ITEM        DESCRIPTION                   USED    AVG    ORDER   END   VALUE OF
                                                  USE    POINT   INV   GOODS
**********************************************************************

22222     MIDDLE CLASS WIDGET             60      60     52      40    2226.4
-----------------------------------------------------------------
                              LOCATION 1233 VALUE OF GOODS     2226.4




**********************************************************************
                              TOTAL VALUE OF INVENTORY   10828.9

INVENTORY REPORT IS COMPLETE
         3 RECORDS PRINTED

BREAK IN 730
OK
```

```
10 REM                     SAVED AT IREPORT4
20 REM *******************************************************************
30 REM                    INITIALIZATION
40 REM *******************************************************************
50 M0=2
60 M1=12
70 M2=8
80 M3=100
90 DIM U(M1),Q(M2),V(M2),CO$(M3),T(M3),F1$(M0),D1$(M0)
100 FOR I=1 TO M3
110    CO$(I)="*"
120 NEXT I
130 F$="MINDEX"
140 REM *******************************************************************
150 REM                    PROCESSING AREA
160 REM *******************************************************************
170 PRINT
180 PRINT
190 PRINT "               INVENTORY REPORT PROGRAM - BY CLASS"
200 PRINT
210 PRINT "ENTER THE MONTH FOR THE REPORT ";
220 INPUT MO$
230 PRINT "ENTER TODAY'S DATE";
240 INPUT D9$
250 PRINT "ALIGN TO TOP-OF-PAGE AND PRESS THE RETURN"
260 INPUT A$
270 PRINT
280 GOSUB 690                    'ACCESS FILES
290 GOSUB 1040                   'INITIALIZE ARRAYS
300 FOR K=1 TO M3
310    IF CO$(K)="*" THEN 520
320    GOSUB  880                'PRINT HEADINGS
330    IF EOF(2) THEN 420
340    GOSUB 770                 'READ FILE
350    IF CO$(K)<>C$ THEN 330
360    UO=B+R-O
370    T(K)=T(K)+CO
380    PRINT I$;;TAB(10);D$;TAB(37);B;TAB(45);R;TAB(52);O;TAB(59);UO;TAB(65);
390    PRINT CO
400    LO=LO+1
410    GOTO 330
420    CLOSE 2
430    GOSUB 740                 'REOPEN FILE
440    PRINT STRING$(72,45)
450    PRINT TAB(30);"INV CLASS ";CO$(K);" COST OF GOODS SOLD ";TAB(62);T(K)
460    TO=TO+T(K)
470    PRINT
480    PRINT
490    PRINT
500 NEXT K
510 REM *******************************************************************
520 REM                    TERMINATION POINT
530 REM *******************************************************************
540 PRINT
550 PRINT
560 PRINT
570 PRINT
580 PRINT STRING$(72,42)
590 PRINT TAB(38);"TOTAL COSTS OF GOODS SOLD ";TAB(62);TO
600 PRINT
610 PRINT "INVENTORY REPORT IS COMPLETE"
620 PRINT "               ";LO;"RECORDS PRINTED"
630 PRINT
640 CLOSE 1,2
650 STOP
```

```
660 REM ***************************************************************
670 REM                    SUBROUTINES FOLLOW
680 REM ***************************************************************
690 REM                    ACCESS FILES
700 OPEN "I",1,F$
710 FOR I=1 TO MO
720    INPUT#1,F1$(I),D1$(I)
730 NEXT I
740 OPEN "I",2,F1$(1)
750 INPUT #2,DO$
760 RETURN


770 REM ******************** READ FILE  **************************
780 INPUT#2,I$,L$,C$,D$
790 FOR I=1 TO M1
800    INPUT#2,U(I)
810 NEXT I
820 INPUT#2,B,R,O
830 FOR I=1 TO M2
840    INPUT#2,Q(I),V(I)
850 NEXT I
860 INPUT#2,RO,CO
870 RETURN


880 REM ******************** PRINT HEADING *********************
890 PRINT
900 PRINT
910 PRINT "                           REPORT 4 "
920 PRINT "     INVENTORY REPORT   -   MONTH OF: ";MO$;TAB(59);"CLASS ";CO$(K)
930 PRINT "               PREPARED: ";D9$
940 PRINT
950 PRINT
960 PRINT STRING$(72,42)
970 PRINT "ITEM";TAB(10);"DESCRIPTION";
980 PRINT TAB(36);"BEGIN";TAB(45);"RCVD";TAB(53);"END";TAB(59);"USED";
990 PRINT TAB(65);"COST OF"
1000 PRINT TAB(36);" INV";TAB(53);"INV";TAB(66);"GOODS"
1010 PRINT STRING$(72,42)
1020 PRINT
1030 RETURN


1040 REM ****************  INITIALIZE CLASS ARRAYS  ***************
1050 IF EOF(2) THEN 1130
1060 GOSUB 770                      'READ FILE
1070 FOR I = 1 TO M3
1080    IF C$ = CO$(I) THEN 1050
1090    IF CO$(I) <>"*" THEN 1120
1100    CO$(I)=C$
1110    GOTO 1050
1120 NEXT I
1130 CLOSE 2
1140 OPEN "I",2,F1$(1)
1150 INPUT#2,DO$
1160 RETURN
```

```
RUN "IREPORT4"


              INVENTORY REPORT PROGRAM - BY CLASS

ENTER THE MONTH FOR THE REPORT ? NOVEMBER
ENTER TODAY'S DATE? 12/06/80
ALIGN TO TOP-OF-PAGE AND PRESS THE RETURN
?




                          REPORT 4
           INVENTORY REPORT   -   MONTH OF: NOVEMBER        CLASS ABCD
                     PREPARED: 12/06/80


********************************************************************
ITEM      DESCRIPTION                 BEGIN    RCVD     END     USED   COST OF
                                      INV               INV            GOODS
********************************************************************

11111     SUPER DELUXE WIDGET          100      15       45      70    850.5
22222     MIDDLE CLASS WIDGET           50      50       40      60    3390.1
-------------------------------------------------------------------
                        INV CLASS ABCD COST OF GOODS SOLD   4240.6




                          REPORT 4
           INVENTORY REPORT   -   MONTH OF: NOVEMBER        CLASS ABXX
                     PREPARED: 12/06/80


********************************************************************
ITEM      DESCRIPTION                 BEGIN    RCVD     END     USED   COST OF
                                      INV               INV            GOODS
********************************************************************

33333     GOLD-PLATED WIDGET            50      10       90     -30   -2652.9
-------------------------------------------------------------------
                        INV CLASS ABXX COST OF GOODS SOLD  -2652.9




********************************************************************
                        TOTAL COSTS OF GOODS SOLD   1587.7

INVENTORY REPORT IS COMPLETE
        3 RECORDS PRINTED

BREAK IN 650
OK
```

```
10 REM                         SAVED AT IREPORT5
20 REM ***********************************************************
30 REM                      INITIALIZATION
40 REM ***********************************************************
50 MO=2
60 M1=12
70 M2=8
80 M3=100
90 DIM U(M1),Q(M2),V(M2),CO$(M3),T(M3),F1$(MO),D1$(MO)
100 FOR I=1 TO M3
110   CO$(I)="*"
120 NEXT I
130 F$="MINDEX"
140 REM ***********************************************************
150 REM                    PROCESSING AREA
160 REM ***********************************************************
170 PRINT
180 PRINT
190 PRINT "                INVENTORY REPORT PROGRAM - BY CLASS"
200 PRINT
210 PRINT "ENTER THE MONTH FOR THE REPORT ";
220 INPUT MO$
230 PRINT "ENTER TODAY'S DATE";
240 INPUT D9$
250 PRINT "ALIGN TO TOP-OF-PAGE AND PRESS THE RETURN"
260 INPUT A$
270 PRINT
280 GOSUB 810                    'ACCESS FILES
290 GOSUB 1160                   'INITIALIZE ARRAYS
300 FOR K=1 TO M3
310   IF CO$(K)="*" THEN 640
320   GOSUB  1000                'PRINT HEADINGS
330   IF EOF(2) THEN 540
340   GOSUB 890                  'READ FILE
350   IF CO$(K)<>C$ THEN 330
360   UO=B+R-O
370   FOR I= 1 TO M1
380     IF U(I)<>0 AND X=0 THEN X=M1-I+1
390     IF X>0 THEN AO=AO+U(I)
400   NEXT I
410   IF X>0 THEN AO=INT(AO/X)
420   IF X=0 THEN AO=0
430   FOR I=1 TO M2
440     VO=VO+Q(I)*V(I)
450   NEXT I
460   T(K)=T(K)+VO
470   PRINT I$;;TAB(10);D$;TAB(37);UO;TAB(45);AO;TAB(51);RO;TAB(59);O;TAB(65);
480   PRINT VO
490   AO=0
500   VO=0
510   X=0
520   LO=LO+1
530   GOTO 330
540   CLOSE 2
550   GOSUB 860                  'REOPEN FILE
560   PRINT STRING$(72,45)
570   PRINT TAB(29);"INV CLASS ";CO$(K);" VALUE OF GOODS ";TAB(62);T(K)
580   TO=TO+T(K)
590   PRINT
600   PRINT
610   PRINT
620 NEXT K
630 REM ***********************************************************
640 REM                    TERMINATION POINT
650 REM ***********************************************************
660 PRINT
670 PRINT
680 PRINT
```

```
690 PRINT
700 PRINT STRING$(72,42)
710 PRINT TAB(38);"TOTAL VALUE OF INVENTORY ";TAB(62);TO
720 PRINT
730 PRINT "INVENTORY REPORT IS COMPLETE"
740 PRINT "              ";LO;"RECORDS PRINTED"
750 PRINT
760 CLOSE 1,2
770 STOP


780 REM ***********************************************************
790 REM                    SUBROUTINES FOLLOW
800 REM ***********************************************************
810 REM                  ACCESS FILES
820 OPEN "I",1,F$
830 FOR I=1 TO MO
840    INPUT#1,F1$(I),D1$(I)
850 NEXT I
860 OPEN "I",2,F1$(1)
870 INPUT #2,DO$
880 RETURN


890 REM ******************** READ FILE  ************************
900 INPUT#2,I$,L$,C$,D$
910 FOR I=1 TO M1
920    INPUT#2,U(I)
930 NEXT I
940 INPUT#2,B,R,O
950 FOR I=1 TO M2
960    INPUT#2,Q(I),V(I)
970 NEXT I
980 INPUT#2,RO,CO
990 RETURN


1000 REM ******************** PRINT HEADING ********************
1010 PRINT
1020 PRINT
1030 PRINT "                        REPORT 5"
1040 PRINT "     INVENTORY REPORT  -   MONTH OF: ";MO$;TAB(60);"CLASS: ";CO$(K)
1050 PRINT "                PREPARED: ";D9$
1060 PRINT
1070 PRINT
1080 PRINT STRING$(72,42)
1090 PRINT "ITEM";TAB(10);"DESCRIPTION";
1100 PRINT TAB(36);"USED";TAB(45);"AVG";TAB(51);"ORDER";TAB(59);"END";
1110 PRINT TAB(64);"VALUE OF"
1120 PRINT TAB(45);"USE";TAB(51);"POINT";TAB(59);"INV";TAB(66);"GOODS"
1130 PRINT STRING$(72,42)
1140 PRINT
1150 RETURN


1160 REM ************   INITIALIZE CLASS ARRAYS  *****************
1170 IF EOF(2) THEN 1250
1180 GOSUB 890                   'READ FILE
1190 FOR I = 1 TO M3
1200    IF C$ = CO$(I) THEN 1170
1210    IF CO$(I) <>"*" THEN 1240
1220    CO$(I)=C$
1230    GOTO 1170
1240 NEXT I
1250 CLOSE 2
1260 OPEN "I",2,F1$(1)
1270 INPUT#2,DO$
1280 RETURN
```

```
RUN "IREPORT5"

                    INVENTORY REPORT PROGRAM - BY CLASS

ENTER THE MONTH FOR THE REPORT ? NOVEMBER
ENTER TODAY'S DATE? 12/06/80
ALIGN TO TOP-OF-PAGE AND PRESS THE RETURN
?




                        REPORT 5
            INVENTORY REPORT   - MONTH OF: NOVEMBER           CLASS: ABCD
                    PREPARED: 12/06/80



*******************************************************************
ITEM      DESCRIPTION                USED   AVG   ORDER  END  VALUE OF
                                            USE   POINT  INV  GOODS
*******************************************************************

11111     SUPER DELUXE WIDGET         70    63     90    45    1377
22222     MIDDLE CLASS WIDGET         60    60     52    40    2226.4
----------------------------------------------------------------
                          INV CLASS ABCD VALUE OF GOODS      3603.4




                        REPORT 5
            INVENTORY REPORT   - MONTH OF: NOVEMBER           CLASS: ABXX
                    PREPARED: 12/06/80



*******************************************************************
ITEM      DESCRIPTION                USED   AVG   ORDER  END  VALUE OF
                                            USE   POINT  INV  GOODS
*******************************************************************

33333     GOLD-PLATED WIDGET         -30   -30     10    90    7225.5
----------------------------------------------------------------
                          INV CLASS ABXX VALUE OF GOODS      7225.5




*******************************************************************
                          TOTAL VALUE OF INVENTORY   10828.9

INVENTORY REPORT IS COMPLETE
        3 RECORDS PRINTED

BREAK IN 770
OK
```

Inventory Analysis

Program Name: ICOMP

This program provides inventory analysis information and can easily be extended to serve other analytical functions. Note that in its present form it can produce both projected-use information (based on weighted averages) and a list of items that have fallen below their reorder point.

Files Affected: None

```
10 REM                    SAVED AT ICOMP
20 REM ****************************************************************
30 REM                    INITIALIZATION
40 REM ****************************************************************
50 MO=2
60 M1=12
70 M2=8
80 DIM U(M1),Q(M2),V(M2),F1$(MO),D1$(MO)
90 F$="MINDEX"
100 REM ****************************************************************
110 REM                   PROCESSING AREA
120 REM ****************************************************************
130 PRINT
140 PRINT
150 PRINT "               INVENTORY ANALYSIS PROGRAM"
160 PRINT
170 PRINT "ENTER THE MONTH FOR THE REPORT ";
180 INPUT MO$
190 PRINT "ENTER TODAY'S DATE";
200 INPUT D9$
210 PRINT "ENTER THE REPORT TO BE PRINTED"
220 PRINT "     1   ALL ITEMS
230 PRINT "     2   ITEMS BELOW REORDER POINT"
240 INPUT A
250 PRINT "ALIGN TO TOP-OF-PAGE AND PRESS THE RETURN"
260 INPUT A$
270 PRINT
280 GOSUB 650                    'ACCESS FILES
290 GOSUB  850                   'PRINT HEADINGS
300 GOSUB 730                    'READ FILE
310 UO=B+R-O
320 FOR I=1 TO M1
330    IF U(I)<>0 AND X=0 THEN X=M1-I+1
340    IF X=0 THEN 380
350    AO=AO+U(I)
360    P9=P9+U(I)*I        'WEIGHTING APPLIED HERE
370    C9=C9+I
380 NEXT I
390 IF X>0 THEN AO=INT(AO/X)
400 IF X>0 THEN P9=INT(P9/C9)    'PROJECTED USE COMPUTED HERE
410 IF A=2 AND O>RO THEN 300
420 PRINT I$;;TAB(10);D$;TAB(37);UO;TAB(45);AO;TAB(52);RO;TAB(59);O;TAB(65);
430 PRINT P9
440 LO=LO+1
450 X=0
460 P9=0
470 C9=0
480 AO=0
490 GOTO 300
500 REM ****************************************************************
510 REM                   TERMINATION POINT
520 REM ****************************************************************
```

```
530 PRINT
540 PRINT STRING$(72,45)
550 PRINT
560 PRINT
570 PRINT "INVENTORY ANALYSIS IS COMPLETE"
580 PRINT "            ";L0;"RECORDS PRINTED"
590 PRINT
600 CLOSE 1,2
610 STOP


620 REM ***************************************************************
630 REM                   SUBROUTINES FOLLOW
640 REM ***************************************************************
650 REM              ACCESS FILES
660 OPEN "I",1,F$
670 FOR I=1 TO M0
680    INPUT#1,F1$(I),D1$(I)
690 NEXT I
700 OPEN "I",2,F1$(1)
710 INPUT #2,D0$
720 RETURN


730 REM ******************** READ FILE  ****************************
740 IF EOF(2) THEN 510
750 INPUT#2,I$,L$,C$,D$
760 FOR I=1 TO M1
770    INPUT#2,U(I)
780 NEXT I
790 INPUT#2,B,R,O
800 FOR I=1 TO M2
810    INPUT#2,Q(I),V(I)
820 NEXT I
830 INPUT#2,R0,C0
840 RETURN


850 REM ******************** PRINT HEADING *******************
860 PRINT
870 PRINT
880 PRINT "     INVENTORY ANALYSIS  -   MONTH OF: ";M0$
890 PRINT "               PREPARED: ";D9$
900 PRINT
910 IF A=2 THEN PRINT "               ITEMS BELOW REORDER POINT"
920 PRINT
930 PRINT STRING$(72,42)
940 PRINT "ITEM";TAB(10);"DESCRIPTION";
950 PRINT TAB(36);"USED";TAB(45);"AVG";TAB(51);"REORDER";TAB(59);"END";
960 PRINT TAB(65);"PROJ."
970 PRINT TAB(45);"USE";TAB(52);"POINT";TAB(59);"INV";TAB(66);"USE"
980 PRINT STRING$(72,42)
990 PRINT
1000 RETURN




RUN "ICOMP"


                    INVENTORY ANALYSIS PROGRAM

ENTER THE MONTH FOR THE REPORT ? NOVEMBER
ENTER TODAY'S DATE? 12/06/80
ENTER THE REPORT TO BE PRINTED
        1   ALL ITEMS
        2   ITEMS BELOW REORDER POINT
? 1
ALIGN TO TOP-OF-PAGE AND PRESS THE RETURN
?
```

```
           INVENTORY ANALYSIS  -  MONTH OF: NOVEMBER
                  PREPARED: 12/06/80


****************************************************************************
ITEM       DESCRIPTION             USED      AVG    REORDER  END    PROJ.
                                             USE     POINT   INV     USE
****************************************************************************

11111      SUPER DELUXE WIDGET      70        63      90      45      62
22222      MIDDLE CLASS WIDGET      60        60      52      40      60
33333      GOLD-PLATED WIDGET      -30       -30      10      90     -30

----------------------------------------------------------------------------


INVENTORY ANALYSIS IS COMPLETE
       3 RECORDS PRINTED

BREAK IN 610
OK
```

```
RUN "ICOMP"

                  INVENTORY ANALYSIS PROGRAM

ENTER THE MONTH FOR THE REPORT ? NOVEMBER
ENTER TODAY'S DATE? 12/06/80
ENTER THE REPORT TO BE PRINTED
        1   ALL ITEMS
        2   ITEMS BELOW REORDER POINT
? 2
ALIGN TO TOP-OF-PAGE AND PRESS THE RETURN
?
```

```
           INVENTORY ANALYSIS  -  MONTH OF: NOVEMBER
                  PREPARED: 12/06/80

              ITEMS BELOW REORDER POINT

****************************************************************************
ITEM       DESCRIPTION             USED      AVG    REORDER  END    PROJ.
                                             USE     POINT   INV     USE
****************************************************************************

11111      SUPER DELUXE WIDGET      70        63      90      45      62
22222      MIDDLE CLASS WIDGET      60        60      52      40      60

----------------------------------------------------------------------------


INVENTORY ANALYSIS IS COMPLETE
       2 RECORDS PRINTED

BREAK IN 610
OK
```

7 Inventory Programs (General)

Reorder Point Computation

Program Name: REORDER

This program accepts keyboard entries of average use and delivery time for various products and computes the minimum inventory levels for reordering replacement materials. Since use and delivery times are considered fixed, the occurrence of above-average demand or delivery delays will result in stock outages. Critical items should have their reorder point adjusted upward to cover contingencies.

Comment: This program can be modified to interface with either the periodic or perpetual inventory systems.

Files Affected: None

```
10 REM           SAVED AT REORDER
20 REM  COMPUTES REORDER POINTS  USING A BASE-STOCK SYSTEM
30 M=100
40 DIM I$(M),U(M),D(M),R(M)
50 X$="******************************************************************"
60 PRINT
70 PRINT
80 PRINT "ENTER THE NUMBER OF DAYS SAFETY STOCK TO MAINTAIN";
90 INPUT S
100 PRINT
110 PRINT "ENTER FOR EACH ITEM:"
120 PRINT TAB(5);"ITEM NAME,AVERAGE DAILY USE,DAYS UNTIL ORDER IS RECEIVED"
130 PRINT
140 PRINT "EXAMPLE        WIDGET CLASS 1,3,15"
150 PRINT
160 PRINT "JUST PRESS THE RETURN WHEN FINISHED"
170 PRINT
180 PRINT "ENTER INFORMATION NOW"
190 PRINT
200 FOR I = 1 TO M
210   I$(I)=""
220   INPUT I$(I),U(I),D(I)
230   IF I$(I)="" THEN 260
240 NEXT I
250 REM ************************************************************
260 REM              PRINT RESULTS
270 REM ************************************************************
```

190

```
280 M1=I-1
290 PRINT "POSITION PAPER NOW"
300 INPUT A$
310 PRINT
320 PRINT
330 PRINT X$
340 PRINT
350 PRINT TAB(10);"ITEM";TAB(40);"AVG USE";TAB(50);"TIME LAG";TAB(60);
360 PRINT "REORDER AT"
370 PRINT
380 FOR I=1 TO M1
390    R(I)=S*U(I)+U(I)*D(I)
400    PRINT I$(I);TAB(40);U(I);TAB(50);D(I);TAB(60);R(I)
410 NEXT I
420 REM *************************************************************
430 REM                  PROGRAM TERMINATION POINT
440 REM *************************************************************
450 PRINT
460 PRINT
470 PRINT "PROCESSING COMPLETE"
480 PRINT
490 STOP
```

```
RUN "REORDER"


ENTER THE NUMBER OF DAYS SAFETY STOCK TO MAINTAIN? 5

ENTER FOR EACH ITEM:
     ITEM NAME,AVERAGE DAILY USE,DAYS UNTIL ORDER IS RECEIVED

EXAMPLE        WIDGET CLASS 1,3,15

JUST PRESS THE RETURN WHEN FINISHED

ENTER INFORMATION NOW

? SUPER WIDGET,3,15
? MIDDLE CLASS WIDGET,2,5
? BUDGET WIDGET,1,2
? SUPPER Q-TYPE WIDGET,1,25
?
POSITION PAPER NOW
?
```

```
*************************************************************

          ITEM                       AVG USE    TIME LAG   REORDER AT

SUPER WIDGET                            3          15         60
MIDDLE CLASS WIDGET                     2          5          20
BUDGET WIDGET                           1          2          7
SUPPER Q-TYPE WIDGET                    1          25         30


PROCESSING COMPLETE

BREAK IN 490
OK
```

```
MAJOR SYMBOL TABLE - REORDER                                    FUNCTIONS USED
I---------------------------------------------------------I    I----------------I
I NAME    .. DESCRIPTION                                   I    I  NAME          I
I---------------------------------------------------------I    I----------------I
I  A$     .. DUMMY ANSWER VARIABLE                         I    I TAB            I
I  D$()   .. DAY ARRAY FOR TIME LAG                        I    I DIM            I
I  I      .. INDEX AND ARRAY POINTER                       I    I----------------I
I  I$()   .. ITEM NAME ARRAY                               I
I  M      .. MAXIMUM NUMBER OF ENTRIES POSSIBLE            I
I  M1     .. NUMBER OF ITEMS ENTERED                       I
I  R()    .. REORDER POINT ARRAY                           I
I  S      .. NUMBER OF DAYS SAFETY STOCK TO KEEP           I
I  U()    .. DAILY USE ARRAY                               I
I  X$     .. LINE OF ASTERISKS                             I
I---------------------------------------------------------I
```

Inventory Turnover Analysis

Program Name: ANALYSIS

This program accepts keyboard entries of inventory on-hand amounts, calculates average inventory (numbers and value), and then determines the inventory turnover ratio, that is, the cost of goods sold divided by the average inventory value. All data is entered in response to program messages.

Comment: This program can be easily extended to interface with either perpetual or periodic inventory systems.

Files Affected: None

```
10 REM          SAVED AT ANALYSIS
20 REM      INVENTORY TURNOVER ANALYSIS PROGRAM
30 REM *******************************************************************
40 X$="*******************************************************"
50 PRINT
60 PRINT
70 PRINT "ENTER THE NUMBER OF MONTHS TO BE ANALYZED";
80 INPUT N
90 DIM O(N)
100 PRINT "ENTER THE PRODUCT NAME";
110 INPUT N$
120 T=0
130 PRINT "ENTER THE TOTAL COST OF GOODS SOLD FOR THE PERIODS";
140 INPUT C
150 PRINT "ENTER THE AMOUNT ON-HAND FOR THE FOLLOWING PERIODS"
160 PRINT
170 PRINT "PERIOD    ON-HAND"
180 FOR I = 1 TO N
190    PRINT I;TAB(10)
```

```
200   INPUT O(I)
210    T=T+O(I)
220 NEXT I
230 PRINT "ENTER THE AVERAGE VALUE OF EACH ITEM";
240 INPUT V
250 A1=T/N
260 A2=V*A1
270 A3=C/A2
280 PRINT
290 REM ***************************************************************
300 REM              PRINT OF RESULTS
310 REM ***************************************************************
320 PRINT X$
330 PRINT
340 PRINT TAB(20);"INVENTORY TURNOVER ANALYSIS"
350 PRINT TAB(25);N$
360 PRINT
370 PRINT TAB(10);"AVG ON-HAND";TAB(25);"AVG VALUE";TAB(40);"TURNOVER"
380 PRINT
390 PRINT TAB(12);A1;TAB(25);A2;TAB(40);A3
400 PRINT
410 PRINT X$
420 PRINT
430 PRINT "ANOTHER PRODUCT? (Y OR N)?";
440 INPUT A$
450 IF A$="Y" THEN 100
460 REM ***************************************************************
470 REM             PROGRAM TERMINATION POINT
480 REM ***************************************************************
490 PRINT
500 PRINT "PROCESSING COMPLETE"
510 PRINT
520 STOP
```

```
RUN "ANALYSIS"


ENTER THE NUMBER OF MONTHS TO BE ANALYZED? 6
ENTER THE PRODUCT NAME? SUPER WIDGETS
ENTER THE TOTAL COST OF GOODS SOLD FOR THE PERIODS? 1200
ENTER THE AMOUNT ON-HAND FOR THE FOLLOWING PERIODS

PERIOD    ON-HAND
  1        ? 10
  2        ? 20
  3        ? 30
  4        ? 40
  5        ? 50
  6        ? 60
ENTER THE AVERAGE VALUE OF EACH ITEM? 10

*****************************************************************

                INVENTORY TURNOVER ANALYSIS
                     SUPER WIDGETS

      AVG ON-HAND     AVG VALUE      TURNOVER

          35             350          3.42857


*****************************************************************
```

```
ANOTHER PRODUCT? (Y OR N)?? Y
ENTER THE PRODUCT NAME? BUDGET WIDGET
ENTER THE TOTAL COST OF GOODS SOLD FOR THE PERIODS? 695
ENTER THE AMOUNT ON-HAND FOR THE FOLLOWING PERIODS

PERIOD     ON-HAND
  1        ? 5
  2        ? 10
  3        ? 15
  4        ? 20
  5        ? 25
  6        ? 30
ENTER THE AVERAGE VALUE OF EACH ITEM? 10

****************************************************************

                    INVENTORY TURNOVER ANALYSIS
                         BUDGET WIDGET

        AVG ON-HAND      AVG VALUE       TURNOVER

           17.5            175           3.97143

****************************************************************

ANOTHER PRODUCT? (Y OR N)?? N

PROCESSING COMPLETE

BREAK IN 520
OK
```

```
  MAJOR SYMBOL TABLE - ANALYSIS                              FUNCTIONS USED
I----------------------------------------------------------I  I-----------------I
I NAME   .. DESCRIPTION                                    I  I  NAME           I
I----------------------------------------------------------I  I-----------------I
I  A$    .. TEMP ANSWER VARIABLE                           I  I TAB             I
I  A1    .. AVERAGE ON-HAND                                I  I DIM             I
I  A2    .. AVERAGE VALUE ON-HAND                          I  I-----------------I
I  A3    .. TURNOVER=COST OF GOODS/AVG INVENTORY           I
I  C     .. COST OF GOODS SOLD                             I
I  I     .. INDEX AND ARRAY POINTER                        I
I  N     .. NUMBER OF MONTHS TO ANALYZE                    I
I  N$    .. PRODUCT NAME                                   I
I  O()   .. ON-HAND ARRAY                                  I
I  T     .. TOTAL ON-HAND                                  I
I  V     .. AVERAGE VALUE OF INVENTORY ITEM                I
I  X$    .. LINE OF ASTERISKS                              I
I----------------------------------------------------------I
```

Inventory Use Projections

Program Name: PROJECT

This program projects inventory usage based upon the least squares regression projection method. All data is entered through the keyboard in response to program messages.

Comment: This program can be extended easily to interface with either the perpetual or periodic inventory systems.

Files Affected: None

```
10 REM            SAVED AT PROJECT
20 REM       INVENTORY USE PROJECTION PROGRAM
30 REM ***********************************************************
40 X$="*********************************************************"
50 PRINT
60 PRINT
70 PRINT "ENTER THE NUMBER OF MONTHS TO BE ANALYZED";
80 INPUT N
90 PRINT "ENTER THE PRODUCT NAME";
100 INPUT N$
110 X1=0
120 Y1=0
130 Z1=0
140 X2=0
150 PRINT "ENTER THE AMOUNT USED FOR THE FOLLOWING PERIODS"
160 PRINT
170 PRINT "PERIOD      ON-HAND"
180 FOR XO=1 TO N
190   PRINT XO;TAB(10);
200   INPUT YO
210   Y1=Y1+YO
220   X1=X1+XO
230   Z1=Z1+XO*YO
240   X2=X2+XO^2
250 NEXT XO
260 PRINT "ENTER THE AVERAGE COST OF THE PRODUCT";
270 INPUT V
280 REM ***********************************************************
290 REM           COMPUTATIONS
300 REM ***********************************************************
310 A=(X2*Y1-X1*Z1)/(N*X2-X1^2)
320 B=(N*Z1-X1*Y1)/(N*X2-X1^2)
330 Y9=A+B*(N+1)
340 A1=Y1/N
350 A2=V*A1
360 PRINT
370 REM ***********************************************************
380 REM             PRINT OF RESULTS
390 REM ***********************************************************
400 PRINT X$
410 PRINT
420 PRINT TAB(20);"INVENTORY USE PROJECTION"
430 PRINT TAB(20);"LEAST SQUARES REGRESSION"
440 PRINT TAB(25);N$
450 PRINT
460 PRINT TAB(10);"AVG USED";TAB(25);"AVG COST";TAB(40);"PROJECTED"
470 PRINT
480 PRINT TAB(12);A1;TAB(25);A2;TAB(40);Y9
490 PRINT
```

```
500 PRINT X$
510 PRINT
520 PRINT "ANOTHER PRODUCT? (Y OR N)?";
530 INPUT A$
540 IF A$="Y" THEN 90
550 REM *****************************************************************
560 REM            PROGRAM TERMINATION POINT
570 REM *****************************************************************
580 PRINT
590 PRINT "PROCESSING COMPLETE"
600 PRINT
610 STOP
```

RUN "PROJECT"

ENTER THE NUMBER OF MONTHS TO BE ANALYZED? 6
ENTER THE PRODUCT NAME? SUPER Q-TYPE WIDGET
ENTER THE AMOUNT USED FOR THE FOLLOWING PERIODS

PERIOD   ON-HAND
1   ? 10
2   ? 20
3   ? 30
4   ? 40
5   ? 50
6   ? 60
ENTER THE AVERAGE COST OF THE PRODUCT? 10

****
                    INVENTORY USE PROJECTION
                    LEAST SQUARES REGRESSION
                      SUPER Q-TYPE WIDGET

       AVG USED   AVG COST   PROJECTED

          35   350   69.9999

****

ANOTHER PRODUCT? (Y OR N)?? Y
ENTER THE PRODUCT NAME? BUDGET WIDGET
ENTER THE AMOUNT USED FOR THE FOLLOWING PERIODS

PERIOD   ON-HAND
1   ? 5
2   ? 10
3   ? 15
4   ? 20
5   ? 25
6   ? 30
ENTER THE AVERAGE COST OF THE PRODUCT? 10

****
                    INVENTORY USE PROJECTION
                    LEAST SQUARES REGRESSION
                        BUDGET WIDGET

       AVG USED   AVG COST   PROJECTED

         17.5   175   34.9999

****

196   BASIC Computer Programs for Business
```
```

```
ANOTHER PRODUCT? (Y OR N)?? N

PROCESSING COMPLETE

BREAK IN 610
OK
```

```
     MAJOR SYMBOL TABLE - PROJECT                              FUNCTIONS USED
I-------------------------------------------------I         I---------------I
I NAME    .. DESCRIPTION                          I         I  NAME         I
I-------------------------------------------------I         I---------------I
I  A      .. VALUE OF Y INTERCEPT                 I         I TAB           I
I  A$     .. TEMP ANSWER VARIABLE                 I         I---------------I
I  A1     .. AVERAGE USE                          I
I  A2     .. AVERAGE COST OF MATERIALS USED       I
I  B      .. SLOPE OF REGRESSION LINE             I
I  N      .. NUMBER OF MONTHS TO USE              I
I  N$     .. PRODUCT NAME                         I
I  V      .. AVERAGE UNIT COST OF THE PRODUCT     I
I  X$     .. LINE OF ASTERISKS                    I
I  XO     .. PERIOD NUMBER                        I
I  X1     .. SUM OF XO                            I
I  X2     .. SUM OF XO SQUARED                    I
I  YO     .. PERIOD USE                           I
I  Y1     .. SUM OF YO                            I
I  Y9     .. PROJECTED USE                        I
I  Z1     .. SUM OF XO TIMES YO                   I
I-------------------------------------------------I
```

Asset Control/Accounting

Program Name: ASSETS

This program uses sequential file handling to perform all functions required for the recording, updating, and printing of assets and for citing those individuals responsible for them, these actions being controlled by the operator's responses to program messages. The first time the program is executed (or when the deletion of all previous entries is desired), the operator must answer "Y" to the question, "ARE YOU INITIALIZING THE SYSTEM (Y OR N)?" Once the system has been initialized, any one of the following six options is available:

Option 1 allows the printing of the file in its current order. If desired, the printing can be in label format.

Option 2 allows the printing of the file grouped by the first L characters of the stock number.

Option 3 allows the printing of the file grouped by the first L characters of the description.

Option 4 allows the printing of the file grouped by the first L characters of the location.

Option 5 allows the printing of the file, in order, by the first L characters of the responsible individual's name.

Option 6 allows the operator to update the files. Individual records can be inserted (code I), deleted (code D), or changed (code C). The insert code requests record information from the operator and then inserts the new record immediately following the current record position. The delete code causes the current record (from the input file) not to be written to the new output file. The change code replaces the current input record with new information prior to writing the record to the file.

Figure 7-1 illustrates the program's options.

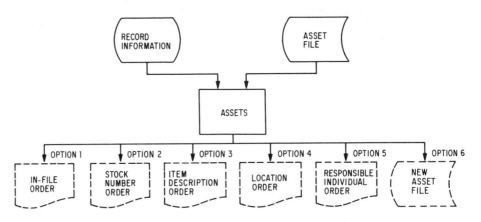

Fig. 7-1 Operation of the asset control/accounting program

Two sequential files are used by this program—one for input, the other for output. Requesting option 6 (updating files) creates an output file containing all new records. Depending on the action codes specified, the records from the input file will be written to the new file in sequential order, replaced by a new record, or ignored and therefore not written to the new file. The format of the files is shown in Fig. 7-2.

Stock number	Item description	Location	Responsible party
I$(1)	I$(2)	I$(3)	I$(4)

Fig. 7-2 Record format

Comment: Using sequential files in this manner allows files to be recovered by stepping back to a previous file and processing only the updates to it.

Suggested enhancement: You may wish to sort the groups before printing. A simple sort of array S$( ) will provide sorted output.

```
10 REM              SAVED AT ASSETS
20 REM                ASSET CONTROL PROGRAM
30 REM ****************************************************************
40 X$="****************************************************************"
50 M=50
60 M1=10000
70 DIM S$(M),H$(10),T(4),I$(4),I1(4)
80 H$(1)="CURRENT FILE CONTENTS"
90 H$(2)="STOCK NUMBER"
100 H$(3)="ITEM DESCRIPTION"
110 H$(4)="LOCATION"
120 H$(5)="RESPONSIBLE PARTY"
130 H$(6)=" "
140 H$(7)="STOCK NBR"
150 H$(8)="ITEM DESCRIPTION"
160 H$(9)="LOCATION"
170 H$(10)="RESPONSIBLE PARTY"
180 T(1)=10
190 T(2)=20
200 T(3)=10
210 T(4)=20
220 PRINT
230 PRINT
240 I=1
250 PRINT "ARE YOU INITIALIZING THE SYSTEM (Y OR N)";
260 INPUT A$
270 PRINT "ENTER FILE NAME OF ASSET FILE";
280 INPUT F$
290 IF A$<>"Y" THEN 400
300 PRINT "WARNING - FILES BY THE NAME OF ";F$;" WILL BE OVERWRITTEN"
310 PRINT "IS THAT WHAT YOU WANT TO DO (Y OR N)";
320 INPUT A$
330 IF A$<>"Y" THEN 730
340 F1$=F$
350 I=2
360 GOSUB 740                    'FILE OPEN
370 GOSUB 2280
380 CLOSE 2
390 I=1
400 GOSUB 740                    'FILE OPEN
410 PRINT
420 PRINT X$
430 PRINT "THE FOLLOWING OPTIONS ARE AVAILABLE:"
440 PRINT TAB(5);"NBR      ACTION"
450 PRINT TAB(5);"1..PRINTING THE FILE IN ITS PRESENT ORDER"
460 PRINT TAB(5);"2..PRINTING THE FILE IN ORDER BY STOCK NUMBER"
470 PRINT TAB(5);"3..PRINTING THE FILE IN ORDER BY ITEM (6 CHAR)"
480 PRINT TAB(5);"4..PRINTING THE ITEM IN ORDER BY LOCATION"
490 PRINT TAB(5);"5..PRINTING THE FILE IN ORDER BY RESPONSIBLE PARTY"
500 PRINT    TAB(5);"--------------------------------------------------"
510 PRINT TAB(5);"6..UPDATING THE FILE"
520 PRINT
530 PRINT "ENTER OPTION NUMBER";
540 O=0
550 INPUT O
560 IF O=1 THEN GOSUB 800              'PRINT FILE
570 IF O=2 THEN GOSUB 1490             'STOCK NUMBER ORDER
580 IF O=3 THEN GOSUB 1610             'ITEM ORDER
590 IF O=4 THEN GOSUB 1730             'LOCATION ORDER
600 IF O=5 THEN GOSUB 1850             'RESPONSIBILITY ORDER
610 IF O=6 THEN GOSUB 1970             'UPDATE FILE
```

```
620 IF O=0 THEN 680
630 IF O=6 THEN 670
640 CLOSE 1,2
650 GOTO 390
660 REM ****************************************************************
670 REM                 PROGRAM TERMINATION POINT
680 REM ****************************************************************
690 PRINT
700 PRINT
710 PRINT "PROCESSING COMPLETE"
720 PRINT
730 STOP


740 REM ****************************************************************
750 REM               FILE OPEN
760 REM ****************************************************************
770 IF I=1 THEN OPEN "I",I,F$,0
780 IF I=2 THEN OPEN "O",I,F1$,0
790 RETURN


800 REM ****************************************************************
810 REM               PRINT FILE
820 REM ****************************************************************
830 I1(1)=1
840 I1(2)=2
850 I1(3)=3
860 I1(4)=4
870 PRINT "SHALL I PRINT IN LABEL FORMAT (Y OR N)";
880 INPUT T$
890 IF T$="N" THEN GOSUB 1310            'HEADING
900 IF EOF(1) THEN 960
910 GOSUB 970                            'INPUT RECORD
920 K1=K1+1
930 IF T$="N" THEN GOSUB 1070            'PRINT LINE
940 IF T$="Y" THEN GOSUB 1190            'PRINT LABEL
950 GOTO 900
960 RETURN


970 REM ****************************************************************
980 REM               INPUT RECORD
990 REM ****************************************************************
1000 INPUT#1,I$(1),I$(2),I$(3),I$(4)
1010 RETURN


1020 REM ****************************************************************
1030 REM               WRITE RECORD
1040 REM ****************************************************************
1050 PRINT#2,I$(1);",";I$(2);",";I$(3);",";I$(4)
1060 RETURN


1070 REM ****************************************************************
1080 REM                 PRINT LINE
1090 REM ****************************************************************
1100 FOR J1=1 TO 4
1110    TO=TO+T(I1(J1))
1120    PRINT I$(I1(J1));TAB(TO);
1130 NEXT J1
1140 IF O=1 THEN PRINT K1;
1150 TO=0
1160 PRINT
1170 RETURN
```

```
1180 REM*******************************************************************
1190 REM                    PRINT LABEL
1200 REM ******************************************************************
1210 N=N+1
1220 IF N>1 THEN  1250
1230 PRINT "ALIGN LABELS NOW";
1240 INPUT A$
1250 PRINT
1260 PRINT I$(1);TAB(10);I$(2)
1270 PRINT I$(3)
1280 PRINT I$(4)
1290 PRINT
1300 RETURN


1310 REM ******************************************************************
1320 REM                    PRINT HEADINGS
1330 REM ******************************************************************
1340 PRINT "POSITION PAPER NOW";
1350 INPUT A$
1360 PRINT
1370 PRINT X$
1380 PRINT
1390 PRINT TAB(10);"ASSET LISTING - IN ORDER BY: ";H$(O)
1400 PRINT
1410 FOR J=1 TO 4
1420    TO=TO+T(I1(J))
1430    PRINT H$(6+I1(J));TAB(TO);
1440 NEXT J
1450 TO=0
1460 PRINT
1470 PRINT
1480 RETURN


1490 REM ******************************************************************
1500 REM             STOCK NUMBER ORDER
1510 REM ******************************************************************
1520 N=1
1530 I1(1)=1
1540 I1(2)=2
1550 I1(3)=3
1560 I1(4)=4
1570 L=6
1580 GOSUB  2500                  'CHECK ARRAY
1590 GOSUB 2630                    'PRINT GROUPED RESULTS
1600 RETURN


1610 REM ******************************************************************
1620 REM             ITEM DESCRIPTION ORDER
1630 REM ******************************************************************
1640 L=6
1650 N=2
1660 I1(1)=2
1670 I1(2)=1
1680 I1(3)=3
1690 I1(4)=4
1700 GOSUB 2500                   'CHECK ARRAY
1710 GOSUB 2630                   'PRINT GROUPED RESULTS
1720 RETURN


1730 REM ******************************************************************
1740 REM             LOCATION ORDER
1750 REM ******************************************************************
1760 L=6
1770 I1(1)=3
```

```
1780 I1(2)=1
1790 I1(3)=2
1800 I1(4)=4
1810 N=3
1820 GOSUB 2500                    'CHECK ARRAY
1830 GOSUB 2630                    'PRINT GROUPED RESULTS
1840 RETURN


1850 REM ****************************************************************
1860 REM                   RESPONSIBILITY ORDER
1870 REM ****************************************************************
1880 L=6
1890 N=4
1900 I1(1)=4
1910 I1(2)=1
1920 I1(3)=2
1930 I1(4)=3
1940 GOSUB 2500                    'CHECK ARRAY
1950 GOSUB 2630                    'PRINT GROUPED RESULTS
1960 RETURN


1970 REM ****************************************************************
1980 REM                   UPDATE FILE
1990 REM ****************************************************************
2000 J1=1
2010 I=2
2020 PRINT "ENTER THE FILE NAME FOR THE UPDATED FILE";
2030 INPUT F1$
2040 GOSUB 740                     'FILE OPEN
2050 PRINT "ENTER THE RECORD # TO PROCESS";
2060 INPUT N1
2070 FOR J=J1 TO N1
2080    IF EOF(1) THEN 2120
2090    GOSUB 970                  'INPUT RECORD
2100    IF J<N1 THEN GOSUB 1020        'WRITE RECORD
2110 NEXT J
2120 J1=N1+1
2130 IF A$="S" THEN 2270
2140 IF EOF(1) THEN PRINT "AT END-OF-FILE";
2150 PRINT " DELETE(D),CHANGE(C),INSERT(I), OR STOP (S)";
2160 INPUT A$
2170 IF A$<>"S" THEN 2210
2180 N1=M1
2190 IF NOT EOF(1) THEN GOSUB 1020                      'WRITE RECORD
2200 GOTO 2070
2210 IF A$="D" THEN 2050
2220 IF A$="I" AND NOT EOF(1) THEN GOSUB 1020    'WRITE RECORD
2230 GOSUB 2380                    '          ACCEPT RECORD
2240 GOSUB 1020                    'WRITE RECORD
2250 IF EOF(1) THEN 2140
2260 GOTO 2050
2270 RETURN


2280 REM ****************************************************************
2290 REM                   INITIALIZE RECORDS
2300 REM ****************************************************************
2310 PRINT "ENTER RECORDS (JUST PRESS RETURN TO STOP)"
2320 I$(1)=""
2330 GOSUB 2380                    'ACCEPT RECORD
2340 IF I$(1)="" THEN 2370
2350 GOSUB 1020                    'WRITE RECORD
2360 GOTO 2320
2370 RETURN
```

```
2380 REM ****************************************************************
2390 REM                    ACCEPT RECORD
2400 REM ****************************************************************
2410 PRINT "ENTER THE STOCK NUMBER";
2420 INPUT I$(1)
2430 PRINT "ENTER THE ITEM DESCRIPTION";
2440 INPUT I$(2)
2450 PRINT "ENTER THE ASSET'S LOCATION";
2460 INPUT I$(3)
2470 PRINT "ENTER THE RESPONSIBLE PARTY";
2480 INPUT I$(4)
2490 RETURN


2500 REM ****************************************************************
2510 REM                    CHECK ARRAY
2520 REM ****************************************************************
2530 K=0
2540 IF EOF(1) THEN 2620
2550 GOSUB 970                    'INPUT RECORD
2560 K=K+1
2570 FOR J=1 TO K
2580   IF S$(J)=LEFT$(I$(N),L) THEN 2610
2590 NEXT J
2600 S$(K)=LEFT$(I$(N),L)
2610 GOTO 2540
2620 RETURN


2630 REM ****************************************************************
2640 REM                    PRINT GROUPED RESULTS
2650 REM ****************************************************************
2660 GOSUB 1310                   'PRINT HEADINGS
2670 I=1
2680 FOR J=1 TO K
2690   CLOSE 1
2700   GOSUB 750                  'OPEN FILE
2710   IF EOF(1) THEN 2750
2720   GOSUB 970                  'INPUT FILE
2730   IF S$(J)=LEFT$(I$(N),L) THEN GOSUB 1070   'PRINT LINE
2740   GOTO 2710
2750   S$(J)="       "
2760 NEXT J
2770 RETURN




RUN "ASSETS"


ARE YOU INITIALIZING THE SYSTEM (Y OR N)? Y
ENTER FILE NAME OF ASSET FILE? AFILE
WARNING - FILES BY THE NAME OF AFILE WILL BE OVERWRITTEN
IS THAT WHAT YOU WANT TO DO (Y OR N)? Y
ENTER RECORDS (JUST PRESS RETURN TO STOP)
ENTER THE STOCK NUMBER? 11111
ENTER THE ITEM DESCRIPTION? 60 X 36 DESK
ENTER THE ASSET'S LOCATION? B624
ENTER THE RESPONSIBLE PARTY? JOHN SMITH
ENTER THE STOCK NUMBER? 22222
ENTER THE ITEM DESCRIPTION? TABLE
ENTER THE ASSET'S LOCATION? B624
ENTER THE RESPONSIBLE PARTY? JOE JONES
ENTER THE STOCK NUMBER? 33333
```

```
ENTER THE ITEM DESCRIPTION? COFFEE POT
ENTER THE ASSET'S LOCATION? B100
ENTER THE RESPONSIBLE PARTY? JOHN SMITH
ENTER THE STOCK NUMBER?
ENTER THE ITEM DESCRIPTION?
ENTER THE ASSET'S LOCATION?
ENTER THE RESPONSIBLE PARTY?


**************************************************************************
THE FOLLOWING OPTIONS ARE AVAILABLE:
     NBR       ACTION
     1..PRINTING THE FILE IN ITS PRESENT ORDER
     2..PRINTING THE FILE IN ORDER BY STOCK NUMBER
     3..PRINTING THE FILE IN ORDER BY ITEM (6 CHAR)
     4..PRINTING THE ITEM IN ORDER BY LOCATION
     5..PRINTING THE FILE IN ORDER BY RESPONSIBLE PARTY
     -----------------------------------------------------------------
     6..UPDATING THE FILE

ENTER OPTION NUMBER? 1
SHALL I PRINT IN LABEL FORMAT (Y OR N)? N
POSITION PAPER NOW?

**************************************************************************
          ASSET LISTING - IN ORDER BY: CURRENT FILE CONTENTS

STOCK NBR ITEM DESCRIPTION    LOCATION  RESPONSIBLE PARTY

11111     60 X 36 DESK        B624      JOHN SMITH             1
22222     TABLE               B624      JOE JONES              2
33333     COFFEE POT          B100      JOHN SMITH             3

**************************************************************************
THE FOLLOWING OPTIONS ARE AVAILABLE:
     NBR       ACTION
     1..PRINTING THE FILE IN ITS PRESENT ORDER
     2..PRINTING THE FILE IN ORDER BY STOCK NUMBER
     3..PRINTING THE FILE IN ORDER BY ITEM (6 CHAR)
     4..PRINTING THE ITEM IN ORDER BY LOCATION
     5..PRINTING THE FILE IN ORDER BY RESPONSIBLE PARTY
     -----------------------------------------------------------------
     6..UPDATING THE FILE

ENTER OPTION NUMBER?

PROCESSING COMPLETE




RUN "ASSETS"


ARE YOU INITIALIZING THE SYSTEM (Y OR N)? N
ENTER FILE NAME OF ASSET FILE? AFILE

**************************************************************************
THE FOLLOWING OPTIONS ARE AVAILABLE:
     NBR       ACTION
     1..PRINTING THE FILE IN ITS PRESENT ORDER
     2..PRINTING THE FILE IN ORDER BY STOCK NUMBER
     3..PRINTING THE FILE IN ORDER BY ITEM (6 CHAR)
     4..PRINTING THE ITEM IN ORDER BY LOCATION
     5..PRINTING THE FILE IN ORDER BY RESPONSIBLE PARTY
     -----------------------------------------------------------------
     6..UPDATING THE FILE
```

```
ENTER OPTION NUMBER? 6
ENTER THE FILE NAME FOR THE UPDATED FILE? NEWAFILE
ENTER THE RECORD # TO PROCESS? 1
  DELETE(D),CHANGE(C),INSERT(I), OR STOP (S)? C
ENTER THE STOCK NUMBER? 11111A
ENTER THE ITEM DESCRIPTION? 60 X 48 DESK
ENTER THE ASSET'S LOCATION? B624
ENTER THE RESPONSIBLE PARTY? JOHN SMITH
ENTER THE RECORD # TO PROCESS? 5
AT END-OF-FILE DELETE(D),CHANGE(C),INSERT(I), OR STOP (S)? I
ENTER THE STOCK NUMBER? 11111B
ENTER THE ITEM DESCRIPTION? 48 X 48 DESK
ENTER THE ASSET'S LOCATION? B624
ENTER THE RESPONSIBLE PARTY? JOE JONES
AT END-OF-FILE DELETE(D),CHANGE(C),INSERT(I), OR STOP (S)? S


PROCESSING COMPLETE

BREAK IN 730
OK




RUN "ASSETS"


ARE YOU INITIALIZING THE SYSTEM (Y OR N)? N
ENTER FILE NAME OF ASSET FILE? NEWAFILE

****************************************************************
THE FOLLOWING OPTIONS ARE AVAILABLE:
     NBR      ACTION
     1..PRINTING THE FILE IN ITS PRESENT ORDER
     2..PRINTING THE FILE IN ORDER BY STOCK NUMBER
     3..PRINTING THE FILE IN ORDER BY ITEM (6 CHAR)
     4..PRINTING THE ITEM IN ORDER BY LOCATION
     5..PRINTING THE FILE IN ORDER BY RESPONSIBLE PARTY
     --------------------------------------------------------
     6..UPDATING THE FILE

ENTER OPTION NUMBER? 1
SHALL I PRINT IN LABEL FORMAT (Y OR N)? N
POSITION PAPER NOW?

****************************************************************

          ASSET LISTING - IN ORDER BY: CURRENT FILE CONTENTS

STOCK NBR ITEM DESCRIPTION     LOCATION  RESPONSIBLE PARTY

11111A    60 X 48 DESK         B624      JOHN SMITH        1
22222     TABLE                B624      JOE JONES         2
33333     COFFEE POT           B100      JOHN SMITH        3
11111B    48 X 48 DESK         B624      JOE JONES         4

****************************************************************
THE FOLLOWING OPTIONS ARE AVAILABLE:
     NBR      ACTION
     1..PRINTING THE FILE IN ITS PRESENT ORDER
     2..PRINTING THE FILE IN ORDER BY STOCK NUMBER
     3..PRINTING THE FILE IN ORDER BY ITEM (6 CHAR)
     4..PRINTING THE ITEM IN ORDER BY LOCATION
     5..PRINTING THE FILE IN ORDER BY RESPONSIBLE PARTY
     --------------------------------------------------------
     6..UPDATING THE FILE
```

```
ENTER OPTION NUMBER? 4
POSITION PAPER NOW?

****************************************************************
           ASSET LISTING - IN ORDER BY: LOCATION

LOCATION   STOCK NBR ITEM DESCRIPTION      RESPONSIBLE PARTY

B624       11111A    60 X 48 DESK          JOHN SMITH
B624       22222     TABLE                 JOE JONES
B624       11111B    48 X 48 DESK          JOE JONES
B100       33333     COFFEE POT            JOHN SMITH

****************************************************************
THE FOLLOWING OPTIONS ARE AVAILABLE:
     NBR       ACTION
     1..PRINTING THE FILE IN ITS PRESENT ORDER
     2..PRINTING THE FILE IN ORDER BY STOCK NUMBER
     3..PRINTING THE FILE IN ORDER BY ITEM (6 CHAR)
     4..PRINTING THE ITEM IN ORDER BY LOCATION
     5..PRINTING THE FILE IN ORDER BY RESPONSIBLE PARTY
     6..UPDATING THE FILE

ENTER OPTION NUMBER? 5
POSITION PAPER NOW?

****************************************************************
           ASSET LISTING - IN ORDER BY: RESPONSIBLE PARTY

RESPONSIBLE PARTY    STOCK NBR ITEM DESCRIPTION     LOCATION

JOHN SMITH           11111A    60 X 48 DESK         B624
JOHN SMITH           33333     COFFEE POT           B100
JOE JONES            22222     TABLE                B624
JOE JONES            11111B    48 X 48 DESK         B624

****************************************************************
THE FOLLOWING OPTIONS ARE AVAILABLE:
     NBR       ACTION
     1..PRINTING THE FILE IN ITS PRESENT ORDER
     2..PRINTING THE FILE IN ORDER BY STOCK NUMBER
     3..PRINTING THE FILE IN ORDER BY ITEM (6 CHAR)
     4..PRINTING THE ITEM IN ORDER BY LOCATION
     5..PRINTING THE FILE IN ORDER BY RESPONSIBLE PARTY
     ----------------------------------------------------
     6..UPDATING THE FILE

ENTER OPTION NUMBER?


PROCESSING COMPLETE

BREAK IN 730
OK
```

```
    MAJOR SYMBOL TABLE - ASSETS                        FUNCTIONS USED
I----------------------------------------------I     I-----------------I
I NAME    .. DESCRIPTION                        I     I   NAME          I
I----------------------------------------------I     I-----------------I
I  A$     .. INPUT ANSWER VARIABLE              I     I OPEN            I
I  F$     .. INPUT FILE NAME                    I     I CLOSE           I
I  F1$    .. OUTPUT FILE NAME                   I     I GOSUB           I
I  H$()   .. HEADING ARRAY                      I     I RETURN          I
I  I      .. FILE NUMBER                        I     I DIM             I
I  I$()   .. DATA FIELDS                        I     I TAB             I
I  I1()   .. ORDER OF PRINTING ARRAY            I     I INPUT#          I
I  J      .. INDEX AND ARRAY POINTER            I     I PRINT#          I
I  J1     .. INDEX AND ARRAY POINTER            I     I EOF(1)          I
I  K      .. COUNTER FOR GROUP VALUE ARRAY      I     I LEFT$           I
I  K1     .. RECORD PRINT COUNTER               I     I-----------------I
I  L      .. LENGTH OF FIELD TO COMPARE         I
I  M      .. MAXIMUM NUMBER OF GROUPS           I
I  M1     .. MAXIMUM NUMBER OF DATA RECORDS     I
I  N      .. GROUPING FIELD                     I
I  N1     .. RECORD POINTER FOR UPDATING        I
I  O      .. OPTION NUMBER                      I
I  S$()   .. GROUP VALUE ARRAY                  I
I  T$     .. PRINT FORMAT 'Y'=LABELS            I
I  T()    .. TAB SIZES FOR DATA FILES           I
I  TO     .. CURRENT TAB POISTION               I
I  X$     .. LINE OF ASTERISKS                  I
I----------------------------------------------I
```

Material Locator

Program Name: WARE-INV

This program uses sequential file handling to perform all required functions for the recording, updating, and printing of the location (warehouse or other) of goods or materials, its actions being controlled by the operator's responses to program messages. The first time the program is executed (or when deletion of all previous entries is desired), the operator must answer "Y" to the question, "ARE YOU INITIALIZING THE SYSTEM (Y OR N)?" Once the system has been initialized, any one of the following five options is available:

Option 1 allows the printing of the file in its current order. If desired, the printing can be in label format.

Option 2 allows the printing of the file grouped by the first L positions of the stock number.

Option 3 allows the printing of the file grouped by the first L positions of the item description.

Option 4 allows the printing of the file grouped by the first L positions of the warehouse location.

Option 5 allows the operator to update the files. Individual records can be inserted (code I), deleted (code D), or changed (code C). The insert code requests record information from the operator and then inserts the new record immediately following the current record position. The delete code causes the current record (from the input file) not to be written to the new output file. The change code replaces the current input record with the new information prior to writing the record to the file.

Figure 7-3 illustrates the program's options.

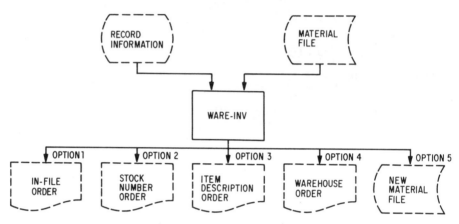

Fig. 7-3 Operation of the material locator program

Two sequential files are used by this program—one for input, the other for output. Requesting option 5 (updating files) creates an output file containing all new records. Depending on the action codes specified by the operator, the records from the input file will be written to the new file in sequential order, replaced by a new record, or ignored and therefore not written to the new file. The format of the files is shown in Fig. 7-4.

Stock number	Item description	Warehouse	Warehouse section/bin
I$(1)	I$(2)	I$(3)	I$(4)

Fig. 7-4 Record format

Comment: Using sequential files in this manner allows files to be recovered by stepping back to a previous file and processing only the updates to it.

Suggested enhancement: You may wish to sort the groups before printing. A simple sort of array S$( ) will provide sorted output.

```
10 REM            SAVED AT WARE-INV
20 REM     WAREHOUSE INVENTORY LOCATION PROGRAM
30 REM ****************************************************************
40 X$="****************************************************************"
50 M=50
60 M1=10000
70 DIM S$(M),H$(8),T(4),I$(4),I1(4)
80 H$(1)="CURRENT FILE CONTENTS"
90 H$(2)="STOCK NUMBER"
100 H$(3)="ITEM DESCRIPTION"
110 H$(4)="WAREHOUSE"
120 H$(5)="STOCK NBR"
130 H$(6)="ITEM DESCRIPTION"
140 H$(7)="WAREHOUSE"
150 H$(8)="SECTION"
160 T(1)=10
170 T(2)=30
180 T(3)=10
190 T(4)=10
200 PRINT
210 PRINT
220 I=1
230 PRINT "ARE YOU INITIALIZING THE SYSTEM (Y OR N)";
240 INPUT A$
250 PRINT "ENTER FILE NAME OF WAREHOUSE FILE";
260 INPUT F$
270 IF A$<>"Y" THEN 380
280 PRINT "WARNING - FILES BY THE NAME OF ";F$;" WILL BE OVERWRITTEN"
290 PRINT "IS THAT WHAT YOU WANT TO DO (Y OR N)";
300 INPUT A$
310 IF A$<>"Y" THEN 690
320 F1$=F$
330 I=2
340 GOSUB 700                    'FILE OPEN
350 GOSUB 2120
360 CLOSE 2
370 I=1
380 GOSUB 700                    'FILE OPEN
390 PRINT
400 PRINT X$
410 PRINT "THE FOLLOWING OPTIONS ARE AVAILABLE:"
420 PRINT TAB(5);"NBR       ACTION"
430 PRINT TAB(5);"1..PRINTING THE FILE IN ITS PRESENT ORDER"
440 PRINT TAB(5);"2..PRINTING THE FILE IN ORDER BY STOCK NUMBER"
450 PRINT TAB(5);"3..PRINTING THE FILE IN ORDER BY ITEM (6 CHAR)"
460 PRINT TAB(5);"4..PRINTING THE ITEM IN ORDER BY WAREHOUSE"
470 PRINT   TAB(5);"-----------------------------------------------"
480 PRINT TAB(5);"5..UPDATING THE FILE"
490 PRINT
500 PRINT "ENTER OPTION NUMBER";
510 O=0
520 INPUT O
530 IF O=1 THEN GOSUB 760        'PRINT FILE
540 IF O=2 THEN GOSUB 1450       'STOCK NUMBER ORDER
550 IF O=3 THEN GOSUB 1570       'ITEM ORDER
560 IF O=4 THEN GOSUB 1690       'WAREHOUSE ORDER
570 IF O=5 THEN GOSUB 1810       'UPDATE FILE
580 IF O=0 THEN 640
590 IF O=5 THEN 630
600 CLOSE 1,2
610 GOTO 370
620 REM ****************************************************************
630 REM            PROGRAM TERMINATION POINT
640 REM ****************************************************************
650 PRINT
660 PRINT
670 PRINT "PROCESSING COMPLETE"
680 PRINT
690 STOP
```

```
700 REM ************************************************************
710 REM              FILE OPEN
720 REM ************************************************************
730 IF I=1 THEN OPEN "I",I,F$,0
740 IF I=2 THEN OPEN "O",I,F1$,0
750 RETURN


760 REM ************************************************************
770 REM              PRINT FILE
780 REM ************************************************************
790 I1(1)=1
800 I1(2)=2
810 I1(3)=3
820 I1(4)=4
830 PRINT "SHALL I PRINT IN LABEL FORMAT (Y OR N)";
840 INPUT T$
850 IF T$="N" THEN GOSUB 1270              'HEADING
860 IF EOF(1) THEN 920
870 GOSUB 930                              'INPUT RECORD
880 K1=K1+1
890 IF T$="N" THEN GOSUB 1030              'PRINT LINE
900 IF T$="Y" THEN GOSUB 1150              'PRINT LABEL
910 GOTO 860
920 RETURN


930 REM ************************************************************
940 REM               INPUT RECORD
950 REM ************************************************************
960 INPUT#1,I$(1),I$(2),I$(3),I$(4)
970 RETURN


980 REM ************************************************************
990 REM              WRITE RECORD
1000 REM ************************************************************
1010 PRINT#2,I$(1);",";I$(2);",";I$(3);",";I$(4)
1020 RETURN


1030 REM ************************************************************
1040 REM               PRINT LINE
1050 REM ************************************************************
1060 FOR J1=1 TO 4
1070    T0=T0+T(I1(J1))
1080    PRINT I$(I1(J1));TAB(T0);
1090 NEXT J1
1100 IF O=1 THEN PRINT K1;
1110 T0=0
1120 PRINT
1130 RETURN


1140 REM ************************************************************
1150 REM               PRINT LABEL
1160 REM ************************************************************
1170 N=N+1
1180 IF N>1 THEN   1210
1190 PRINT "ALIGN LABELS NOW";
1200 INPUT A$
1210 PRINT
1220 PRINT I$(1);TAB(10);I$(2)
1230 PRINT I$(3)
1240 PRINT I$(4)
1250 PRINT
1260 RETURN
```

```
1270 REM *************************************************************
1280 REM                  PRINT HEADINGS
1290 REM *************************************************************
1300 PRINT "POSITION PAPER NOW";
1310 INPUT A$
1320 PRINT
1330 PRINT X$
1340 PRINT
1350 PRINT TAB(10);"ASSET LISTING - IN ORDER BY: ";H$(O)
1360 PRINT
1370 FOR J=1 TO 4
1380   TO=TO+T(I1(J))
1390   PRINT H$(4+I1(J));TAB(TO);
1400 NEXT J
1410 TO=0
1420 PRINT
1430 PRINT
1440 RETURN


1450 REM *************************************************************
1460 REM               STOCK NUMBER ORDER
1470 REM *************************************************************
1480 N=1
1490 I1(1)=1
1500 I1(2)=2
1510 I1(3)=3
1520 I1(4)=4
1530 L=6
1540 GOSUB  2340              'CHECK ARRAY
1550 GOSUB  2470              'PRINT GROUPED RESULTS
1560 RETURN


1570 REM *************************************************************
1580 REM              ITEM DESCRIPTION ORDER
1590 REM *************************************************************
1600 L=6
1610 N=2
1620 I1(1)=2
1630 I1(2)=1
1640 I1(3)=3
1650 I1(4)=4
1660 GOSUB 2340              'CHECK ARRAY
1670 GOSUB 2470              'PRINT GROUPED RESULTS
1680 RETURN


1690 REM *************************************************************
1700 REM              WAREHOUSE LOCATION ORDER
1710 REM *************************************************************
1720 L=6
1730 I1(1)=3
1740 I1(2)=4
1750 I1(3)=1
1760 I1(4)=2
1770 N=3
1780 GOSUB 2340              'CHECK ARRAY
1790 GOSUB 2470              'PRINT GROUPED RESULTS
1800 RETURN


1810 REM *************************************************************
1820 REM              UPDATE FILE
1830 REM *************************************************************
1840 J1=1
1850 I=2
```

```
1860 PRINT "ENTER THE FILE NAME FOR THE UPDATED FILE";
1870 INPUT F1$
1880 GOSUB 700                    'FILE OPEN
1890 PRINT "ENTER THE RECORD # TO PROCESS";
1900 INPUT N1
1910 FOR J=J1 TO N1
1920   IF EOF(1) THEN 1960
1930   GOSUB 930                   'INPUT RECORD
1940   IF J<N1 THEN GOSUB 980             'WRITE RECORD
1950 NEXT J
1960 J1=N1+1
1970 IF A$="S" THEN 2110
1980 IF EOF(1) THEN PRINT "AT END-OF-FILE";
1990 PRINT " DELETE(D),CHANGE(C),INSERT(I), OR STOP (S)";
2000 INPUT A$
2010 IF A$<>"S" THEN 2050
2020 N1=M1
2030 IF NOT EOF(1) THEN GOSUB 980                  'WRITE RECORD
2040 GOTO 1910
2050 IF A$="D" THEN 1890
2060 IF A$="I" AND NOT EOF(1) THEN GOSUB 980    'WRITE RECORD
2070 GOSUB 2220          '        ACCEPT RECORD
2080 GOSUB 980                    'WRITE RECORD
2090 IF EOF(1) THEN 1980
2100 GOTO 1890
2110 RETURN


2120 REM ***********************************************************
2130 REM               INITIALIZE RECORDS
2140 REM ***********************************************************
2150 PRINT "ENTER RECORDS (JUST PRESS RETURN TO STOP)"
2160 I$(1)=""
2170 GOSUB 2220                   'ACCEPT RECORD
2180 IF I$(1)="" THEN 2210
2190 GOSUB 980                    'WRITE RECORD
2200 GOTO 2160
2210 RETURN


2220 REM ***********************************************************
2230 REM               ACCEPT RECORD
2240 REM ***********************************************************
2250 PRINT "ENTER THE STOCK NUMBER";
2260 INPUT I$(1)
2270 PRINT "ENTER THE ITEM DESCRIPTION";
2280 INPUT I$(2)
2290 PRINT "ENTER THE WAREHOUSE LOCATION";
2300 INPUT I$(3)
2310 PRINT "ENTER THE SECTION OF THE WAREHOUSE";
2320 INPUT I$(4)
2330 RETURN


2340 REM ***********************************************************
2350 REM               CHECK ARRAY

2360 REM ***********************************************************
2370 K=0
2380 IF EOF(1) THEN 2460
2390 GOSUB 930                    'INPUT RECORD
2400 K=K+1
2410 FOR J=1 TO K
2420   IF S$(J)=LEFT$(I$(N),L) THEN 2450
2430 NEXT J
2440 S$(K)=LEFT$(I$(N),L)
2450 GOTO 2380
2460 RETURN
```

```
2470 REM *********************************************************
2480 REM               PRINT GROUPED RESULTS
2490 REM *********************************************************
2500 GOSUB 1270                    'PRINT HEADINGS
2510 I=1
2520 FOR J=1 TO K
2530   CLOSE 1
2540   GOSUB 710                   'OPEN FILE
2550   IF EOF(1) THEN 2590
2560   GOSUB 930                   'INPUT FILE
2570   IF S$(J)=LEFT$(I$(N),L) THEN GOSUB 1030  'PRINT LINE
2580   GOTO 2550
2590   S$(J)="        "
2600 NEXT J
2610 RETURN




RUN "WARE-INV


ARE YOU INITIALIZING THE SYSTEM (Y OR N)? Y
ENTER FILE NAME OF WAREHOUSE FILE? WFILE
WARNING - FILES BY THE NAME OF WFILE WILL BE OVERWRITTEN
IS THAT WHAT YOU WANT TO DO (Y OR N)? Y
ENTER RECORDS (JUST PRESS RETURN TO STOP)
ENTER THE STOCK NUMBER? 11111
ENTER THE ITEM DESCRIPTION? SUPER DELUXE WIDGET
ENTER THE WAREHOUSE LOCATION? A
ENTER THE SECTION OF THE WAREHOUSE? 1234
ENTER THE STOCK NUMBER? 22222
ENTER THE ITEM DESCRIPTION? MIDDLE CLASS WIDGET
ENTER THE WAREHOUSE LOCATION? B
ENTER THE SECTION OF THE WAREHOUSE? 5678
ENTER THE STOCK NUMBER? 33333
ENTER THE ITEM DESCRIPTION? BUDGET WIDGET
ENTER THE WAREHOUSE LOCATION? A
ENTER THE SECTION OF THE WAREHOUSE? 6663
ENTER THE STOCK NUMBER?
ENTER THE ITEM DESCRIPTION?
ENTER THE WAREHOUSE LOCATION?
ENTER THE SECTION OF THE WAREHOUSE?

*********************************************************
THE FOLLOWING OPTIONS ARE AVAILABLE:
     NBR      ACTION
     1..PRINTING THE FILE IN ITS PRESENT ORDER
     2..PRINTING THE FILE IN ORDER BY STOCK NUMBER
     3..PRINTING THE FILE IN ORDER BY ITEM (6 CHAR)
     4..PRINTING THE ITEM IN ORDER BY WAREHOUSE
     ----------------------------------------------------
     5..UPDATING THE FILE

ENTER OPTION NUMBER? 1
SHALL I PRINT IN LABEL FORMAT (Y OR N)? N
POSITION PAPER NOW?


*********************************************************

        ASSET LISTING - IN ORDER BY: CURRENT FILE CONTENTS

STOCK NBR ITEM DESCRIPTION              WAREHOUSE SECTION

11111      SUPER DELUXE WIDGET          A         1234      1
22222      MIDDLE CLASS WIDGET          B         5678      2
33333      BUDGET WIDGET                A         6663      3
```

Inventory Programs (General)   213

```
******************************************************************
THE FOLLOWING OPTIONS ARE AVAILABLE:
     NBR        ACTION
     1..PRINTING THE FILE IN ITS PRESENT ORDER
     2..PRINTING THE FILE IN ORDER BY STOCK NUMBER
     3..PRINTING THE FILE IN ORDER BY ITEM (6 CHAR)
     4..PRINTING THE ITEM IN ORDER BY WAREHOUSE
     -----------------------------------------------------
     5..UPDATING THE FILE

ENTER OPTION NUMBER? 2
POSITION PAPER NOW?




******************************************************************
          ASSET LISTING - IN ORDER BY: STOCK NUMBER

STOCK NBR ITEM DESCRIPTION                WAREHOUSE SECTION

11111     SUPER DELUXE WIDGET            A        1234
22222     MIDDLE CLASS WIDGET            B        5678
33333     BUDGET WIDGET                  A        6663

******************************************************************
THE FOLLOWING OPTIONS ARE AVAILABLE:
     NBR        ACTION
     1..PRINTING THE FILE IN ITS PRESENT ORDER
     2..PRINTING THE FILE IN ORDER BY STOCK NUMBER
     3..PRINTING THE FILE IN ORDER BY ITEM (6 CHAR)
     4..PRINTING THE ITEM IN ORDER BY WAREHOUSE
     -----------------------------------------------------
     5..UPDATING THE FILE

ENTER OPTION NUMBER? 4
POSITION PAPER NOW?




******************************************************************
          ASSET LISTING - IN ORDER BY: WAREHOUSE

WAREHOUSE SECTION    STOCK NBR ITEM DESCRIPTION

A        1234        11111     SUPER DELUXE WIDGET
A        6663        33333     BUDGET WIDGET
B        5678        22222     MIDDLE CLASS WIDGET

******************************************************************
THE FOLLOWING OPTIONS ARE AVAILABLE:
     NBR        ACTION
     1..PRINTING THE FILE IN ITS PRESENT ORDER
     2..PRINTING THE FILE IN ORDER BY STOCK NUMBER
     3..PRINTING THE FILE IN ORDER BY ITEM (6 CHAR)
     4..PRINTING THE ITEM IN ORDER BY WAREHOUSE
     -----------------------------------------------------
     5..UPDATING THE FILE

ENTER OPTION NUMBER?


PROCESSING COMPLETE

BREAK IN 690
OK
```

```
RUN "WARE-INV"


ARE YOU INITIALIZING THE SYSTEM (Y OR N)? N
ENTER FILE NAME OF WAREHOUSE FILE? WFILE

*****************************************************************
THE FOLLOWING OPTIONS ARE AVAILABLE:
     NBR       ACTION
     1..PRINTING THE FILE IN ITS PRESENT ORDER
     2..PRINTING THE FILE IN ORDER BY STOCK NUMBER
     3..PRINTING THE FILE IN ORDER BY ITEM (6 CHAR)
     4..PRINTING THE ITEM IN ORDER BY WAREHOUSE
     ----------------------------------------------------------
     5..UPDATING THE FILE

ENTER OPTION NUMBER? 5
ENTER THE FILE NAME FOR THE UPDATED FILE? NEW-FILE
ENTER THE RECORD # TO PROCESS? 2
 DELETE(D),CHANGE(C),INSERT(I), OR STOP (S)? I
ENTER THE STOCK NUMBER? 222222A
ENTER THE ITEM DESCRIPTION? NEW MODEL GOLD WIDGET
ENTER THE WAREHOUSE LOCATION? C
ENTER THE SECTION OF THE WAREHOUSE? 674
ENTER THE RECORD # TO PROCESS? 54
AT END-OF-FILE DELETE(D),CHANGE(C),INSERT(I), OR STOP (S)? S


PROCESSING COMPLETE

BREAK IN 690
OK




RUN "WARE-INV"


ARE YOU INITIALIZING THE SYSTEM (Y OR N)? N
ENTER FILE NAME OF WAREHOUSE FILE? NEW-FILE

*****************************************************************
THE FOLLOWING OPTIONS ARE AVAILABLE:
     NBR       ACTION
     1..PRINTING THE FILE IN ITS PRESENT ORDER
     2..PRINTING THE FILE IN ORDER BY STOCK NUMBER
     3..PRINTING THE FILE IN ORDER BY ITEM (6 CHAR)
     4..PRINTING THE ITEM IN ORDER BY WAREHOUSE
     ----------------------------------------------------------
     5..UPDATING THE FILE

ENTER OPTION NUMBER? 1
SHALL I PRINT IN LABEL FORMAT (Y OR N)? Y
ALIGN LABELS NOW?


11111      SUPER DELUXE WIDGET
A
1234


22222      MIDDLE CLASS WIDGET
B
5678
```

```
222222A   NEW MODEL GOLD WIDGET
C
674


33333     BUDGET WIDGET
A
6663


***************************************************************
THE FOLLOWING OPTIONS ARE AVAILABLE:
     NBR       ACTION
     1..PRINTING THE FILE IN ITS PRESENT ORDER
     2..PRINTING THE FILE IN ORDER BY STOCK NUMBER
     3..PRINTING THE FILE IN ORDER BY ITEM (6 CHAR)
     4..PRINTING THE ITEM IN ORDER BY WAREHOUSE
     -----------------------------------------------------
     5..UPDATING THE FILE

ENTER OPTION NUMBER?


PROCESSING COMPLETE

BREAK IN 690
OK
```

```
     MAJOR SYMBOL TABLE - WARE-INV                    FUNCTIONS USED
I-----------------------------------------------I   I---------------I
I NAME   .. DESCRIPTION                         I   I  NAME         I
I-----------------------------------------------I   I---------------I
I  A$    .. INPUT ANSWER VARIABLE               I   I OPEN          I
I  F$    .. INPUT FILE NAME                     I   I CLOSE         I
I  F1$   .. OUTPUT FILE NAME                    I   I GOSUB         I
I  H$()  .. HEADING ARRAY                       I   I RETURN        I
I  I     .. FILE NUMBER                         I   I DIM           I
I  I$()  .. DATA FIELDS                         I   I TAB           I
I  I1()  .. ORDER OF PRINTING ARRAY             I   I INPUT#        I
I  J     .. INDEX AND ARRAY POINTER             I   I PRINT#        I
I  J1    .. INDEX AND ARRAY POINTER             I   I EOF(1)        I
I  K     .. COUNTER FOR GROUP VALUE ARRAY       I   I LEFT$         I
I  K1    .. RECORD PRINT COUNTER                I   I---------------I
I  L     .. LENGTH OF FIELD TO COMPARE          I
I  M     .. MAXIMUM NUMBER OF GROUPS            I
I  M1    .. MAXIMUM NUMBER OF DATA RECORDS      I
I  N     .. GROUPING FIELD                      I
I  N1    .. RECORD POINTER FOR UPDATING         I
I  O     .. OPTION NUMBER                       I
I  S$()  .. GROUP VALUE ARRAY                   I
I  T$    .. PRINT FORMAT 'Y'=LABELS             I
I  T()   .. TAB SIZES FOR DATA FILES            I
I  TO    .. CURRENT TAB POISTION                I
I  X$    .. LINE OF ASTERISKS                   I
I-----------------------------------------------I
```

III
Production Planning and Control

8 Production Programs (General)

Job Costing

Program Name: JOBCOST

This program accepts overhead, fixed, and variable costs from the terminal to compute component and overall costs for each quantity of production scheduled. These figures can then be used to assist in product pricing. All necessary data should be gathered in advance; it is entered at the terminal in response to program prompting.

Files Affected: None

```
10 REM             SAVED AT JOBCOST
20 REM    COMPUTES COST OF JOB INCLUDING OVERHEAD,FIXED, AND VARIABLE COSTS
30 REM ****************************************************************
40 M=25
50 I=1
60 J=1
70 DIM F(M),F$(M),V(M),V$(M)
80 X$="****************************************************************"
90 REM                  ENTER INITIALIZING INFORMATION
100 REM ****************************************************************
110 PRINT "ENTER THE AMOUNT OF OVERHEAD DOLLARS TO APPLY";
120 INPUT O
130 PRINT "ENTER FIXED COSTS THAT APPLY AND THE TYPE OF COST"
140 PRINT "EXAMPLE  1000,SET UP CHARGES"
150 INPUT F(I),F$(I)
160 IF F(I)=0 THEN 190
170 I=I+1
180 GOTO 150
190 PRINT "ENTER VARIABLE COSTS THAT APPLY AND THE TYPE OF COST"
200 PRINT "EXAMPLE 10,MATERIALS"
210 INPUT V(J),V$(J)
220 IF V(J)=0 THEN 250
230 J=J+1
240 GOTO 210
250 PRINT "DO YOU WANT TO PRINT COSTS FOR A RANGE OF QUANTITIES (Y OR N)";
260 INPUT A$
270 IF A$="Y" THEN 330
280 PRINT "ENTER QUANTITY TO BE COSTED";
290 INPUT Q1
300 Q2=Q1
```

```
310 S=1
320 GOTO 400
330 PRINT "ENTER BEGINNING QUANTITY";
340 INPUT Q1
350 PRINT "ENTER ENDING QUANTITY";
360 INPUT Q2
370 PRINT "ENTER INTERVAL BETWEEN PRINTS";
380 INPUT S
390 REM *****************************************************************
400 REM                         DISPLAY RESULTS
410 REM *****************************************************************
420 PRINT
430 J1=J-1
440 I1=I-1
450 PRINT X$
460 PRINT
470 PRINT TAB(15);"JOB COST"
480 PRINT
490 PRINT "OVERHEAD";TAB(30);O
500 PRINT
510 PRINT "FIXED COSTS"
520 FOR I=1 TO I1
530    PRINT " ";F$(I);TAB(30);F(I)
540    F9=F9+F(I)
550 NEXT I
560 PRINT TAB(30);"----------"
570 PRINT "TOTAL FIXED COSTS";TAB(30);F9
580 PRINT
590 PRINT "VARIABLE COSTS"
600 FOR J=1 TO J1
610    PRINT " ";V$(J);TAB(30);V(J)
620    V9=V9+V(J)
630 NEXT J
640 PRINT TAB(30);"----------"
650 PRINT "VARIABLE COSTS PER UNIT";TAB(30);V9
660 PRINT
670 PRINT X$
680 PRINT
690 REM ****************PRINT A RANGE OF COSTS   *****************
700 PRINT "QUANTITY";TAB(10);"OVERHEAD";TAB(20);"FIXED";
710 PRINT TAB(30);"VARIABLE";TAB(40);"TOT COSTS";TAB(50);"COST/UNIT"
720 PRINT
730 FOR K=Q1 TO Q2 STEP S
740    T1=K*V9
750    T=O+F9+T1
760    PRINT K;TAB(10);O;TAB(20);F9;TAB(30);T1;TAB(40);T;TAB(50);T/K
770 NEXT K
780 PRINT X$
790 REM *****************************************************************
800 REM                    PROGRAM TERMINATION POINT
810 REM *****************************************************************
820 PRINT
830 PRINT
840 PRINT "PROCESSING COMPLETE"
850 PRINT
860 STOP
```

```
RUN "JOBCOST"
ENTER THE AMOUNT OF OVERHEAD DOLLARS TO APPLY? 1000
ENTER FIXED COSTS THAT APPLY AND THE TYPE OF COST
EXAMPLE  1000,SET UP CHARGES
? 1000,SET UP CHARGES
?
ENTER VARIABLE COSTS THAT APPLY AND THE TYPE OF COST
EXAMPLE 10,MATERIALS
? 10,MATERIALS
? 10,OTHER VARIABLE
?
DO YOU WANT TO PRINT COSTS FOR A RANGE OF QUANTITIES (Y OR N)? Y
ENTER BEGINNING QUANTITY? 100
ENTER ENDING QUANTITY? 200
ENTER INTERVAL BETWEEN PRINTS? 10


*****************************************************************

                   JOB COST

OVERHEAD                        1000

FIXED COSTS
  SET UP CHARGES                1000
                            ---------------
TOTAL FIXED COSTS               1000

VARIABLE COSTS
  MATERIALS                      10
  OTHER VARIABLE                 10
                            ---------------
VARIABLE COSTS PER UNIT         20

*****************************************************************

QUANTITY  OVERHEAD   FIXED     VARIABLE   TOT COSTS COST/UNIT

  100      1000      1000       2000       4000      40
  110      1000      1000       2200       4200      38.1818
  120      1000      1000       2400       4400      36.6667
  130      1000      1000       2600       4600      35.3846
  140      1000      1000       2800       4800      34.2857
  150      1000      1000       3000       5000      33.3333
  160      1000      1000       3200       5200      32.5
  170      1000      1000       3400       5400      31.7647
  180      1000      1000       3600       5600      31.1111
  190      1000      1000       3800       5800      30.5263
  200      1000      1000       4000       6000      30
*****************************************************************


PROCESSING COMPLETE

BREAK IN 860
OK
```

```
MAJOR SYMBOL TABLE - JOBCOST                              FUNCTIONS USED
I-------------------------------------------------------I     I-----------------I
I NAME    .. DESCRIPTION                                I     I NAME          I
I-------------------------------------------------------I     I-----------------I
I  A$     .. OPTION-ANSWER VARIABLE                     I     I TAB           I
I  F$()   .. FIXED COST NAME ARRAY                      I     I DIM           I
I  F()    .. FIXED COST ARAY                            I     I-----------------I
I  F9     .. TOTAL FIXED COSTS                          I
I  I      .. INDEX TO FIXED COSTS                       I
I  I1     .. NUMBER OF FIXED COSTS ENTERED              I
I  J      .. INDEX TO VARIABLE COSTS                    I
I  J1     .. NUMBER OF VARIABLE COSTS ENTERED           I
I  M      .. MAXIMUM ARRAY SIZE                         I
I  O      .. OVERHEAD  COSTS                            I
I  Q1     .. BEGIN PRINT QUANTITY                       I
I  Q2     .. END PRINT QUANTITY                         I
I  S      .. PRINT INTERVAL                             I
I  T      .. TOTAL COSTS                                I
I  T1     .. TOTAL VARIABLE COSTS                       I
I  V$()   .. VARIABLE COST NAME ARRAY                   I
I  V()    .. VARIABLE COST ARRAY                        I
I  V9     .. TOTAL VARIABLE COSTS PER UNIT              I
I  X$     .. LINE OF ASTERISKS                          I
I-------------------------------------------------------I
```

Bill of Materials

Program Name: BILL-MAT

This program performs all functions necessary to maintain a random-access disk file containing the material requirements for multiple products. Individual material components and assemblies can be entered in the file and recalled when required. To execute this program, the operator need only respond to the program messages (Fig. 8-1). When a

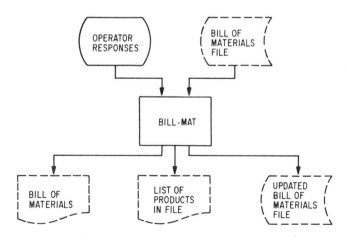

Fig. 8-1 Operation of the bill of materials program

product number that does not exist in the file is entered, the operator has the option of adding it to the file, printing it, and then storing the bill of materials. If it is found to exist in the file already, the operator has the option of printing it anyway or deleting it.

One random-access file is used by the program, its name defined by the operator. The contents are shown in Fig. 8-2.

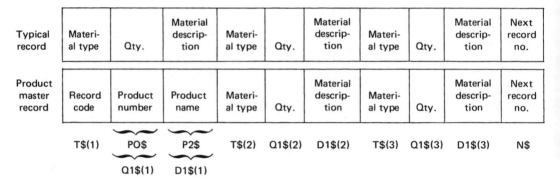

Fig. 8-2 Record format

```
10 REM              SAVED AT BILL-MAT
20 REM              BILL OF MATERIALS PROGRAM
30 REM**********************************************************
40 M=50
50 DIM Q$(M),D$(M),T$(M)
60 DIM T1$(4),Q1$(4),D1$(4)
70 X$="**********************************************************"
80 PRINT "ENTER THE NAME OF THE BILL OF MATERIALS FILE";
90 INPUT F$
100 GOSUB 620                      'FILE OPEN
110 M0=LOF(1)
120 DIM P1$(M0),S(M0)
130 GOSUB 710                      'TABLE BUILD
140 PRINT "ENTER PRODUCT NUMBER";
150 P$=""
160 INPUT P$
170 IF P$="" THEN 520
180 P$=P$+SPACE$(8-LEN(P$))
190 FOR I=1 TO M1
200   IF P$=P1$(I) THEN 370
210 NEXT I
220 PRINT "PRODUCT NOT IN FILE - DO YOU WISH TO CONTINUE (Y OR N)";
230 INPUT A$
240 IF A$<>"Y" THEN 140
250 REM ********************************************************
260 REM            PRODUCT NOT FOUND
270 REM ********************************************************
280 GOSUB 1550                     'ENTER INFO
290 PRINT "SHALL I PRINT THE BILL OF MATERIALS (Y OR N)";
300 INPUT A$
310 IF A$="Y" THEN GOSUB 1710      'FORMATTED PRINT
320 PRINT "SHALL I PLACE THE PRODUCT IN THE FILE (Y OR N)";
330 INPUT A$
340 IF A$="Y" THEN GOSUB 1020      'FILE WRITE
350 GOTO 140
```

```
360 REM ************************************************************
370 REM                  PRODUCT FOUND
380 REM ************************************************************
390 PRINT "PRODUCT FOUND -SHALL I PRINT IT (Y OR N)";
400 INPUT A$
410 IF A$<>"N" THEN 460
420 PRINT "SHALL I DELETE IT (Y OR N)";
430 INPUT A$
440 IF A$="Y" THEN GOSUB 1930    'DELETE PRODUCT
450 GOTO 140
460 PRINT
470 K=S(I)
480 GOSUB 1340                   'BUILD TABLE FOR PRINT
490 GOSUB 1710                   'FORMATTED PRINT
500 GOTO 140
510 REM ************************************************************
520 REM             PROGRAM TERMINATION POINT
530 REM ************************************************************
540 LSET T1$(1)=" "
550 LSET N$=MKI$(L)
560 PUT#1,1
570 PRINT
580 PRINT
590 PRINT "PROCESSING COMPLETE"
600 PRINT
610 STOP


620 REM************************************************************
630 REM             FILE OPEN AND DEFINE
640 REM ************************************************************
650 OPEN "R",1,F$,0
660 FOR I=1 TO 4
670    FIELD#1,(I-1)*31 AS X1$,1 AS T1$(I),6  AS Q1$(I),24 AS D1$(I)
680 NEXT I
690 FIELD#1,1 AS X1$,8 AS P0$,22 AS P2$,84 AS X1$,2 AS N$
700 RETURN


710 REM ************************************************************
720 REM                  BUILD  PRODUCT TABLE
730 REM ************************************************************
740 J=1
750 FOR K=1 TO M0
760    IF K>LOF(1) THEN 830
770    GOSUB 960              'FILE READ
780    IF T1$(1)<>"*" THEN 820
790    P1$(J)=P0$
800    S(J)=K
810    J=J+1
820 NEXT K
830 M1=J-1
840 PRINT TAB(5);M1;"PRODUCTS ARE IN THE FILE"
850 PRINT "SHALL I PRINT A LIST OF ALL PRODUCTS (Y OR N)";
860 INPUT A$
870 IF A$="Y" THEN GOSUB 2150           'PRODUCT LIST
880 REM ******   INITIALIZE LAST RECORD COUNTER   **********
890 L=1
900 IF M1=0 THEN 940
910 K=1
920 GOSUB 970                           'FILE READ
930 L=CVI(N$)
940 PRINT
950 RETURN


960 REM ************************************************************
970 REM                      FILE READ
980 REM ************************************************************
990 GET#1,K
1000 RETURN
```

```
1010 REM *******************************************************************
1020 REM              FILE WRITE
1030 REM *******************************************************************
1040 M4=M3/4
1050 IF M4<>INT(M4) THEN M4=INT(M4+1)
1060 N=0
1070 K=2
1080 FOR I=M4 TO 1 STEP -1
1090   FOR J=K TO LOF(1)
1100     K=J
1110     IF J=LOF(1) THEN 1150
1120     IF J=L+1 THEN 1150
1130     GOSUB 970                       'FILE READ
1140     IF T1$(1)<>" " THEN 1210
1150     FOR J1=1 TO 4
1160       LSET T1$(J1)=T$((I-1)*4+J1)
1170       LSET Q1$(J1)=Q$((I-1)*4+J1)
1180       LSET D1$(J1)=D$((I-1)*4+J1)
1190     NEXT J1
1200     GOTO 1220
1210   NEXT J
1220   IF J<L THEN 1250
1230   L=L+1
1240   J=L
1250   K=J
1260   LSET N$=MKI$(N)
1270   N=K
1280   IF T1$(1)<>"*" THEN 1310
1290   LSET P0$=P$
1300   LSET P2$=N2$
1310   PUT#1,K
1320 NEXT I
1330 RETURN


1340 REM *******************************************************************
1350 REM          BUILD ARRAY FROM FILE FOR PRINTING
1360 REM *******************************************************************
1370 J1=1
1380 IF K<=0 THEN 1530
1390 GOSUB 970                           'FILE READ
1400 N=CVI(N$)
1410 FOR I1=1 TO 4
1420   IF T1$(I1)="S" THEN 1530
1430   IF T1$(I1)<>"*" THEN 1460
1440   P$=P0$
1450   N2$=P2$
1460   T$(J1)=T1$(I1)
1470   Q$(J1)=Q1$(I1)
1480   D$(J1)=D1$(I1)
1490   J1=J1+1
1500 NEXT I1
1510 K=N
1520 GOTO 1380
1530 M3=J1-1
1540 RETURN


1550 REM *******************************************************************
1560 REM              ENTER NEW PRODUCT INFORMATION
1570 REM *******************************************************************
1580 PRINT "ENTER PRODUCT NAME";
1590 INPUT N2$
1600 LSET P2$=N2$
1610 PRINT "ENTER MATERIAL TYPE CODE,QTY,DESCRIPTION -RETURN WHEN DONE"
1620 T$(1)="*"
1630 LSET P0$=P$
1640 FOR I=2 TO M
```

```
1650    T$(I)=""
1660    INPUT T$(I),Q$(I),D$(I)
1670    IF T$(I)="" THEN 1690
1680 NEXT I
1690 M3=I-1
1700 RETURN


1710 REM *********************************************************
1720 REM                   FORMATTED PRINT    FROM ARRAY
1730 REM *********************************************************
1740 J1=1
1750 PRINT "POSITION PAPER NOW";
1760 INPUT A$
1770 PRINT X$
1780 PRINT
1790 PRINT TAB(10);"BILL OF MATERIALS"
1800 PRINT
1810 PRINT TAB(5);"PRODUCT ";P$;TAB(20);N2$
1820 PRINT
1830 PRINT TAB(5);"TYPE";TAB(15);"QTY";TAB(25);"ITEM"
1840 PRINT TAB(5);"-----";TAB(14);"--------";TAB(22);"------------------------------------"
1850 FOR I=2 TO M3
1860    PRINT TAB(7);T$(I);TAB(15);Q$(I);TAB(22);D$(I)
1870 NEXT I
1880 PRINT
1890 PRINT X$
1900 PRINT
1910 PRINT
1920 RETURN


1930 REM *********************************************************
1940 REM                   DELETE PRODUCT
1950 REM *********************************************************
1960 A$=""
1970 PRINT "ARE YOU CERTAIN THAT YOU WANT TO DELETE ";P1$(I);" (Y OR N)";
1980 INPUT A$
1990 IF A$<>"Y" THEN 2140
2000 K=S(I)
2010 GOSUB 970                                      'FILE READ
2020 N=CVI(N$)
2030 FOR I=1 TO 3
2040    LSET T1$(I)=" "
2050    LSET Q1$(I)=" "
2060    LSET D1$(I)=" "
2070 NEXT I
2080 LSET N$=MKI$(0)
2090 PUT#1,K
2100 IF N<=0 THEN 2130
2110 K=N
2120 GOTO 2010
2130 PRINT "PRODUCT ";P1$(I);" HAS BEEN DELETED"
2140 RETURN


2150 REM *********************************************************
2160 REM                   PRODUCT LIST
2170 REM *********************************************************
2180 PRINT
2190 PRINT X$
2200 PRINT
2210 PRINT "PRODUCT        REC #"
2220 PRINT
2230 FOR I=1 TO M1
2240    PRINT P1$(I);TAB(12);S(I)
2250 NEXT I
2260 PRINT
2270 PRINT X$
2280 RETURN
```

```
RUN "BILL-MAT"
ENTER THE NAME OF THE BILL OF MATERIALS FILE? MAT-FILE
        0 PRODUCTS ARE IN THE FILE
SHALL I PRINT A LIST OF ALL PRODUCTS (Y OR N)? N

ENTER PRODUCT NUMBER? A111
PRODUCT NOT IN FILE - DO YOU WISH TO CONTINUE (Y OR N)? Y
ENTER PRODUCT NAME? SUPER DELUXE WIDGET
ENTER MATERIAL TYPE CODE,QTY,DESCRIPTION -RETURN WHEN DONE
? A,1,MATERIAL ASSEMBLY #1
? A,2,MATERIAL ASSEMBLY #2
? C,4,RAW MAT COMPONENT #1
? C,3,RAW MAT COMPONENT #2
?
SHALL I PRINT THE BILL OF MATERIALS (Y OR N)? Y
POSITION PAPER NOW?


*************************************************************

          BILL OF MATERIALS

     PRODUCT A111      SUPER DELUXE WIDGET

     TYPE       QTY        ITEM
     ----       -------    -----------------------
       A          1        MATERIAL ASSEMBLY #1
       A          2        MATERIAL ASSEMBLY #2
       C          4        RAW MAT COMPONENT #1
       C          3        RAW MAT COMPONENT #2


*************************************************************


SHALL I PLACE THE PRODUCT IN THE FILE (Y OR N)? Y
ENTER PRODUCT NUMBER? A112
PRODUCT NOT IN FILE - DO YOU WISH TO CONTINUE (Y OR N)? Y
ENTER PRODUCT NAME? WORLD SERIES HOT DOG
ENTER MATERIAL TYPE CODE,QTY,DESCRIPTION -RETURN WHEN DONE
? C,1,HOT DOG
? C,1,ROLL
? C,1 TSP,MUSTARD
?
SHALL I PRINT THE BILL OF MATERIALS (Y OR N)? Y
POSITION PAPER NOW?


*************************************************************

          BILL OF MATERIALS

     PRODUCT A112      WORLD SERIES HOT DOG

     TYPE       QTY        ITEM
     ----       -------    -----------------------
       C          1        HOT DOG
       C          1        ROLL
       C        1 TSP      MUSTARD


*************************************************************


SHALL I PLACE THE PRODUCT IN THE FILE (Y OR N)? Y
ENTER PRODUCT NUMBER?


PROCESSING COMPLETE

BREAK IN 610
```

226   BASIC Computer Programs for Business

```
RUN "BILL-MAT"
ENTER THE NAME OF THE BILL OF MATERIALS FILE? MAT-FILE
       2 PRODUCTS ARE IN THE FILE
SHALL I PRINT A LIST OF ALL PRODUCTS (Y OR N)? N

ENTER PRODUCT NUMBER? A112
PRODUCT FOUND -SHALL I PRINT IT (Y OR N)? Y

POSITION PAPER NOW?


*********************************************************************
          BILL OF MATERIALS

     PRODUCT A112     WORLD SERIES HOT DOG

     TYPE      QTY        ITEM
     ----      ---        ----
       C        1         HOT DOG
       C        1         ROLL
       C        1 TSP     MUSTARD

*********************************************************************


ENTER PRODUCT NUMBER? A113
PRODUCT NOT IN FILE - DO YOU WISH TO CONTINUE (Y OR N)? N
ENTER PRODUCT NUMBER?


PROCESSING COMPLETE

BREAK IN 610
OK
```

```
  MAJOR SYMBOL TABLE - BILL-MAT                          FUNCTIONS USED
I---------------------------------------------------I    I-----------------I
I NAME    .. DESCRIPTION                            I    I  NAME           I
I---------------------------------------------------I    I-----------------I
I A$      .. INPUT ANSWER VARIABLE                  I    I DIM             I
I D$()    .. DESCRIPTION OF MATERIAL ARRAY          I    I GOSUB           I
I D1$()   .. DESCRIPTION ARRAY - IN FILE            I    I RETURN          I
I F$      .. FILE NAME                              I    I PUT             I
I I       .. INDEX AND ARRAY POINTER                I    I GET             I
I I1      .. INDEX AND ARRAY POINTER                I    I CVI             I
I J       .. INDEX AND ARRAY POINTER                I    I MKI$            I
I J1      .. INDEX AND ARRAY POINTER                I    I TAB             I
I K       .. RECORD # TO BE READ                    I    I INT             I
I L       .. LAST RECORD # USED                     I    I LSET            I
I LOF(1).. LAST RECORD NUMBER USED IN FILE 1        I    I LEN             I
I M       .. MAX NUMBER OF MATERIALS PER PRODUCT    I    I FIELD           I
I M0      .. MAX NUMBER OF PRODUCTS IN FILE         I    I SPACE$          I
I M1      .. NUMBER OF PRODUCTS IN THE FILE         I    I LOF(1)          I
I M3      .. NUMBER OF MATERIAL ITEMS ENTERED       I    I-----------------I
I M4      .. NUMBER OF RECORDS TO BE WRITTEN        I
I N       .. NEXT RECORD NUMBER                     I
I N$      .. CHARACTER STRING OF NEXT RECORD        I
I N2$     .. INPUT PRODUCT NAME                     I
I P$      .. INPUT PRODUCT NAME                     I
I P0$     .. PRODUCT NUMBER - IN FILE               I
```

```
I   P1$()  .. PRODUCT NAME ARRAY                    I
I   P2$    .. PRODUCT NAME - IN FILE                I
I   Q$()   .. QTY ARRAY                             I
I   Q1$()  .. QTY ARRAY - IN FILE                   I
I   S()    .. PRODUCT RECORD # ARRAY                I
I   T$()   .. TYPE ARRAY                            I
I   T1$()  .. TYPE ARRAY - IN FILE                  I
I   X$     .. LINE OF ASTERISKS                     I
I   X1$    .. DUMMY VARIABLE                        I
I-----------------------------------------------------I
```

Production Scheduling

Program Name: SCHEDULE

This program, which records and displays the scheduled use of critical items, can be applied to a wide variety of problems involving the allocation and scheduling of any scarce resource. It contains all of the functions necessary to operate such a system. It is executed by entering the appropriate option number in response to the program message.

The operation of the system requires three distinct steps:

1. *Initialization of the system:* The initialization option must be executed for each separate scheduling period (that is, month). This option creates, and initializes, a file for that period. The file is created as "Pxxx", where "xxx" is the abbreviation of the month.
2. *Scheduling resources:* Resources (machines) are scheduled for specific time periods through the execution of Option 2. This option allocates individual one-hour segments to jobs and records the scheduling in the file.
3. *Printing (querying) schedules:* Option 3 allows the review of schedules to determine available time and to assist in providing separate and combined schedules.

The flowchart in Fig. 8-3 illustrates the typical processing of the scheduling system.

The scheduling program requires just one file for its operation, a file created and initialized by Option 1. It is a random-access file named "Pxxx", where "xxx" is a three-letter, month-name abbreviation; for example, PAPR indicates the April file. All records have the identical format shown in Fig. 8-4.

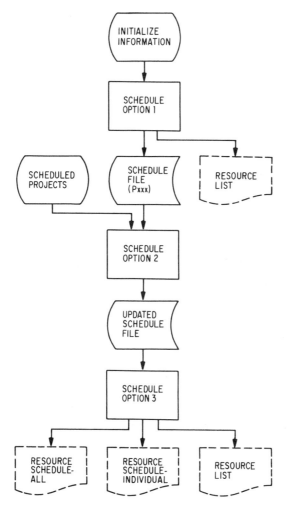

Fig. 8-3 Operation of the scheduling program

Suggested enhancement: Since scheduling records contain eight-character project names for specific time periods, an additional option can be implemented to display the scheduled accomplishment of all tasks.

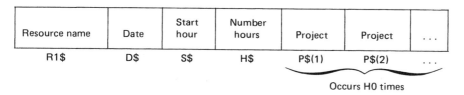

Resource name	Date	Start hour	Number hours	Project	Project	. . .
R1$	D$	S$	H$	P$(1)	P$(2)	. . .

Occurs H0 times

Fig. 8-4 Record format

```
10 REM            SAVED AT SCHEDULE
20 REM    PRODUCTION SCHEDULING SYTEM
30 REM ******************************************************************
40 X$="*****************************************************************"
50 HO=12
60 M=100
70 DIM R$(M),P$(12)
80 PRINT "ENTER THE MONTH NAME ABBREVIATION I.E. JAN";
90 INPUT M$
100 DATA JAN,31,FEB,29,MAR,31,APR,30,MAY,31,JUN,30
110 DATA JUL,31,AUG,31,SEP,30,OCT,31,NOV,30,DEC,31
120 FOR I=1 TO 12
130   READ M1$,D1
140   IF M1$=M$ THEN 180
150 NEXT I
160 PRINT "INVALID MONTH ABBREVIATION - TRY AGAIN"
170 GOTO 80
180 PRINT
190 F$="P"+M$
200 GOSUB 1560              'OPEN FILE
210 N1=D1
220 N2=N1
230 REM ******************************************************************
240 REM          CHOOSE PROCESSING OPTION
250 REM ******************************************************************
260 PRINT "THE FOLLOWING OPTIONS ARE AVAILABLE:"
270 PRINT TAB(5);"1...INITIALIZING FILES"
280 PRINT TAB(5);"2...SCHEDULING RESOURCES"
290 PRINT TAB(5);"3...PRINTING SCHEDULES"
300 PRINT
310 PRINT "ENTER THE OPTION NUMBER DESIRED -PRESS RETURN TO STOP";
320 INPUT O
330 IF O=1 THEN GOSUB 440             'INITIALIZE FILES
340 IF O=2 THEN GOSUB 750             'SCHEDULE ENTRIES
350 IF O=3 THEN GOSUB 1090            'PRINT SCHEDULE
360 REM ******************************************************************
370 REM               PROGRAM TERMINATION POINT
380 REM ******************************************************************
390 CLOSE 1
400 PRINT
410 PRINT "PROCESSING COMPLETE"
420 PRINT
430 STOP


440 REM ******************************************************************
450 REM    1    FILE INITIALIZATION
460 REM ******************************************************************
470 PRINT "ENTER THE STARTING HOUR FOR THE SCHEDULE I.E. 0800";
480 INPUT S
490 PRINT "ENTER THE NUMBER OF HOURS PER DAY TO SCHEDULE";
500 INPUT H
510 IF H<=HO THEN 540
520 PRINT "THE MAXIMUM NUMBER OF HOURS IN EACH FILE IS 12"
530 GOTO 490
540 PRINT "THE FILE NAME WILL BE CREATED AS ";F$
550 PRINT "ENTER THE RESOURCES TO BE INCLUDED IN THE FILE"
560 PRINT "JUST PRESS THE RETURN - WHEN FINISHED"
570 PRINT
580 FOR I=1 TO M
590   INPUT R$(I)
600   IF R$(I)="" THEN 620
610 NEXT I
620 REM ******************************************************************
630 REM             PROCESSING TO FILE
640 REM ******************************************************************
650 PRINT "FILES ARE BEING INITIALIZED"
660 M=I-1
```

```
670 GOSUB   1720                    'INITIALIZE RECORD
680 FOR I=1 TO M
690    GOSUB 1810                   'WRITE RECORD
700 NEXT I
710 R$(I)="END"
720 N2=1
730 GOSUB 1810                      'WRITE END RECORD
740 RETURN


750 REM ***************************************************************
760 REM     2       SCHEDULE ENTRY
770 REM ***************************************************************
780 GOSUB 1960                      'CREATE RESOURCE TABLE
790 PRINT "SHALL I PRINT THE RESOURCES IN THE FILE (Y OR N)";
800 INPUT A$
810 IF A$="Y" THEN GOSUB 2070           'PRINT TABLE
820 PRINT "SHALL I PRINT THE RECORD (Y OR N)";
830 INPUT A1$
840 PRINT "ENTER THE MACHINE NUMBER TO BE SCHEDULED -RETURN TO STOP";
850 M3=0
860 INPUT M3
870 IF M3=0 THEN 1080
880 PRINT "ENTER THE DAY TO BE SCHEDULED";
890 INPUT D3
900 K=(M3-1)*N1+D3
910 GOSUB 1640                      'READ FILE
920 H1$=R1$
930 IF A1$<>"Y" THEN   970
940 GOSUB 2250                      'PRINT HEADING
950 GOSUB 2170                      'PRINT RECORD
960 PRINT
970 PRINT "ENTER THE HOUR TO SCHEDULE AND THE TASK I.E 0800,TASK1";
980 H2=0
990 INPUT H2,T$
1000 IF H2=0 THEN 1080
1010 H2=INT(H2/100)
1020 H1=S/100
1030 H3=H2-H1+1
1040 LSET P$(H3)=T$
1050 IF A1$="Y" THEN GOSUB 2170 'PRINT RECORD
1060 GOSUB 1910                     'FILE WRITE
1070 GOTO 840
1080 RETURN


1090 REM ***************************************************************
1100 REM     3       PRINT SCHEDULE
1110 REM ***************************************************************
1120 H2$="DAY"
1130 GOSUB 1960                     'CREATE RESOURCE TABLE
1140 PRINT "SHALL I PRINT THE RESOURCE TABLE (Y OR N)";
1150 INPUT A$
1160 IF A$="Y" THEN GOSUB 2070          'PRINT TABLE
1170 PRINT "SHALL I PRINT ALL RESOURCES (Y OR N)";
1180 INPUT A$
1190 PRINT "ENTER THE FIRST AND LAST DAY TO BE PRINTED I.E. 1,10";
1200 INPUT J0,J1
1210 IF A$="Y" THEN 1400
1220 REM ********* PRINT INDIVIDUAL RESOURCE  ******************
1230 PRINT "ENTER THE MACHINE NUMBER TO BE PRINTED - 0 TO STOP";
1240 M3=0
1250 INPUT M3
1260 PRINT
1270 IF M3=0 THEN 1540
1280 K=(M3-1)*N1+1
1290 GOSUB 1640                     'FILE READ
1300 H1$=R1$
```

```
1310 GOSUB 2260                    'PRINT HEADING
1320 FOR J=J0 TO J1
1330    K=(M3-1)*N1+J
1340    GOSUB 1640                 'FILE READ
1350    PRINT D;
1360    GOSUB 2170                 'PRINT RECORD
1370 NEXT J
1380 PRINT X$
1390 GOTO 1230
1400 REM ************ PRINT ALL ENTRIES   *************************
1410 H1$="COMBINED "
1420 FOR J=J0 TO J1
1430    D=J
1440    H2$="MCH"
1450    GOSUB 2250                 'PRINT HEADING
1460    FOR I1=1 TO M
1470       K=((I1-1)*N1)+J
1480       GOSUB 1640              'FILE READ
1490       PRINT I1;
1500       GOSUB 2170              'PRINT LINE
1510       PRINT
1520    NEXT I1
1530 NEXT J
1540 RETURN


1550 REM ************************************************************
1560 REM               FILE OPEN AND DEFINE
1570 REM ************************************************************
1580 OPEN "R",1,F$,0
1590 FIELD#1,26 AS R1$,2 AS D$,2 AS S$,2 AS H$
1600 FOR I=1 TO H0
1610    FIELD#1,32+(I-1)*8 AS X1$,8 AS P$(I)
1620 NEXT I
1630 RETURN


1640 REM ************************************************************
1650 REM                   FILE READ
1660 REM ************************************************************
1670 GET#1,K
1680 H=CVI(H$)
1690 S=CVI(S$)
1700 D=CVI(D$)
1710 RETURN


1720 REM ************************************************************
1730 REM               RECORD INITIALIZE
1740 REM ************************************************************
1750 LSET S$=MKI$(S)
1760 LSET H$=MKI$(H)
1770 FOR I=1 TO H
1780    LSET P$(I)="          "
1790 NEXT I
1800 RETURN


1810 REM ************************************************************
1820 REM               INITIALIZE FILE WRITE
1830 REM ************************************************************
1840 LSET R1$=R$(I)
1850 FOR J=1 TO N2
1860    LSET D$=MKI$(J)
1870    K=(I-1)*N1+J
1880    PUT#1,K
1890 NEXT J
1900 RETURN
```

```
1910 REM ***************************************************************
1920 REM                FILE WRITE ROUTINE
1930 REM ***************************************************************
1940 PUT#1,K
1950 RETURN


1960 REM ***************************************************************
1970 REM               CREATE RESOURCE TABLE
1980 REM ***************************************************************
1990 FOR I=1 TO M
2000    K=(I-1)*N1+1
2010    GOSUB 1640                      'FILE READ
2020    IF LEFT$(R1$,3)="END" THEN 2050
2030    R$(I)=R1$
2040 NEXT I
2050 M=I-1
2060 RETURN


2070 REM ***************************************************************
2080 REM               PRINT RESOURCE TABLE
2090 REM ***************************************************************
2100 PRINT
2110 PRINT "NBR   RESOURCE"
2120 PRINT
2130 FOR I=1 TO M
2140    PRINT I;TAB(5);R$(I)
2150 NEXT I
2160 RETURN


2170 REM ***************************************************************
2180 REM           PRINT INDIVIDUAL RESOURCE SCHEDULE
2190 REM ***************************************************************
2200 FOR I=1 TO H
2210    PRINT TAB((I-1)*9+3);P$(I);
2220 NEXT I
2230 PRINT
2240 RETURN


2250 REM ***************************************************************
2260 REM               PRINT HEADING
2270 REM ***************************************************************
2280 PRINT X$
2290 PRINT
2300 PRINT TAB(10);H1$;"SCHEDULE";D;M$
2310 PRINT
2320 PRINT H2$;
2330 FOR I=1 TO H
2340    PRINT TAB((I-1)*9+3);S+(100*(I-1));
2350 NEXT I
2360 PRINT
2370 PRINT
2380 RETURN
```

```
RUN "SCHEDULE"
ENTER THE MONTH NAME ABBREVIATION I.E. JAN? APR

THE FOLLOWING OPTIONS ARE AVAILABLE:
     1...INITIALIZING FILES
     2...SCHEDULING RESOURCES
     3...PRINTING SCHEDULES

ENTER THE OPTION NUMBER DESIRED -PRESS RETURN TO STOP? 1
ENTER THE STARTING HOUR FOR THE SCHEDULE I.E. 0800? 0800
ENTER THE NUMBER OF HOURS PER DAY TO SCHEDULE? 8
THE FILE NAME WILL BE CREATED AS PAPR
ENTER THE RESOURCES TO BE INCLUDED IN THE FILE
JUST PRESS THE RETURN - WHEN FINISHED

? MACHINE TYPE 1
? MACHINE TYPE 2
? MACHINE TYPE 3
?
FILES ARE BEING INITIALIZED

PROCESSING COMPLETE

BREAK IN 430
OK


RUN "SCHEDULE"
ENTER THE MONTH NAME ABBREVIATION I.E. JAN? APR

THE FOLLOWING OPTIONS ARE AVAILABLE:
     1...INITIALIZING FILES
     2...SCHEDULING RESOURCES
     3...PRINTING SCHEDULES

ENTER THE OPTION NUMBER DESIRED -PRESS RETURN TO STOP? 2
SHALL I PRINT THE RESOURCES IN THE FILE (Y OR N)? Y

NBR    RESOURCE

 1     MACHINE TYPE 1
 2     MACHINE TYPE 2
 3     MACHINE TYPE 3
SHALL I PRINT THE RECORD (Y OR N)? N
ENTER THE MACHINE NUMBER TO BE SCHEDULED -RETURN TO STOP? 1
ENTER THE DAY TO BE SCHEDULED? 1
ENTER THE HOUR TO SCHEDULE AND THE TASK I.E 0800,TASK1? 0800,TASK 1
ENTER THE MACHINE NUMBER TO BE SCHEDULED -RETURN TO STOP? 2
ENTER THE DAY TO BE SCHEDULED? 1
ENTER THE HOUR TO SCHEDULE AND THE TASK I.E 0800,TASK1? 0900,TASK 2
ENTER THE MACHINE NUMBER TO BE SCHEDULED -RETURN TO STOP? 1
ENTER THE DAY TO BE SCHEDULED? 2
ENTER THE HOUR TO SCHEDULE AND THE TASK I.E 0800,TASK1? 1400,TASK 3
ENTER THE MACHINE NUMBER TO BE SCHEDULED -RETURN TO STOP? 2
ENTER THE DAY TO BE SCHEDULED? 2
ENTER THE HOUR TO SCHEDULE AND THE TASK I.E 0800,TASK1? 1000,TASK 4
ENTER THE MACHINE NUMBER TO BE SCHEDULED -RETURN TO STOP?

PROCESSING COMPLETE

BREAK IN 430
OK
```

```
RUN "SCHEDULE"
ENTER THE MONTH NAME ABBREVIATION I.E. JAN? APR

THE FOLLOWING OPTIONS ARE AVAILABLE:
     1...INITIALIZING FILES
     2...SCHEDULING RESOURCES
     3...PRINTING SCHEDULES

ENTER THE OPTION NUMBER DESIRED -PRESS RETURN TO STOP? 3
SHALL I PRINT THE RESOURCE TABLE (Y OR N)? N
SHALL I PRINT ALL RESOURCES (Y OR N)? Y
ENTER THE FIRST AND LAST DAY TO BE PRINTED I.E. 1,10? 1,2
*************************************************************************

          COMBINED SCHEDULE 1 APR

MCH 800      900      1000      1100      1200      1300      1400      1500

  1 TASK 1

  2           TASK 2

  3

*************************************************************************

          COMBINED SCHEDULE 2 APR

MCH 800      900      1000      1100      1200      1300      1400      1500

  1                                                      TASK 3

  2                     TASK 4

  3


PROCESSING COMPLETE

BREAK IN 430
OK
```



```
RUN "SCHEDULE"
ENTER THE MONTH NAME ABBREVIATION I.E. JAN? APR

THE FOLLOWING OPTIONS ARE AVAILABLE:
     1...INITIALIZING FILES
     2...SCHEDULING RESOURCES
     3...PRINTING SCHEDULES

ENTER THE OPTION NUMBER DESIRED -PRESS RETURN TO STOP? 3
SHALL I PRINT THE RESOURCE TABLE (Y OR N)? Y

NBR    RESOURCE

  1    MACHINE TYPE 1
  2    MACHINE TYPE 2
  3    MACHINE TYPE 3
SHALL I PRINT ALL RESOURCES (Y OR N)? N
ENTER THE FIRST AND LAST DAY TO BE PRINTED I.E. 1,10? 1,4
ENTER THE MACHINE NUMBER TO BE PRINTED - 0 TO STOP? 1
```

Production Programs (General)   235

```
****************************************************************************
                MACHINE TYPE 1             SCHEDULE 1 APR

DAY 800      900      1000     1100     1200     1300      1400      1500

  1 TASK 1
  2                                                      TASK 3
  3
  4
****************************************************************************
ENTER THE MACHINE NUMBER TO BE PRINTED - 0 TO STOP?


PROCESSING COMPLETE

BREAK IN 430
OK
```

MAJOR SYMBOL TABLE — SCHEDULE

NAME	DESCRIPTION
A$	ANSWER VARIABLE
A1$	ANSWER VARIABLE
D	DAY OF THE MONTH
D$	CHARACTER REPRESENTATION OF D
D1	NUMBER OF DAYS IN THE MONTH
F$	FILE NAME
H	NUMBER OF HOURS SHEDULED IN FILE
H$	CHARACTER REPRESENTATION OF H
H0	MAXIMUM HOURS STORED IN FILE
H1	TIME/100 =HOUR NUMBER
H1$	HEADING INFORMATION
H2	HOUR TO BE SCHEDULED
H3	ARRAY POSITION FOR SCHEDULE ENTRY
I	INDEX AND ARRAY POINTER
I1	INDEX AND ARRAY POINTER
J	INDEX AND ARRAY POINTER
J0	FIRST DAY TO PRINT
J1	LAST DAY TO PRINT
K	RECORD NUMBER TO BE READ
M	MAXIMUM NUMBER OF RESOURCES(MACHINES)
M$	ABBREVIATED MONTH NAME
M1$	STANDARD MONTH ABBREVIATIONS
M3	NUMBER OF RESOURCES(MACHINES)
N1	NUMBER OF RECORDS FOR EACH RESOURCE
N2	NUMBER OF RECORDS FOR EACH RESOURCE
O	OPTION NUMBER
P$()	PROJECTS SCHEDULED
R$()	NAME OF RESOURCES
R1$	NAME OF RESOURCE-IN FILE
S	STARTING HOUR FOR THE SCHEDULE
S$	CHARACTER REPRESENTATION OF S
X$	LINE OF ASTERISKS
X1$	DUMMY VARIABLE

FUNCTIONS USED

NAME
TAB
OPEN
CLOSE
GOSUB
RETURN
DIM
CVI
GET
PUT
LSET
MKI$
LEFT$
INT
FIELD

Job Routing

Program Name: JOBROUT

This program performs all functions necessary to maintain a random-access disk file containing job-routing information for multiple products. The individual processes and tasks to be performed for the completion of any project can be entered into the file and recalled whenever required.

To execute this program, the operator need only respond to the program messages (Fig. 8-5). When a product number that does not exist in the file is entered, the operator has the option of adding it to the file, printing it, and/or storing the routing information. If it is found to exist in the file already, the operator has the option of printing it anyway or deleting it.

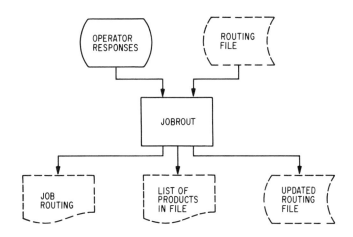

Fig. 8-5 Operation of the job routing program

One random-access file is used by the program. Its name is defined by the operator; its contents are shown in Fig. 8-6.

Typical record	Process code	De-scription		Process code	De-scription	Process code	De-scription	Next record no.
Product master record	Record code	Product number	Product name	Process code	De-scription	Process code	De-scription	Next record no.
	T$(1)	PO$	P2$	T$(2)	F1$(2)	T$(3)	F1$(3)	N$
		F1$(1)						

Fig. 8-6 Record format

```
10 REM              SAVED AT JOBROUT
20 REM              JOB ROUTING PROGRAM
30 REM**************************************************************
40 M=50
50 DIM R2$(M),D$(M)
60 DIM T$(3),F1$(3)
70 X$="**************************************************************"
80 PRINT "ENTER THE NAME OF THE ROUTING FILE";
90 INPUT F$
100 GOSUB 630                    'FILE OPEN
110 M0=LOF(1)
120 DIM P1$(M0),S(M0)
130 GOSUB 720                    'TABLE BUILD
140 PRINT "ENTER PRODUCT NUMBER";
150 P$=""
160 INPUT P$
170 IF P$="" THEN 530
180 P$=P$+SPACE$(8-LEN(P$))
190 FOR I=1 TO M1
200   IF P$=P1$(I) THEN 370
210 NEXT I
220 PRINT "PRODUCT NOT IN FILE - DO YOU WISH TO CONTINUE (Y OR N)";
230 INPUT A$
240 IF A$<>"Y" THEN 140
250 REM ***************************************************************
260 REM              PRODUCT NOT FOUND
270 REM ***************************************************************
280 GOSUB 1630                    'ENTER INFO
290 PRINT "SHALL I PLACE THE PRODUCT IN THE FILE (Y OR N)";
300 INPUT A$
310 IF A$="Y" THEN GOSUB 1030    'FILE WRITE
320 PRINT "SHALL I PRINT THE JOB ROUTING (Y OR N)";
330 INPUT A$
340 IF A$="Y" THEN GOSUB 1850    'FORMATTED PRINT
350 GOTO 140
360 REM ***************************************************************
370 REM              PRODUCT FOUND
380 REM ***************************************************************
390 PRINT "PRODUCT FOUND -SHALL I PRINT IT (Y OR N)";
400 INPUT A$
410 IF A$<>"N" THEN 460
420 PRINT "SHALL I DELETE IT (Y OR N)";
430 INPUT A$
440 IF A$="Y" THEN GOSUB 2050    'DELETE PRODUCT
450 GOTO 140
460 PRINT
470 PRINT "POSITION PAPER NOW";
480 INPUT A$
490 K=S(I)
500 GOSUB 1340                    'PRINT ROUTING
510 GOTO 140
520 REM ***************************************************************
530 REM              PROGRAM TERMINATION POINT
540 REM ***************************************************************
550 LSET T$(1)="   "
560 LSET N$=MKI$(L)
570 PUT#1,1
580 PRINT
590 PRINT
600 PRINT "PROCESSING COMPLETE"
610 PRINT
620 STOP


630 REM**************************************************************
640 REM              FILE OPEN AND DEFINE
650 REM **************************************************************
660 OPEN "R",1,F$,0
```

```
670 FOR I=1 TO 3
680   FIELD#1,(I-1)*42 AS X1$,2 AS T$(I),40 AS F1$(I)
690 NEXT I
700 FIELD#1,2 AS X1$,8 AS P0$,32 AS P2$,84 AS X1$,2 AS N$
710 RETURN


720 REM ***********************************************************
730 REM                   BUILD  PRODUCT TABLE
740 REM ***********************************************************
750 J=1
760 FOR K=1 TO M0
770   IF K>LOF(1) THEN 840
780   GOSUB 970                    'FILE READ
790   IF T$(1)<>"* " THEN 830
800   P1$(J)=P0$
810   S(J)=K
820   J=J+1
830 NEXT K
840 M1=J-1
850 PRINT TAB(5);M1;"PRODUCTS ARE IN THE FILE"
860 PRINT "SHALL I PRINT A LIST OF ALL PRODUCTS (Y OR N)";
870 INPUT A$
880 IF A$="Y" THEN GOSUB 2250              'PRODUCT LIST
890 REM *******   INITIALIZE LAST RECORD COUNTER  **********
900 L=1
910 IF M1=0 THEN 950
920 K=1
930 GOSUB 980                        'FILE READ
940 L=CVI(N$)
950 PRINT
960 RETURN


970 REM ***********************************************************
980 REM                      FILE READ
990 REM ***********************************************************
1000 GET#1,K
1010 RETURN


1020 REM ***********************************************************
1030 REM               FILE WRITE
1040 REM ***********************************************************
1050 M4=M3/3
1060 IF M4<>INT(M4) THEN M4=INT(M4+1)
1070 N=0
1080 K=2
1090 FOR I=M4 TO 1 STEP -1
1100   FOR J=K TO LOF(1)
1110     K=J
1120     IF J=LOF(1) THEN 1160
1130     IF J=L+1 THEN 1160
1140     GOSUB 980                  'FILE READ
1150     IF T$(1)<>"  " THEN 1210
1160     FOR J1=1 TO 3
1170       LSET T$(J1)=R2$((I-1)*3+J1)
1180       LSET F1$(J1)=D$((I-1)*3+J1)
1190     NEXT J1
1200     GOTO 1220
1210   NEXT J
1220   IF J<L THEN 1250
1230   L=L+1
1240   J=L
1250   K=J
1260   LSET N$=MKI$(N)
1270   N=K
1280   IF T$(1)<>"* " THEN 1310
```

```
1290    LSET PO$=P$
1300    LSET P2$=N2$
1310    PUT#1,K
1320 NEXT I
1330 RETURN


1340 REM **********************************************************
1350 REM                    PRINT ROUTING
1360 REM **********************************************************
1370 J1=0
1380 PRINT X$
1390 PRINT
1400 IF K<=0 THEN 1580
1410 GOSUB 980                              'FILE READ
1420 N=CVI(N$)
1430 FOR I1=1 TO 3
1440    IF T$(I1)="ST" THEN 1570
1450    IF T$(I1)<>"* " THEN PRINT TAB(2);J1;TAB(12);T$(I1);TAB(20);F1$(I1)
1460    IF T$(I1)<>"* " THEN 1510
1470    PRINT "PRODUCT ";PO$;TAB(20);P2$
1480    PRINT
1490    PRINT"STEP #";TAB(10);"PROCESS";TAB(22);"TASK(S)"
1500    PRINT "-------";TAB(10);"----------";TAB(20);"------------------------"
1510    R2$(J1)=T$(I1)
1520    D$(J1)=F1$(I1)
1530    J1=J1+1
1540 NEXT I1
1550 K=N
1560 GOTO 1400
1570 PRINT
1580 M3=J1-1
1590 PRINT X$
1600 PRINT
1610 PRINT
1620 RETURN


1630 REM **********************************************************
1640 REM            ENTER NEW PRODUCT INFORMATION
1650 REM **********************************************************
1660 PRINT "ENTER PRODUCT NAME";
1670 INPUT N2$
1680 PRINT "ENTER ROUTING CODE,PROCESS DESCRIPTION -RETURN WHEN DONE"
1690 R2$(1)="* "
1700 LSET PO$=P$
1710 FOR I=2 TO M
1720    R2$(I)=""
1730    INPUT R2$(I),D$(I)
1740    IF R2$(I)="" THEN 1760
1750 NEXT I
1760 M3=I-1
1770 REM ************* PRINT/VERIFY *****************************
1780 PRINT
1790 PRINT "PROCESS      FUNCTION PERFORMED"
1800 FOR I=2 TO M3
1810    PRINT TAB(5);R2$(I);TAB(10);D$(I)
1820 NEXT I
1830 PRINT
1840 RETURN
1850 REM **********************************************************
1860 REM                    FORMATTED PRINT
1870 REM **********************************************************
1880 J1=1
1890 PRINT "POSITION PAPER NOW";
1900 INPUT A$
1910 PRINT X$
1920 PRINT
```

```
1930 PRINT "PRODUCT ";PO$;TAB(20);P2$
1940 PRINT
1950 PRINT "STEP #";TAB(10);"PROCESS";TAB(22);"TASK(S)"
1960 PRINT "-------";TAB(10);"-------";TAB(20);"--------------------------------"
1970 FOR I=2 TO M3
1980   PRINT TAB(2);I-1;TAB(12);R2$(I);TAB(20);D$(I)
1990 NEXT I
2000 PRINT
2010 PRINT X$
2020 PRINT
2030 PRINT
2040 RETURN


2050 REM ****************************************************************
2060 REM                    DELETE PRODUCT
2070 REM ****************************************************************
2080 A$=""
2090 PRINT "ARE YOU CERTAIN THAT YOU WANT TO DELETE ";P1$(I);" (Y OR N)";
2100 INPUT A$
2110 IF A$<>"Y" THEN 2240
2120 K=S(I)
2130 GOSUB 980                                    'FILE READ
2140 N=CVI(N$)
2150 FOR I=1 TO 3
2160   LSET T$(I)="    "
2170   LSET F1$(I)="    "
2180 NEXT I
2190 LSET N$=MKI$(0)
2200 PUT#1,K
2210 IF N<=0 THEN 2240
2220 K=N
2230 GOTO 2130
2240 RETURN


2250 REM ****************************************************************
2260 REM                    PRODUCT LIST
2270 REM ****************************************************************
2280 PRINT
2290 PRINT X$
2300 PRINT
2310 PRINT "PRODUCT        REC #"
2320 PRINT
2330 FOR I=1 TO M1
2340   PRINT P1$(I);TAB(12);S(I)
2350 NEXT I
2360 PRINT
2370 PRINT X$
2380 RETURN




RUN "JOBROUT"
ENTER THE NAME OF THE ROUTING FILE? ROUTFILE
      0 PRODUCTS ARE IN THE FILE
SHALL I PRINT A LIST OF ALL PRODUCTS (Y OR N)? N

ENTER PRODUCT NUMBER? 1122
PRODUCT NOT IN FILE - DO YOU WISH TO CONTINUE (Y OR N)? Y
ENTER PRODUCT NAME? SUPER WIDGET - GOLD
ENTER ROUTING CODE,PROCESS DESCRIPTION -RETURN WHEN DONE
? A,PROCESS AT MACHINE #1
? B,PROCESS AT MACHINE #2
? A,SECOND PROCESS ON MACHINE #1
?
```

```
PROCESS      FUNCTION PERFORMED
     A      PROCESS AT MACHINE #1
     B      PROCESS AT MACHINE #2
     A      SECOND PROCESS ON MACHINE #1

SHALL I PLACE THE PRODUCT IN THE FILE (Y OR N)? Y
SHALL I PRINT THE JOB ROUTING (Y OR N)? N
ENTER PRODUCT NUMBER? 3344
PRODUCT NOT IN FILE - DO YOU WISH TO CONTINUE (Y OR N)? Y
ENTER PRODUCT NAME? W-TYPE WIDGET
ENTER ROUTING CODE,PROCESS DESCRIPTION -RETURN WHEN DONE
? C,PROCESS AT MACHINE #3
? D,PROCESS AT MACHINE #4
? 3,SPECIAL PAINT APPLICATION
? E,VARNISH STAND
?

PROCESS      FUNCTION PERFORMED
     C      PROCESS AT MACHINE #3
     D      PROCESS AT MACHINE #4
     3      SPECIAL PAINT APPLICATION
     E      VARNISH STAND

SHALL I PLACE THE PRODUCT IN THE FILE (Y OR N)? Y
SHALL I PRINT THE JOB ROUTING (Y OR N)? Y
POSITION PAPER NOW?

******************************************************************

PRODUCT 3344         W-TYPE WIDGET

STEP #     PROCESS      TASK(S)
-------    -------      ------------------
    1         C         PROCESS AT MACHINE #3
    2         D         PROCESS AT MACHINE #4
    3         3         SPECIAL PAINT APPLICATION
    4         E         VARNISH STAND


******************************************************************


ENTER PRODUCT NUMBER?


PROCESSING COMPLETE

BREAK IN 620
OK
```
```
RUN "JOBROUT"
ENTER THE NAME OF THE ROUTING FILE? ROUTFILE
     2 PRODUCTS ARE IN THE FILE
SHALL I PRINT A LIST OF ALL PRODUCTS (Y OR N)? N

ENTER PRODUCT NUMBER? 3344
PRODUCT FOUND -SHALL I PRINT IT (Y OR N)? Y

POSITION PAPER NOW?
```

```
*********************************************************************
PRODUCT 3344        W-TYPE WIDGET

STEP #      PROCESS      TASK(S)
------      -------      -------
  1           C          PROCESS AT MACHINE #3
  2           D          PROCESS AT MACHINE #4
  3           3          SPECIAL PAINT APPLICATION
  4           E          VARNISH STAND
  5
*********************************************************************


ENTER PRODUCT NUMBER? 1122
PRODUCT FOUND -SHALL I PRINT IT (Y OR N)? N
SHALL I DELETE IT (Y OR N)? Y
ARE YOU CERTAIN THAT YOU WANT TO DELETE 1122     (Y OR N)? Y
ENTER PRODUCT NUMBER?


PROCESSING COMPLETE

BREAK IN 620
OK
```

MAJOR SYMBOL TABLE - JOBROUT		FUNCTIONS USED	
NAME	**DESCRIPTION**	**NAME**	
A$	INPUT ANSWER VARIABLE	DIM	
D$()	DESCRIPTION OF PROCESS ARRAY	GOSUB	
F$	FILE NAME	PUT	
F1$()	PROCESS DESCRIPTION - IN FILE	GET	
I	INDEX AND ARRAY POINTER	RETURN	
I1	INDEX AND ARRAY POINTER	CVI	
J	INDEX AND ARRAY POINTER	MKI$	
J1	INDEX AND ARRAY POINTER	TAB	
K	RECORD # TO BE READ	INT	
L	LAST RECORD # USED	LSET	
LOF(1)	LAST RECORD NUMBER OF FILE 1	LEN	
M	MAX NUMBER OF STOPS(PROCESSES) PER JOB	FIELD	
M0	MAXIMUM NUMBER OF PRODUCTS IN FILE	SPACE$	
M1	NUMBER OF PRODUCTS IN FILE	OPEN	
M3	NUMBER OF PROCESSES ENTERED	LOF(1)	
M4	NUMBER OF RECORDS TO BE WRITTEN		
N	NEXT RECORD NUMBER		
N$	CHARACTER STRING OF NEXT RECORD #		
N2$	INPUT PRODUCT NAME		
P$	INPUT PRODUCT NAME		
P0$	PRODUCT NUMBER - IN FILE		
P1$()	PRODUCT NAME ARRAY		
P2$	PRODUCT NAME - IN FILE		
R2$()	PROCESS(STOP) CODE ARRAY		
S()	PRODUCT RECORD # ARRAY		
T$()	PROCESS CODE - IN FILE		
X$	LINE OF ASTERISKS		
X1$	DUMMY VARIABLE		

Equipment Maintenance Scheduling

Program Name: MAINT

This program uses sequential file handling to perform all required functions for the recording, updating, and display of scheduled maintenance on machines and other equipment. It will be useful both to the small production shop and to other businesses concerned with equipment maintenance.

The program is controlled by the operator's responses to program messages. The first time the program is executed (or when deletion of all previous entries is desired), the operator must answer "Y" to the question, "ARE YOU INITIALIZING THE SYSTEM (Y OR N)?" Once the system has been initialized, four options are available through keyboard selection:

Option 1 allows a formatted print of the current contents of the file.

Option 2 allows the printing of all maintenance scheduled for a specified date.

Option 3 allows the printing of all maintenance scheduled for a specified machine.

Option 4 allows the entry and update of maintenance information in the file. Individual records can be inserted (code I), deleted (code D), or changed (code C). The insert code requests record information from the operator and then inserts it after the current record position. The delete code causes the current input record (from the input file) not to be written to the output file. The change code replaces the current input record with the new information requested from the operator.

Figure 8-7 illustrates the program's options.

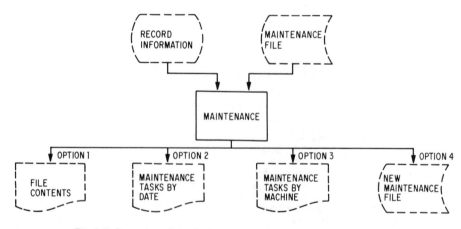

Fig. 8-7 Operation of the equipment maintenance scheduling program

Two sequential files are used by this program, one for input and the second for output. Requesting Option 4 (updating files) creates an output file containing the new records. Depending on the action codes specified by the operator, the records from the input file will be written to the new file in sequential order, replaced by a new record, or ignored and therefore not written to the new file. The format of the files is shown in Fig. 8-8.

Comment: The use of sequential files in this manner allows files to be recovered by stepping back to a previous file and processing only the updates to it.

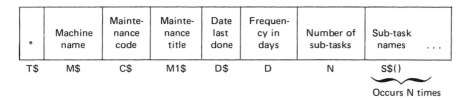

*	Machine name	Mainte-nance code	Mainte-nance title	Date last done	Frequen-cy in days	Number of sub-tasks	Sub-task names	
T$	M$	C$	M1$	D$	D	N	S$( )	...

Occurs N times

Fig. 8-8 Record format

```
10 REM              SAVED AT MAINT
20 REM          MAINTENANCE SCHEDULING PROGRAM
30 REM *******************************************************************
40 X$="*****************************************************************"
50 M=25
60 M2=10000
70 DIM S$(M),DO(12)
80 FOR I = 1 TO 12
90    READ DO(I)
100 NEXT I
110 DATA 31,28,31,30,31,30,31,31,30,31,30,31
120 PRINT "ENTER TODAY'S DATE MM/DD/YY";
130 INPUT DO$
140 PRINT
150 PRINT
160 PRINT "ARE YOU INITIALIZING THE SYSTEM (Y OR N)";
170 INPUT A1$
180 IF A1$<>"Y" THEN 240
190 F1$="NULL"
200 GOSUB 1710              'OPEN OUTPUT
210 CLOSE 2
220 F$=F1$
230 GOTO 260
240 PRINT "ENTER THE NAME OF THE MAINTENANCE FILE";
250 INPUT F$
260 GOSUB 1600              'OPEN INPUT
270 PRINT
280 PRINT X$
290 PRINT
300 PRINT "THE FOLLOWING OPTIONS ARE AVAILABLE:"
310 PRINT
320 PRINT TAB(5);"1..CURRENT FILE CONTENTS"
330 PRINT TAB(5);"2..MAINTENANCE TASK LIST - SPECIFIC DATE"
340 PRINT TAB(5);"3..MAINTENANCE SCHEDULE - BY MACHINE"
```

```
350 PRINT "-------------------------------------------------------------"
360 PRINT TAB(5);"4..UPDATE FILES"
370 PRINT
380 PRINT "ENTER OPTION NUMBER";
390 O=0
400 INPUT O
410 IF O=1 THEN GOSUB 570
420 IF O=2 THEN GOSUB 790        'DATE LIST
430 IF O=3 THEN GOSUB 1070       'MACHINE SCHEDULE
440 IF O=4 THEN GOSUB 1310       'UPDATE FILES
450 CLOSE
460 IF O>=4 THEN 490
470 IF O<>0 THEN 260
480 REM ************************************************************
490 REM              PROGRAM TERMINATION POINT
500 REM ************************************************************
510 PRINT
520 PRINT
530 PRINT "PROCESSING COMPLETE"
540 PRINT
550 STOP


560 REM ************************************************************
570 REM              PRINT CURRENT CONTENTS
580 REM ************************************************************
590 PRINT "POSITION PAPER NOW";
600 INPUT A$
610 PRINT
620 K=1
630 PRINT

640 PRINT X$
650 PRINT
660 PRINT TAB(10);"CURRENT MAINTENANCE FILE CONTENTS"
670 PRINT
680 PRINT "#";TAB(3);"MACHINE";TAB(12);"MAINT CODE";TAB(30);"MAINT";
690 PRINT TAB(45);"LAST DATE";TAB(55);"FREQUENCY"
700 PRINT "-- --------";TAB(12);"----------";TAB(25);"----------";
710 PRINT TAB(45);"---------";TAB(55);"---------"
720 PRINT
730 IF EOF(1) THEN 770
740 GOSUB 2300                    'READ RECORD
750 GOSUB 1750                    'PRINT RECORD
760 GOTO 730
770 RETURN

780 REM ************************************************************
790 REM                    DATE LIST
800 REM ************************************************************
810 PRINT "ENTER THE DATE TO BE PRINTED";
820 INPUT D$
830 GOSUB 2530                    'DECODE DATE
840 M9=M1
850 D9=D1
860 Y9=Y1
870 PRINT "POSITION PAPER NOW";
880 INPUT A$
890 PRINT
900 PRINT X$
910 PRINT
920 PRINT TAB(10);"MAINTENANCE LIST FOR ";D$
930 PRINT
940 PRINT TAB(2);"CODE";TAB(10);"MACHINE";TAB(20);"LAST DONE";
950 PRINT TAB(30);"MAINT. TASK";TAB(50);"DATE ACCOMP."
960 PRINT TAB(2);"-----";TAB(10);"--------";TAB(20);"---------";
970 PRINT TAB(30);"------------";TAB(50);"---------"
980 PRINT
990 IF EOF(1) THEN 1050
```

```
1000 GOSUB 2300                    'READ RECORD
1010 GOSUB 2530                    'DECODE DATE
1020 GOSUB 2610                    'FIND NEXT DATE
1030 IF D2=D9 AND M1 =M9 AND Y1=Y9 THEN GOSUB 1890        'PRINT RECORD
1040 GOTO 990
1050 RETURN


1060 REM *****************************************************************
1070 REM                  MACHINE SCHEDULE
1080 REM *****************************************************************
1090 PRINT "ENTER THE MACHINE TO BE PRINTED";
1100 INPUT M9$
1110 PRINT "POSITION PAPER NOW";
1120 INPUT A$
1130 PRINT
1140 PRINT X$
1150 PRINT
1160 PRINT TAB(10);"MAINTENANCE SCHEDULE FOR ";M$
1170 PRINT
1180 PRINT TAB(3);"MACHINE";TAB(12);"MAINT CODE";TAB(30);"MAINT";
1190 PRINT TAB(45);"LAST DATE";TAB(55);"FREQUENCY"
1200 PRINT TAB(3);"--------";TAB(12);"------------";TAB(25);"----------------";
1210 PRINT TAB(45);"---------";TAB(55);"----------"
1220 IF EOF(1) THEN 1290
1230 GOSUB 2300                    'READ RECORD
1240 GOSUB 2540                    'DECODE DATE
1250 GOSUB 2610                    'FIND NEXT DATE
1260 D5$=STR$(M1)+"/"+STR$(D2)+"/"+STR$(Y1)
1270 IF M9$=M$ THEN GOSUB 1750   'PRINT RECORD
1280 GOTO 1220
1290 RETURN


1300 REM *****************************************************************
1310 REM                  UPDATE FILES
1320 REM *****************************************************************
1330 GOSUB 1660                    'OPEN OUTPUT FILE
1340 J1=1
1350 PRINT "ENTER THE RECORD # TO PROCESS";
1360 INPUT N1
1370 FOR J=J1 TO N1
1380    IF EOF(1) THEN 1420
1390    GOSUB 2300                 'READ RECORD
1400    IF J<N1 THEN GOSUB 2390   'WRITE RECORD
1410 NEXT J
1420 J1=N1+1
1430 IF A$="S" THEN 1580
1440 IF EOF(1) THEN PRINT "AT END-OF-FILE";
1450 IF NOT EOF(1) THEN PRINT " DELETE(D),CHANGE(C)";
1460 PRINT ", INSERT(I), OR STOP (S)";
1470 INPUT A$
1480 IF A$<>"S" THEN 1520
1490 N1=M2
1500 IF NOT EOF(1) THEN GOSUB 2390        'WRITE RECORD
1510 GOTO 1370
1520 IF A$="D" THEN 1350
1530 IF A$="I" AND NOT EOF(1) THEN GOSUB 2390    'WRITE RECORD
1540 GOSUB 1990                   'ACCEPT INPUT
1550 GOSUB 2390               'WRITE RECORD
1560 IF EOF(1) THEN 1440
1570 GOTO 1350
1580 RETURN


1590 REM *****************************************************************
1600 REM               OPEN AND DEFINE  INPUT FILES
1610 REM *****************************************************************
1620 OPEN "I",1,F$,0
1630 INPUT#1,D0$
1640 RETURN
```

```
1650 REM ***********************************************************
1660 REM               OPEN AND DEFINE OUTPUT FILES
1670 REM ***********************************************************
1680 PRINT "ENTER THE NAME OF THE OUTPUT MAINTENANCE FILE"
1690 PRINT "*** WARNING *** THE FILE CONTENTS WILL BE DESTROYED"
1700 INPUT F1$
1710 OPEN "O",2,F1$,0
1720 PRINT#2,DO$
1730 RETURN

1740 REM ***********************************************************
1750 REM               PRINT RECORD
1760 REM ***********************************************************
1770 IF O=1 THEN PRINT K;
1780 PRINT TAB(5);M$;TAB(15);C$;TAB(25);M1$;TAB(45);D$;TAB(55);D;
1790 IF O=3 THEN PRINT TAB(60);D5$;
1800 PRINT
1810 K=K+1
1820 IF N=0 THEN 1860
1830 FOR I=1 TO N
1840   PRINT TAB(27);S$(I)
1850 NEXT I
1860 PRINT
1870 RETURN

1880 REM ***********************************************************
1890 REM               PRINT DATE LIST -SCHEDULE
1900 REM ***********************************************************
1910 PRINT TAB(5);C$;TAB(10);M$;TAB(20);D$;TAB(30);M1$;TAB(50);"(
1920 IF N=0 THEN 1960
1930 FOR I=1 TO N
1940   PRINT TAB(30);S$(I);TAB(62);"()"
1950 NEXT I
1960 PRINT
1970 RETURN

1980 REM ***********************************************************
1990 REM               ACCEPT INPUT
2000 REM ***********************************************************
2010 PRINT "ENTER MACHINE NAME";
2020 M$=""
2030 INPUT M$
2040 IF M$="" THEN 2280
2050 PRINT "ENTER MAINTENANCE CODE (RETURN FOR NEXT MACHINE)";
2060 C$=""
2070 INPUT C$
2080 IF C$="" THEN 2010
2090 PRINT "ENTER THE NAME OF THE MAINTENANCE";
2100 INPUT M1$
2110 PRINT "ENTER DATE LAST ACCOMPLISHED (MM/DD/YY)";
2120 INPUT D$
2130 M1=VAL(LEFT$(D$,2))
2140 IF M1<=12 THEN 2170
2150 PRINT "INCORRECT DATE FORMAT "
2160 GOTO 2110
2170 PRINT "ENTER THE NUMBER OF DAYS BETWEEN ACCOMPLISHMENT";
2180 INPUT D
2190 PRINT "ENTER THE NUMBER OF MAINTENANCE SUBTASKS TO BE RECORDED";
2200 N=0
2210 INPUT N
2220 IF N=0 THEN 2280
2230 PRINT "ENTER THE INDIVIDUAL SUB TASKS NOW"
2240 FOR I=1 TO N
2250   PRINT I;"...";
2260   INPUT S$(I)
2270 NEXT I
2280 RETURN
```

```
2290 REM ***************************************************************
2300 REM                 READ RECORD
2310 REM ***************************************************************
2320 INPUT#1,T$,M$,C$,M1$,D$,D,N
2330 IF N=0 THEN 2370
2340 FOR I=1 TO N
2350   INPUT#1,S$(I)
2360 NEXT I
2370 RETURN

2380 REM ***************************************************************
2390 REM                 WRITE RECORD
2400 REM ***************************************************************
2410 PRINT#2,"*"
2420 PRINT#2,M$
2430 PRINT#2,C$
2440 PRINT#2,M1$
2450 PRINT#2,D$
2460 PRINT#2,D
2470 PRINT#2,N
2480 IF N=0 THEN 2520
2490 FOR I=1 TO N
2500   PRINT#2,S$(I)
2510 NEXT I
2520 RETURN

2530 REM ***************************************************************
2540 REM                 DECODE DATE
2550 REM ***************************************************************
2560 M1=VAL(LEFT$(D$,2))
2570 D1=VAL(MID$(D$,4,2))
2580 Y1=VAL(RIGHT$(D$,2))
2590 RETURN

2600 REM ***************************************************************
2610 REM                 FIND NEXT DATE
2620 REM ***************************************************************
2630 D2=D1+D
2640 IF D2<=DO(M1) THEN 2710
2650 D2=D2-DO(M1)
2660 M1=M1+1
2670 IF M1<13 THEN 2640
2680 M1=1
2690 Y1=Y1+1
2700 GOTO 2640
2710 RETURN




RUN "MAINT"
ENTER TODAY'S DATE MM/DD/YY? 02/28/81


ARE YOU INITIALIZING THE SYSTEM (Y OR N)? Y

***************************************************************

THE FOLLOWING OPTIONS ARE AVAILABLE:

    1..CURRENT FILE CONTENTS
    2..MAINTENANCE TASK LIST - SPECIFIC DATE
    3..MAINTENANCE SCHEDULE - BY MACHINE
----------------------------------------------------------------
    4..UPDATE FILES
```

```
ENTER OPTION NUMBER? 4
ENTER THE NAME OF THE OUTPUT MAINTENANCE FILE
*** WARNING *** THE FILE CONTENTS WILL BE DESTROYED
? M-FILE
ENTER THE RECORD # TO PROCESS? 1
AT END-OF-FILE, INSERT(I), OR STOP (S)? I
ENTER MACHINE NAME? MACHINE 1
ENTER MAINTENANCE CODE (RETURN FOR NEXT MACHINE)? A
ENTER THE NAME OF THE MAINTENANCE? ANNUAL SERVICE
ENTER DATE LAST ACCOMPLISHED (MM/DD/YY)? 03/01/80
ENTER THE NUMBER OF DAYS BETWEEN ACCOMPLISHMENT? 365
ENTER THE NUMBER OF MAINTENANCE SUBTASKS TO BE RECORDED? 5
ENTER THE INDIVIDUAL SUB TASKS NOW
  1 ...? CHANGE BELT
  2 ...? LUBE GEAR 1
  3 ...? OIL SHAFT
  4 ...? CHANGE BULB
  5 ...? CLEAN SHELF
AT END-OF-FILE, INSERT(I), OR STOP (S)? S


PROCESSING COMPLETE

BREAK IN 550
OK
```

```
RUN "MAINT"
ENTER TODAY'S DATE MM/DD/YY? 02/28/81


ARE YOU INITIALIZING THE SYSTEM (Y OR N)? N
ENTER THE NAME OF THE MAINTENANCE FILE?     M-FILE

**********************************************************************

THE FOLLOWING OPTIONS ARE AVAILABLE:

      1..CURRENT FILE CONTENTS
      2..MAINTENANCE TASK LIST - SPECIFIC DATE
      3..MAINTENANCE SCHEDULE - BY MACHINE
--------------------------------------------------------------------
      4..UPDATE FILES

ENTER OPTION NUMBER? 1
POSITION PAPER NOW?


**********************************************************************
          CURRENT MAINTENANCE FILE CONTENTS

#  MACHINE  MAINT CODE        MAINT          LAST DATE FREQUENCY
-- --------- ----------   ---------------    --------- ---------

1   MACHINE 1 A           ANNUAL SERVICE     03/01/80    365
                          CHANGE BELT
                          LUBE GEAR 1
                          OIL SHAFT
                          CHANGE BULB
                          CLEAN SHELF
```

```
****************************************************************

THE FOLLOWING OPTIONS ARE AVAILABLE:

     1..CURRENT FILE CONTENTS
     2..MAINTENANCE TASK LIST - SPECIFIC DATE
     3..MAINTENANCE SCHEDULE - BY MACHINE
------------------------------------------------------------
     4..UPDATE FILES

ENTER OPTION NUMBER? 2
ENTER THE DATE TO BE PRINTED? 03/01/81
POSITION PAPER NOW?

****************************************************************

         MAINTENANCE LIST FOR 03/01/81

  CODE    MACHINE   LAST DONE MAINT. TASK        DATE ACCOMP.
  ----    -------   --------- ----------         -----------

   A    MACHINE 1 03/01/80  ANNUAL SERVICE      (        )
                            CHANGE BELT                    ( )
                            LUBE GEAR 1                     ( )
                            OIL SHAFT                       ( )
                            CHANGE BULB                     ( )
                            CLEAN SHELF                     ( )

****************************************************************

THE FOLLOWING OPTIONS ARE AVAILABLE:

     1..CURRENT FILE CONTENTS
     2..MAINTENANCE TASK LIST - SPECIFIC DATE
     3..MAINTENANCE SCHEDULE - BY MACHINE
------------------------------------------------------------
     4..UPDATE FILES

ENTER OPTION NUMBER? 3
ENTER THE MACHINE TO BE PRINTED? MACHINE 1
POSITION PAPER NOW?

****************************************************************

         MAINTENANCE SCHEDULE FOR MACHINE 1

  MACHINE   MAINT CODE       MAINT        LAST DATE FREQUENCY
  -------   ----------    ----------      --------- ---------
   MACHINE 1 A            ANNUAL SERVICE  03/01/80   365  3/ 1/ 81
                          CHANGE BELT
                          LUBE GEAR 1
                          OIL SHAFT
                          CHANGE BULB
                          CLEAN SHELF

****************************************************************

THE FOLLOWING OPTIONS ARE AVAILABLE:

     1..CURRENT FILE CONTENTS
     2..MAINTENANCE TASK LIST - SPECIFIC DATE
     3..MAINTENANCE SCHEDULE - BY MACHINE
------------------------------------------------------------
     4..UPDATE FILES

ENTER OPTION NUMBER?

PROCESSING COMPLETE

BREAK IN 550
OK
```

NAME	DESCRIPTION		NAME
A1$	ANSWER VARIABLE		DIM
C$	MAINTENANCE CODE		GOSUB
D	DAYS BETWEEN ACCOMPLISHMENT		RETURN
D$	DATE OF LAST ACCOMPLISHMENT		OPEN
D0$	CURRENT DATE		CLOSE
D0()	NUMBER OF DAYS IN EACH MONTH		VAL
D1	DAYS FROM FILE		TAB
D2	DAYS INTO THE NEXT MONTH		EOF(1)
D5$	DATE OF NEXT SCHEDULED ACCOMPLISHMENT		LEFT$
D9	INPUT DAY FOR COMPARE		RIGHT$
F$	INPUT FILE NAME		MID$
F1$	OUTPUT FILE NAME		STR$
I	INDEX AND ARRAY POINTER		
J	INDEX AND ARRAY POINTER		
J1	RECORD COUNTER		
K	COUNTER FOR RECORDS		
M	MAXIMUM NUMBER OF SUB-TASKS		
M$	MACHINE NAME		
M1	MONTH FROM FILE		
M1$	MAINTENANCE TITLE		
M2	MAXIMUM NUMBER OF RECORDS IN FILE		
M9	INPUT MONTH FOR COMPARE		
M9$	NAME OF MACHINE TO PRINT		
N	NUMBER OF SUB-TASKS		
N1	RECORD TO PROCESS		
O	OPTION NUMBER		
S$()	SUB-TASK NAMES		
X$	LINE OF ASTERISKS		
Y1	YEAR FROM FILE		
Y9	INPUT YEAR FOR COMPARE		

Production Lot Size Computation

Program Name: PRODSIZE

This program computes and prints information concerning ideal production-lot sizes for inventory items and identifies the costs associated with these runs. All data is entered in response to program prompting.

Files Affected: None

```
10 REM          SAVED AT PRODSIZE
20 REM ****************************************************************
30 PRINT "COMPUTATION OF ECONOMIC PRODUCTION SIZE"
40 PRINT "ENTER SET UP COSTS ";
50 INPUT S
60 PRINT "ENTER USAGE PER TIME PERIOD ";
70 INPUT U
80 PRINT "ENTER HOLDING COSTS PER TIME PERIOD ";
90 INPUT H
100 PRINT "ENTER  PRODUCTION LEVEL PER TIME PERIOD ";
110 INPUT P
120 PRINT
130 PRINT "*******************************************"
140 PRINT
150 PRINT "       ECONOMIC PRODUCTION SIZE"
160 PRINT
170 PRINT
180 Q=SQR((2*S*U)/H)*(1/(SQR(1-(U/P))))
190 C=SQR(2*S*U*H)*SQR(1-(U/P))
200 PRINT "PRODUCTION SIZE ";TAB(20);Q;"UNITS"
210 PRINT "COST OF PRODUCTION RUN";TAB(20);"$";C
220 PRINT
230 PRINT "*******************************************"
240 REM ************* TERMINATION POINT  ************************
250 PRINT
260 STOP
```

```
RUN "PRODSIZE"
COMPUTATION OF ECONOMIC PRODUCTION SIZE
ENTER SET UP COSTS ? 5
ENTER USAGE PER TIME PERIOD ? 100
ENTER HOLDING COSTS PER TIME PERIOD ? .4
ENTER  PRODUCTION LEVEL PER TIME PERIOD ? 500

*********************************************

       ECONOMIC PRODUCTION SIZE


PRODUCTION SIZE      55.9017 UNITS
COST OF PRODUCTION RUN$ 17.8885

*********************************************

BREAK IN 260
OK
```

```
   MAJOR SYMBOL TABLE - PRODSIZE                              FUNCTIONS USED
I----------------------------------------------------------I   I-------------I
I NAME   .. DESCRIPTION                                    I   I  NAME       I
I----------------------------------------------------------I   I-------------I
I  C     .. COST OF PRODUCTION RUN                         I   I TAB         I
I  H     .. HOLDING/CARRYING COSTS PER TIME PERIOD         I   I SQR         I
I  P     .. PRODUCTION CAPACITY PER TIME PERIOD            I   I-------------I
I  Q     .. OPTIMAL PRODUCTION LOT SIZE                    I
I  S     .. SET UP COSTS                                   I
I  U     .. USAGE PER TIME PERIOD                          I
I----------------------------------------------------------I
```

Production Programs (General)   253

Production Cost Computation No. 1

Program Name: COST-1

This program computes the cost of a given production run. All data is input at the terminal in response to program messages.

Files Affected: None

```
10 REM          SAVED AT COST-1
20 REM ****************** PROCESSING AREA  ********************
30 PRINT
40 PRINT "COMPUTES COST OF PRODUCTION QUANTITY"
50 PRINT
60 PRINT "ENTER FIXED COSTS ";
70 INPUT F
80 PRINT "ENTER VARIABLE COSTS PER UNIT ";
90 INPUT V
100 PRINT "ENTER QUANTITY DESIRED ";
110 INPUT Q
120 REM *************** CALCULATE COSTS   ************************
130 V1=V*Q
140 C=F+V1
150 U=C/Q
160 PRINT
170 PRINT "********************************"
180 PRINT "COST OF PRODUCING ";Q;" UNITS"
190 PRINT
200 PRINT "FIXED COSTS";TAB(15);"$";F
210 PRINT "VARIABLE COSTS";TAB(15);"$";V1
220 PRINT "-----------------------------"
230 PRINT "TOTAL COSTS";TAB(15);"$";C
240 PRINT
250 PRINT "UNIT COST";TAB(15);"$";U;"EACH"
260 PRINT "********************************"
270 PRINT
280 REM ******************* TERMINATION POINT  *****************
290 STOP
```

```
RUN "COST-1"

COMPUTES COST OF PRODUCTION QUANTITY

ENTER FIXED COSTS ? 2050
ENTER VARIABLE COSTS PER UNIT ? 5.15
ENTER QUANTITY DESIRED ? 1000

********************************
COST OF PRODUCING  1000   UNITS

FIXED COSTS    $ 2050
VARIABLE COSTS $ 5150
--------------------------------
TOTAL COSTS    $ 7200

UNIT COST      $ 7.2 EACH
********************************

BREAK IN 290
OK
```

```
      MAJOR SYMBOL TABLE - COST-1                   FUNCTIONS USED
I----------------------------------------I     I----------------I
I NAME    .. DESCRIPTION                  I     I  NAME          I
I----------------------------------------I     I----------------I
I  C      .. TOTAL COSTS                  I     I TAB            I
I  F      .. FIXED COSTS FOR RUN          I     I----------------I
I  Q      .. QUANTITY DESIRED             I
I  U      .. UNIT COSTS                   I
I  V      .. VARIABLE COSTS PER UNIT      I
I  V1     .. TOTAL VARIABLE COSTS         I
I----------------------------------------I
```

Production Cost Computation No. 2

Program Name: COST-2

This program computes fixed and variable costs for a production process when the costs of two production quantities are known. It assumes a straight-line relationship of these costs with all costs identifiable as either fixed or variable. The program also produces a cost breakdown of the two types of costs.

Files Affected: None

```
10 REM            SAVED AT COST-2
20 REM ***************** PROCESSING AREA  ***********************
30 PRINT
40 PRINT
50 PRINT "COMPUTES FIXED AND VARIABLE COSTS WHEN THE COSTS FOR"
60 PRINT "TWO PRODUCTION QUANTITIES ARE KNOWN"
70 PRINT
80 PRINT "ENTER FOR PRODUCTION QUANTITY 1"
90 PRINT "COSTS AND QUANTITY (I.E. 1500,5000)";
100 INPUT C1,Q1
110 PRINT
120 PRINT "ENTER FOR PRODUCTION QUANTITY 2"
130 PRINT "COSTS AND QUANTITY (I.E. 2000,7500)";
140 INPUT C2,Q2
150 REM *************** CALCULATE COSTS  ***********************
160 V=(C2-C1)/(Q2-Q1)
170 F=C1-V*Q1
180 PRINT
190 PRINT "******************************************"
200 PRINT "COST BREAKDOWN OF FIXED AND VARIABLE COSTS"
210 PRINT
220 PRINT "FIXED COSTS";TAB(15);"$";F
230 PRINT "VARIABLE COSTS";TAB(15);"$";V;" EACH"
240 PRINT "******************************************"
250 PRINT
260 REM ****************** TERMINATION POINT  ******************
270 STOP
```

```
RUN "COST-2"

COMPUTES FIXED AND VARIABLE COSTS WHEN THE COSTS FOR
TWO PRODUCTION QUANTITIES ARE KNOWN

ENTER FOR PRODUCTION QUANTITY 1
COSTS AND QUANTITY (I.E. 1500,5000)? 1500,5000

ENTER FOR PRODUCTION QUANTITY 2
COSTS AND QUANTITY (I.E. 2000,7500)? 2000,7500

*********************************************
COST BREAKDOWN OF FIXED AND VARIABLE COSTS

FIXED COSTS    $ 500
VARIABLE COSTS $ .2   EACH
*********************************************

BREAK IN 270
OK
```

```
    MAJOR SYMBOL TABLE - COST-2              FUNCTIONS USED
I-----------------------------------I   I----------------I
I NAME    .. DESCRIPTION            I   I  NAME          I
I-----------------------------------I   I----------------I
I  C1     .. COST OF QUANTITY 1     I   I TAB            I
I  Q1     .. QUANTITY 1             I   I----------------I
I  C2     .. COST OF QUANTITY 2     I
I  Q2     .. QUANTITY 2             I
I  V      .. VARIABLE COSTS         I
I  F      .. FIXED COSTS            I
I-----------------------------------I
```

Analysis of Production Alternatives

Program Name: COST-3

This program compares alternative production methods in terms of fixed and variable cost structures. The number of alternatives and the costs of each are entered at the terminal in response to program prompting. The output consists of a schedule of profit/loss figures for each alternative, the schedule being printed for the range of values specified by the operator.

Files Affected: None

```
10 REM             SAVED AT COST-3
20 REM ***************** PROCESSING AREA   ***********************
30 PRINT
40 PRINT "COMPARES ALTERNATIVE METHODS OF PRODUCTION"
50 PRINT
60 PRINT "ENTER THE NUMBER OF ALTERNATIVES TO BE CONSIDERED ";
70 INPUT N
80 PRINT
90 DIM F(N),V(N),P(N),C(N),R(N),A(N)
100 FOR M=1 TO N
110    PRINT "ENTER FIXED COSTS FOR METHOD ";M;
120    INPUT F(M)
130    PRINT "ENTER VARIABLE COSTS PER UNIT FOR METHOD";M;
140    INPUT V(M)
150    PRINT "ENTER UNIT PRICE FOR METHOD";M;
160    INPUT P(M)
170    PRINT
180 NEXT M
190 PRINT "ENTER BEGINNING QUANTITY FOR COMPUTATIONS";
200 INPUT Q1
210 PRINT "ENTER ENDING QUANTITY FOR COMPUTATIONS";
220 INPUT Q2
230 PRINT "ENTER STEP INCREMENTS TO BE PRINTED";
240 INPUT S
250 PRINT
260 PRINT
270 PRINT "********************************************************"
280 PRINT
290 PRINT "PROFIT/LOSS COMPARISON TABLE"
300 PRINT
310 PRINT "QUANTITY";
320 FOR M=1 TO N
330    PRINT TAB(10*M);"METHOD";M;
340 NEXT M
350 PRINT
360 PRINT
370 REM ***************** CALCULATION AND PRINTING LOOP  *********
380 FOR Q=Q1 TO Q2 STEP S
390    PRINT Q;
400    FOR M=1 TO N
410       R(M)=P(M)*Q
420       C(M)=F(M)+(V(M)*Q)
430       A(M)=R(M)-C(M)
440       PRINT TAB(10*M);A(M);
450    NEXT M
460    PRINT
470 NEXT Q
480 PRINT
490 PRINT "********************************************************"
500 REM ***************** TERMINATION POINT   *******************
510 PRINT
520 STOP


RUN "COST-3"

COMPARES ALTERNATIVE METHODS OF PRODUCTION

ENTER THE NUMBER OF ALTERNATIVES TO BE CONSIDERED ? 2

ENTER FIXED COSTS FOR METHOD   1 ? 600
ENTER VARIABLE COSTS PER UNIT FOR METHOD 1 ? .75
ENTER UNIT PRICE FOR METHOD 1 ? 1.00

ENTER FIXED COSTS FOR METHOD   2 ? 1000
ENTER VARIABLE COSTS PER UNIT FOR METHOD 2 ? .50
ENTER UNIT PRICE FOR METHOD 2 ? 1.10
```

```
ENTER BEGINNING QUANTITY FOR COMPUTATIONS? 100
ENTER ENDING QUANTITY FOR COMPUTATIONS? 2500
ENTER STEP INCREMENTS TO BE PRINTED? 100


**********************************************************

PROFIT/LOSS COMPARISON TABLE

QUANTITY   METHOD 1   METHOD 2

    100      -575       -940
    200      -550       -880
    300      -525       -820
    400      -500       -760
    500      -475       -700
    600      -450       -640
    700      -425       -580
    800      -400       -520
    900      -375       -460
   1000      -350       -400
   1100      -325       -340
   1200      -300       -280
   1300      -275       -220
   1400      -250       -160
   1500      -225       -100
   1600      -200        -40
   1700      -175         20
   1800      -150         80
   1900      -125        140
   2000      -100        200
   2100       -75        260
   2200       -50        320
   2300       -25        380
   2400         0        440
   2500        25        500


**********************************************************

BREAK IN 520
OK
```

MAJOR SYMBOL TABLE - COST-3		FUNCTIONS USED	
NAME	**DESCRIPTION**	**NAME**	
A()	.. PROFIT/LOSS ARRAY	TAB	
C(0	.. TOTAL COST ARRAY	DIM	
F()	.. FIXED COST ARRAY		
M	.. METHOD/ALTERNATIVE NUMBER		
N	.. NUMBER OF ALTERNATIVES TO COMPARE		
P()	.. UNIT PRICE ARRAY		
Q	.. QUANTITY TO BE PRINTED		
Q1	.. BEGINNING QUANTITY TO PRINT		
Q2	.. ENDING QUANTITY TO PRINT		
R()	.. REVENUE ARRAY		
S	.. STEP INCREMENT FOR PRINTING		
V()	.. VARIABLE COST ARRAY		

Production Cost Comparison

Program Name: COST-4

This program prepares another form for comparison of alternative production methods in terms of their fixed and variable cost structures. The number of alternatives and the costs of each are entered at the terminal in response to program prompting. The output is a schedule of production cost figures for each alternative and is printed for the range of values specified by the operator during program initialization.

Files Affected: None

```
10 REM              SAVED AT COST-4
20 REM ****************** PROCESSING AREA  ***********************
30 PRINT
40 PRINT "COMPARES ALTERNATIVE METHODS OF PRODUCTION"
50 PRINT
60 PRINT "ENTER THE NUMBER OF ALTERNATIVES TO BE CONSIDERED ";
70 INPUT N
80 PRINT
90 DIM F(N),V(N),C(N)
100 FOR M=1 TO N
110    PRINT "ENTER FIXED COSTS FOR METHOD ";M;
120    INPUT F(M)
130    PRINT "ENTER VARIABLE COSTS PER UNIT FOR METHOD";M;
140    INPUT V(M)
150    PRINT
160 NEXT M
170 PRINT "ENTER BEGINNING QUANTITY FOR COMPUTATIONS";
180 INPUT Q1
190 PRINT "ENTER ENDING QUANTITY FOR COMPUTATIONS";
200 INPUT Q2
210 PRINT "ENTER STEP INCREMENTS TO BE PRINTED";
220 INPUT S
230 PRINT
240 PRINT
250 PRINT "*****************************************************"
260 PRINT
270 PRINT "TOTAL COST COMPARISON SCHEDULE"
280 PRINT
290 PRINT "QUANTITY";
300 FOR M=1 TO N
310    PRINT TAB(10*M);"METHOD";M;
320 NEXT M
330 PRINT
340 PRINT
350 REM ****************** CALCULATION AND PRINTING LOOP  *********
360 FOR Q=Q1 TO Q2 STEP S
370    PRINT Q;
380    FOR M=1 TO N
390      C(M)=F(M)+(V(M)*Q)
400      PRINT TAB(10*M);C(M);
410    NEXT M
420    PRINT
430 NEXT Q
440 PRINT
450 PRINT "*****************************************************"
460 REM ****************** TERMINATION POINT  ******************
470 PRINT
480 STOP
```

```
RUN "COST-4"

COMPARES ALTERNATIVE METHODS OF PRODUCTION

ENTER THE NUMBER OF ALTERNATIVES TO BE CONSIDERED ? 2

ENTER FIXED COSTS FOR METHOD   1 ? 600
ENTER VARIABLE COSTS PER UNIT FOR METHOD 1 ? .75

ENTER FIXED COSTS FOR METHOD   2 ? 1000
ENTER VARIABLE COSTS PER UNIT FOR METHOD 2 ? .5

ENTER BEGINNING QUANTITY FOR COMPUTATIONS? 100
ENTER ENDING QUANTITY FOR COMPUTATIONS? 2500
ENTER STEP INCREMENTS TO BE PRINTED? 100


****************************************************

TOTAL COST COMPARISON SCHEDULE

QUANTITY   METHOD 1   METHOD 2

   100        675       1050
   200        750       1100
   300        825       1150
   400        900       1200
   500        975       1250
   600       1050       1300
   700       1125       1350
   800       1200       1400
   900       1275       1450
  1000       1350       1500
  1100       1425       1550
  1200       1500       1600
  1300       1575       1650
  1400       1650       1700
  1500       1725       1750
  1600       1800       1800
  1700       1875       1850
  1800       1950       1900
  1900       2025       1950
  2000       2100       2000
  2100       2175       2050
  2200       2250       2100
  2300       2325       2150
  2400       2400       2200
  2500       2475       2250

****************************************************

BREAK IN 480
OK
```

```
MAJOR SYMBOL TABLE - COST-4                              FUNCTIONS USED
I-----------------------------------------------------I  I---------------I
I NAME  .. DESCRIPTION                                I  I NAME          I
I-----------------------------------------------------I  I---------------I
I F()   .. FIXED COST ARRAY                           I  I TAB           I
I V()   .. VARIABLE COST ARRAY                        I  I DIM           I
I C()   .. TOTAL COSTS ARRAY                          I  I---------------I
I N     .. NUMBER OF ALTERNATIVES TO COMPARE          I
I M     .. METHOD/ALTERNATIVE NUMBER                  I
I Q1    .. BEGINNING QUANTITY TO BE PRINTED           I
I Q2    .. ENDING QUANTITYY TO BE PRINTED             I
I Q     .. QUANTITY BEING PRINTED                     I
I S     .. STEP INCREMENT FOR PRINTING                I
I-----------------------------------------------------I
```

Appendix
Language Features Used

All programs in this book were developed, tested, and run on an Altair 8800b Microcomputer System operating under Altair's Revision 4.1 of their Disk Extended BASIC.

Since many of the programs use disk-file handling procedures and other features of the BASIC language that differ from manufacturer to manufacturer, every attempt has been made to minimize this potential source of difficulty. When possible, features that could present compatibility problems (such as file handling routines) have been isolated into separate subroutines to minimize conversion requirements. Each program contains a symbol table and a table of functions used to help clarify problem areas.

To further your understanding of the features used in the programs and to provide information that will help you overcome any compatibility problems, language features are discussed in some detail in this Appendix.

GENERAL

Variable names   All variable names have been defined as either *numeric* or *alphanumeric*. Alphanumeric data names are terminated with a dollar sign, $; that is, A0 is numeric whereas A0$ is alphanumeric.

Arrays   Arrays have been defined with DIM statements. Altair BASIC (by default) will treat any variable as a twelve-position array. Care has been taken to insure that all variables have been explicitly dimensioned, however. Variable dimensioning using a previously defined variable name as the dimension size of the array is also allowed. If this usage causes problems, replace the variable name in the statement with the number that the variable name was assigned.

File handling of random files   Altair BASIC requires all random-file records to be 128 characters long. A smaller record size will be accepted, but disk utilization remains at 128 characters. The buffer (input-output) area for random files is defined separately from all other character variables. Therefore, explicit action is required to define the character names associated with the random record. This is accomplished by means of the FIELD function. All character names in the record are defined using FIELD to indicate their names, size, and location in the record. Note that all items to be placed in the random buffer area have to be moved to that area using the LSET command instead of the normal LET or default assignment. Since Altair BASIC allows only character data to be placed in the buffer, all numeric data names are converted prior to being moved to the buffer. MKS$ and MKI$ are the functions used to perform this task. The reverse functions, CVS and CVI, are used to decode the record items for later use as numeric variables.

FUNCTIONS USED

ABS   This function returns the absolute value of x. For example, ABS (−1)=1=ABS(1).

CLOSE   This function closes all files; CLOSE x closes file number x. An end-of-file record is written to the file when the CLOSE command is executed on a file that is open for output or use as a random file.

CVI   This function converts a field that has been previously encoded to the character value of an integer using the MKI$ function. It is used exclusively for returning items from a random-file input buffer.

CVS   This function converts a real number field that has been previously encoded to its character representation using the MKS$ function. It is used exclusively for returning numeric (real numbers) from a random-file input buffer.

DIM   This function dimensions a variable name. For example, DIM A(12) provides a numeric field A that consists of 12 variable length address locations. The sixth location is addressed as A(6).

EOF   This function checks the status of a file to determine if it is at an end-of-file condition. For example, EOF(1) is true if file number one has previously input its last record.

FIELD   This function defines the variable names that are contained in a random-file input-output buffer. It defines the name, size, and location of the variables in the buffer. For example, FIELD #1,2 AS X$, 4 AS Z$, defines the buffer as containing X$ in the first two positions and Z$ in the third through sixth positions.

GET   This command returns a record from the random file; for example, GET #1,7 returns the record number seven from the random file that has been opened as file number one.

GOSUB   This instruction causes branching to a subroutine. GOSUB 500, for instance, would take the next instruction from line number 500 and continue from that point until a RETURN statement is encountered. The RETURN statement would cause control to return to the first instruction immediately following the GOSUB.

INT   This function causes the truncation of all decimal positions, leaving only the whole number; consequently, INT(12.34)= 12.

INPUT #   This command causes input to come from the file number following the #. INPUT # 1, X$, for instance, reads the next item from file number one and places it into variable name X$.

KILL   This function deletes a file from the disk. KILL "XXX" will delete the entire file XXX from the disk, for example.

*LEFT$*   This function returns the leftmost I positions from a character variable. LEFT$(X$,2), for instance, returns the two leftmost characters of the variable X$.

LEN   This function computes the length of the variable specified.

LOF   This function returns the last record number used in a random file. For example, LOF(1) returns the record number of the last available record in file number one.

LSET   This assignment statement causes data to be placed in the random-file buffer. LSET X$= Z$ will assign the value stored at Z$ to the variable location defined as X$ in a FIELD statement.

*MID$*   This function returns characters from the specified locations in a character string. MID$(X$,3,2), for instance, returns two characters from the string X$, starting from the third character location. When X$= "ABCDEFG," MID$(X$,3,2)=CD.

MKI$ This function converts an integer to a two-character field for storage in a random-file buffer.

MKS$ This function converts a real number into a four-character representation for storage in a random-file buffer.

NAME   This function renames a file; for example, NAME "X" AS "Y" changes file X to file Y in the disk directory. It is a permanent change.

OPEN   This function causes a disk file to be made available for input (I), output (O), or both (R). The form of the command is OPEN x, y, f, d where x indicates whether the file is input, output or random; y is the file number for later use in input/output commands; f is the file name; and d is the disk number. OPEN "I," 1, "XXX," O opens the file named XXX on disk number zero as input and associates it with file number one.

PRINT #   This command causes a record to be written to the file number that follows the # sign.

PUT #   This command causes a record to be written to a random file.

Like the GET command, PUT#1,7 will write the random-file buffer for file one to the seventh record position of that file.

RETURN This command returns to the next instruction following the last GOSUB.

*RIGHT$* This function returns the rightmost positions of a character variable. RIGHT$(X$,2), for instance, returns the last two characters in the field named X$.

*SPACE$* This function returns a specified number of blanks. SPACE$(15) returns fifteen blanks.

SQR This function returns the square root of the argument.

STR$ This function returns the character representation of the argument.

TAB TAB(x) causes the printer (terminal) to move to position x.

VAL This function returns the numeric value of the character variable specified. If the field is not numeric, the value is 0.